The
Father of Waters

The
Father of Waters

A Mississippi River Chronicle

text by *Norah Deakin Davis*
photographs by *Joseph Holmes*

SIERRA CLUB BOOKS
SAN FRANCISCO

The Sierra Club, founded in 1892 by John Muir, has devoted itself to the study and protection of the earth's scenic and ecological resources—mountains, wetlands, woodlands, wild shores and rivers, deserts and plains. The publishing program of the Sierra Club offers books to the public as a nonprofit educational service in the hope that they may enlarge the public's understanding of the Club's basic concerns. The point of view expressed in each book, however, does not necessarily represent that of the Club. The Sierra Club has some fifty chapters coast to coast, in Canada, Hawaii, and Alaska. For information about how you may participate in its programs to preserve wilderness and the quality of life, please address inquiries to Sierra Club, 530 Bush Street, San Francisco, California 94108.

COPYRIGHT 1982 IN ALL COUNTRIES OF THE INTERNATIONAL COPYRIGHT UNION
BY NORAH DEAKIN DAVIS AND JOSEPH HOLMES

LIBRARY OF CONGRESS CATALOGING IN PUBLICATION DATA
Davis, Norah Deakin, 1941-
The father of waters.
Includes index.
1. Mississippi River—Description and travel.
2. Stream ecology—Mississippi River.   3. Davis, Norah
Deakin, 1941-   I. Title
F355.D38   917.7'0433   82-3295
ISBN: 0-87156-318-5   AACR2

Book, case and jacket design by Paula Schlosser, San Francisco.

Printed by Dai Nippon Printing Company, Ltd., Tokyo, Japan.

10   9   8   7   6   5   4   3   2   1

To Dick

Who all his life has delighted in the mystery of living waters.

N.D.

CONTENTS

PREFACE

---◆---

To one who resides beside a river, its restless flowing can be as compelling as an eddy is for a piece of driftwood. A moving stream awakens the nomad in us. Its waters flow, as a riverboat captain once said, "out of the mystery above, into the mystery below." Who can watch the Mississippi without feeling the pull?

It took a year and a half of planning and organization to put our fifteen people afloat. The idea for a canoe expedition and history class on the Mississippi originated with two college teachers, Stephen Andersen and Robert Weyeneth, who describe themselves as obsessed with rivers and who outfit rafting trips when they're not in the classroom.

Dr. Stephen Andersen, who teaches resource economics at an environmental college, became interested in the Mississippi because it is an accessible river, and one that is free of the crowding that has led to reservation systems on some streams. Camping is easy on its many islands and sandbars. And its dams, unlike those on other long rivers in the lower forty-eight, do not require lengthy portages. With the dams on the Missouri, by contrast, the canoeist must arrange the complicated logistics of shuttles.

Steve Andersen was also intrigued by the Mississippi's role in our nation's economic history. No other American river has the Mississippi's historical breadth. The highway of our frontier witnessed the birth and coming of age of a nation. To travel our greatest river is to embark on a journey four centuries long. It was this voyage that lured the expedition's coleader, Bob Weyeneth, an historian. Together, Bob and Steve launched our expedition.

Many historical events, as Aldo Leopold has said, are biotic interactions between people and nature. The Mississippi's human story is partly explained by the facts of ecological history. It was that interplay between a nation and its river that would be my focus—the biography of the Mississippi. Just as the human part in that biography brought in Bob Weyeneth, the natural history attracted Dr. Barbara Gudmundson, a botanist and water-resources ecologist, who joined the trip along with her daughter, Marti, a college student. Barbara, who works as a consultant in Minneapolis, the northernmost city on the Mississippi, conducted a water-quality analysis down the length of the river.

Steve and Bob designed an interdisciplinary course on the river's natural history, its economic history, and, as Mark Twain says, its "historical history." It was an unusual course; field studies are common in subjects like geology and archaeology, but history and economics usually stay indoors. To make a floating classroom work for these subjects, the students who joined the expedition were required to do advance research on individual projects, such as the evolution of transportation on the Mississippi. During the voyage each student did a weekly presentation on the subject selected and led the class in visits to appropriate riverside attractions.

Many of the students came from states that border the Mississippi, such as Illinois and Minnesota. One student, Ellen Kleyman, grew up in St. Louis, which is also my hometown. Universities and colleges from both ends of the continent were represented, including College of the Atlantic in Maine, the school that sponsored the trip.

College of the Atlantic sent along a recent graduate, Alexandra Brown, who is a registered Maine guide. She supervised the preparation of the canoes and paddles, and she taught the expedition members the kneeling posture and rolling motion used by the voyageurs and present-day northwoods canoeists. The technique, which differs substantially from the arm paddling taught by the Red Cross, involves the whole body and thus allows greater power and longer paddling.

Steve and Bob selected three twenty-two-foot wood-and-canvas canoes built in New Brunswick, Canada. Such freighter canoes, though heavy on portages, are sufficiently seaworthy to take the waves produced by barges using the Mississippi. A kayak and a small canoe to provide space for visitors completed our flotilla.

The main group paddled from northern Minnesota to Hannibal—eleven hundred miles in sixty-seven days. Those who had the time, Barbara Gudmundson and five students, then continued downriver either as guests of a barge company or by working their way on the *Mississippi Queen*, sister boat to the *Delta Queen*—the steamboat that took President Carter on his 1979 river excursion.

While Barbara and the others went on by barge or steamboat, another student, Clint Schemmer, and the expedition photographer, Joseph Holmes, joined me on a more leisurely continuation of the journey. We did the next seven hundred miles by outboard—stopping wherever we pleased—then finished the final five hundred more quickly by barge and freighter. In the nineteenth century every imaginable kind of craft traveled the Mississippi: bullboats, flatboats, keelboats, steamboats. Today river traffic includes all the various vessels used by members of our expedition plus quite a few others, such as johnboats, houseboats, ferries, tugboats, and even rafts. I found as the speed of my craft increased, I experienced a feeling of increased distance from the river. Yet the power of the Mississippi is such that it can be sensed even aboard a ship. As our 893-foot freighter turned out of its berth at New Orleans, I could feel the great river's current swinging the ship as truly as the tiny stream twenty-three hundred miles to the north had spun our canoes.

Acknowledgments

———————————◆———————————

AMONG ALL THOSE WHO HELPED me travel the river, I wish to give special thanks to the members of the canoe expedition: Dr. Stephen O. Andersen, Robert R. Weyeneth, Jay Bickford, Alexandra Brown, Tina Green, Dr. Barbara Gudmundson, Marti Gudmundson, Joseph Holmes, Ellen Kleyman, Jeff McGuire, Nan Moyer, Rodd Pemble, Clinton H. Schemmer, Marianne Stam, and Hobson Woodward. As a riverman once observed, when you stay on a stream for a long time, you begin to see things in reverse. You exist on a continent of your own; you are stationary and the shores do the moving. You wonder, he said, when you step ashore which is the reality.

I am especially indebted to my colleagues at College of the Atlantic: Marcia H. Dorr and Marcia L. Dworak for library assistance; Penny E. Grover, Bernice M. Sylvester, and Laura E. Woolley for secretarial help; and Dr. William H. Drury, Dr. Susan Mehrtens, and Lucille J. Honig for their helpful comments on the manuscript. Susan Wight and Robert Woodward of Bangor Public Library also gave invaluable assistance. I cannot thank the many hundreds of people along the river individually, but I do want to mention Keith Larson and Don Rimbach for their generous help and to express my gratitude to the many members and officers of the Sierra Club who gave their time.

Norah Deakin Davis

I WOULD LIKE TO THANK the many people who helped make possible my journey down the Mississippi and the work you see here. The fifteen other members of the College of the Atlantic 1979 Mississippi River canoe expedition deserve more thanks than I can give for their amazing energy in a difficult undertaking. Special thanks are due to Stephen O. Andersen and Robert R. Weyeneth for their leadership down the river's upper half, and Katherine J. Patey for inspiration and assistance. Norah Davis and Clint Schemmer went on to provide critical assistance on the lower river. Many kind people along the entire river generously contributed what they could. The designer, Paula Schlosser, and the staff of Sierra Club Books also deserve thanks for their considerable efforts in bringing the work to its final form.

Joseph E. Holmes

The River

Down the Yellowstone, the Milk, the White and Cheyenne;
The Cannonball, the Musselshell, the James and the Sioux;
Down the Judith, the Grand, the Osage, and the Platte,
The Skunk, the Salt, the Black, and Minnesota;
Down the Rock, the Illinois, and the Kankakee
The Allegheny, the Monongahela, Kanawha, and Muskingum;
Down the Miami, the Wabash, the Licking and the Green,
The Cumberland, the Kentucky, and the Tennessee;
Down the Ouachita, the Wichita, the Red, and Yazoo—
Down the Missouri, three thousand miles from the Rockies;
    Down the Ohio, a thousand miles from the Alleghenies;
Down the Arkansas, fifteen hundred miles from the Great Divide;
    Down the Red, a thousand miles from Texas;
Down the great Valley, twenty-five hundred miles from Minnesota,
    Carrying every rivulet and brook, creek and rill,
Carrying all the rivers that run down two-thirds the continent—
    The Mississippi runs to the Gulf.

PARE LORENTZ, *THE RIVER,*
A NEW DEAL–ERA FILM ON FLOOD CONTROL

*I*N THE DAYS OF THE STEAMBOAT, the Mississippi River took on the proportions of a legend. The river that splices the nation together deserves its legendary character. It drains thirty-one states and two Canadian provinces. Its watershed, shaped like a huge funnel, stretches from the Alleghenies to the Rocky Mountains. Its 500 veins and capillaries reach to within 250 miles of the Atlantic Ocean and five hundred miles of the Pacific, making its drainage basin the fourth largest in the world.

Had America been explored from the west, the Mississippi might also have had the distinction of being the world's third longest river. If the explorers and fur traders had come from the Pacific coast, they would have met the Missouri before the upper Missis-

sippi and taken the former to be the main stem, giving us a considerably longer Missis-sippi than our present 2,322 miles.

That the upper Mississippi did come to be called the main branch is curious. The Ohio contributes more water, and the Missouri is longer, has more northerly headwaters, and supplies the famous café au lait color. The upper Mississippi may have won simply because of its central status. More likely it was a mere historical accident.

The Mississippi is nevertheless one of the longest rivers in the world, and also one of the deepest. Aboard a towboat on the lower river, I saw the depth finder register 440 feet. Yet more than the river's size, the legend of the Mississippi is based on its impact on the American soul. The river flows through our music and folklore, and it sings in the images of our painters and poets. For four centuries it has lured those who are inclined to set themselves adrift.

First came explorers seeking to learn what path the river takes and what country it sees. Then came gentlemen travelers filled with curiosity about river life, who returned home filled with praise for its scenery. Their accounts enticed wandering artists who hoped to capture that beauty and naturalists intent on surveying the flora and fauna. Always the Mississippi drew to itself those seeking their limits, or eager to feel the heart of the continent, or just yearning to flow.

Our Mississippi is a river to inspire poetry—about the wild rice marsh of the far north or the sunset at Natchez or the anhinga gliding over a Louisiana cypress. It is a river to inspire pride—a Midwesterner's satisfaction at living on the Mississippi, not some lesser stream like the Colorado or Hudson. And it is a river that demands respect—or should we say awe—for its enormous potential for destruction.

Death has always been a part of the river. We sent our settlers down the Mississippi on flatboats, to die of yellow fever and malaria. Our jazz was born in the agonies of Africans who gave their lives clearing canebrakes and planting sugarcane. Our nation learned shame in 1838 when the surviving Cherokees crossed the Father of Waters, banished for all time from their homeland. Mothers and children perished at Vicksburg as they sought refuge from the fusillade of the ironclads, hiding in caves in a bluff above the river. Those who traveled by steamboat died by the hundreds in boiler explosions, until the great "floating wedding cakes" were themselves done in—by the railroad. In World War I we turned again to the water highway, this time to move the materials of death. And in 1927 when the Mississippi raged out of its banks, hundreds of us drowned or starved.

After that, we walled it in with a thirty-foot-high levee twice as long as the Great Wall of China. When that was done, we tried to forget.

From bridges far above the river, we tossed careless glances at the water. We built suburbs with drive-in convenience and moved our towns back from the levee. Only the occasional fisherman knew of an overgrown dirt road to the water's edge. Now and then a boy from a small town in Iowa worked a stretch on the river as a deckhand. But otherwise we lived within a few miles of the great highway of our past and were scarcely conscious of its existence.

During three decades of light rainfall, a whole generation grew up in the Mississippi's floodplain with a merely abstract understanding of the river's strength. Even the U.S. Army Corps of Engineers became complacent, until in 1973 the Old Man reminded us of his existence with another granddaddy flood.

Then we began noticing. Where once had been deep water, now willows were growing. Where once had been sloughs filled with catfish, now there were mud flats. Where hardwoods draped with grapevines had sent their roots deep in the black alluvial soil, now soybeans marched in rows. Where yesterday we had feared to swim because of sewage, today we feared to swim because of carcinogens.

We have always taxed the river's tolerances. In less than three decades we stripped the forests from its northern banks. We mined iron ore from its upper reaches, coal and lead from its midsection, and oil and gas from its delta. We built levees so we could drain its swamps to grow our cotton. We turned its living waters into a series of impoundments, creating wetlands that we are now destroying with silt. Never has a river been so changed in such a brief moment of time.

The Mississippi River is an ecological microcosm of the entire continent. What we have done to one we have done to the other.

"MISSISSIPPI" IS A WORD, as Walt Whitman once said, that "rolls a stream three thousand miles long." It is one river, but it is also six. Traditionally the Mississippi has been divided—at Cairo, Illinois—into two, the upper river and the lower. Tradition aside, to journey today from the Minnesota headwaters to the Gulf of Mexico is to see six rivers: an infancy, an adolescence, a young adulthood, a ripe maturity, a senescence, and a final merging.

What is most surprising about all six sections is how wild the shores appear from a boat; the river is wilderness-like the entire way. The uppermost stretch, from the headwaters to the first village, is sixty miles of pristine stream in a country of cool Canadian

THE FALLS OF ST. ANTHONY, 1853

forests and glacial lakes. This segment is a candidate for federal wilderness designation. Environmentalists are also seeking wild and scenic status for the next section, the 427 miles down to Minneapolis. Here forested country inhabited by Chippewa Indians opens onto an occasional pasture, grazed by the cows of farmers with names like Svenson and Olsen. In these infant and adolescent stages, the Mississippi flows through several lakes and drops 700 feet.

Only below Minneapolis and St. Paul does the water become deep enough for large boats and commercial barge traffic. A system of dams maintains navigable depth. From here to St. Louis, the first big tributaries enter: the Minnesota, Des Moines, and Missouri from the west, and the St. Croix, Chippewa, Wisconsin, and Illinois from the east. Rich prairie farms, owned by families of German ancestry, produce corn and soybeans. The scenic sloughs and islands of the Upper Mississippi River Wild Life and Fish Refuge stretch along 284 miles of this section. Its sandbars and wooded bluffs are among the most beautiful river scenery in the world.

The bluffs continue below St. Louis, but after the Missouri bootheel—the protuberance on the southeast corner of the state—the river wanders in giant loops through flat lowlands. The only plateaus in this fourth section are at Memphis and Vicksburg. Though the channel is heavily used by barges, the river feels lonesome and remote. The occasional town is hidden behind woods or grassy levees, as are the cotton, soybeans, and rice grown by descendants of the original Anglo-Saxon settlers. The Kaskaskia, Ohio, Hatchie, and Yazoo enter from the east, and on the west the Meramec, St. Francis, and

Arkansas are tributaries, while the Atchafalaya is a major distributary, draining a large portion of the water of the Mississippi in an independent route to the sea.

At Baton Rouge, where French influence begins to predominate, the industrial river commences and continues nearly to the gulf. The contrasts along this brief stretch are startling: groves of orange trees and live oaks nestle among chemical plants and oil refineries. From Baton Rouge on down, the Mississippi is deep enough for ocean-going ships.

At the very end, the river breaks free from the stench of refineries and enters a remote wilderness of salt marshes, visited only by fishermen, rangers, and fur trappers. The channel forks, dividing into several "passes" or branches that conduct it through the tall grasses to the sea. Here and there on the mud flats an oil rig stands silent as great flocks of snow geese swirl around it.

The Mississippi, in its journey to the sea, flows through ten states with a population of forty million people. It touches upon cultures as disparate as that of the Finnish farmer of Minnesota and the Cajun trapper of Louisiana. It starts in a climate where winter temperatures plunge to forty below. It ends in the subtropics where rainfall averages sixty inches a year. When Christmas oranges are being harvested in New Orleans, wintergreen berries are already buried beneath two feet of snow in Minnesota. The geology, the flora, the fauna, and the human impact are each distinctive from one region to the next on this big river. It was this rich diversity that we came to see.

THE TRUE AGE OF THE MISSISSIPPI is shrouded by thousands of centuries of erosion. We do know that four hundred million years ago the Mississippi Valley lay silent beneath a Paleozoic sea. Sediment eroded from ancient continents accumulated on that ocean floor, compressing to create dolomite, limestone, sandstone, and shale. Beneath the Paleozoic waters the sedimentary bedrock of the valley formed.

Down through the ages the sea rose and fell many times. As the shallow water came and went, the mineral riches of the Mississippi Valley accumulated—vast deposits of iron, lead, and oil. During the early Mesozoic the continent was uplifted again, exposing the bedrock to the forces of erosion. Millions of years passed while the sandstone and limestone weathered to form the bluffs that line the upper river. At the same time, the vegetation in the valley's bogs was decaying into peat and coal.

Ancient segments of the Mississippi flowed in the same general region as they do today, but the present course was not established until the last of the glaciers retreated. The ice came many times. A million and a half years ago, a mere moment, the Nebraskan ice sheet flowed down out of Canada to be followed by the Kansan, the Illinoian, and most recently, the Wisconsin glaciations. Walls of ice two miles thick advanced as far south as Missouri.

Each time the ice came, the water level in the ocean was lowered hundreds of feet. As the eternal cold gripped the upper half of the Mississippi Valley, the shallow sea that covered the lower valley departed. The land was left exposed, and rainwater began the work of "ironing flat . . . the wrinkled fabric of the earth." An extensive drainage system formed, with the Mississippi collecting all the waters from many rivers and streams. As the Mississippi adjusted to its lowered outlet, it cut a deeply entrenched bed. The entrenchment followed the Mississippi Embayment, a structural trough in the bedrock formed by downwarping and slipping of the plates of the earth's crust.

During interglacial periods, melting water raised the sea level and water poured up the entrenched riverbed from the south. Greatly shortened, the Mississippi deposited its sediment load and built up its bed to adjust to the higher base level of the outlet. The river developed a meandering course, winding sinuously through thick deposits of sediment.

A cyclical pattern of valley entrenchment and valley filling was established. The Mississippi Embayment was eroded by the river during times of low sea level, and covered with alluvial deposits when the sea was high. And as the ice sheets came and went, tectonic activity was complicating the geologic story. Uplift raised the alluvial deposits, creating terraces that became the walls of the next entrenchment. Today the lower valley has four terraces, representing four former floodplains.

While the glaciers were altering the lower Mississippi by changing the sea level, to the north the grinding ice was eroding and flattening the land. Each time the climate warmed, meltwater poured from the retreating glacier. The glacial torrent, far larger than today's river, scoured a trench eight hundred feet deep. The present course of the Mississippi follows the valley of that ancient glacial river. The meltwater also left behind thick deposits of glacial drift—terraces of coarse sand and gravel. Layers of windblown silt, or loess, were deposited on adjacent uplands.

In its uppermost reaches, the Mississippi exhibits the unintegrated drainage of a river system recently released from glaciation. The river has not had enough time to develop a systematic, branching network of tributaries. It wanders from basin to basin, in and out of swamps and "kettle" lakes. Kettle or pit lakes result when a glacier leaves behind an immense block of ice. The block melts slowly, leaving a hole as the surrounding terrain fills with drift.

When the river reaches southwestern Wisconsin, it flows for a time through the so-called "driftless" area. This is a pocket of land that lacks almost all direct topographical effects of glaciation. It is thought to have been spared because it lies to the lee of a highland that blocked the southward movement of ice.

By the time the Mississippi enters Illinois and Iowa, it is sweeping through fertile black soil formed on relatively unweathered glacial till. The early settlers were drawn to this rich farmland. Thus our population patterns, like the land, were shaped by a glacier that retreated ten thousand years ago. South of the terminal moraine that marks the end of recent glaciation, the soil is gray clay. It is less productive because more time has elapsed since the ground was glaciated, and so it has had deep weathering.

In Missouri, the Mississippi reaches the land of limestone caverns. Though St. Paul has a number of caves, the climax of the underground realm comes between Hannibal and St. Louis. Caves like the one that Twain made famous were formed by groundwater carrying carbon dioxide and organic acids, which dissolved the limestone along its fracture lines. Cape Girardeau in southern Missouri marks the end of the bluffs and the beginning of a floodplain of enormous extent, ranging from 25 miles wide near Natchez to 125 miles at Helena, Arkansas. During the Pleistocene the Mississippi flowed down the western edge of its valley, on the far side of Crowley's Ridge in Arkansas. The Ohio River paralleled it down the east side, refusing to join the Mississippi until they both reached northern Louisiana. Today they merge near Cairo in southern Illinois.

Here begins the restless river, the river that is continually creating sandbars and then changing its mind and taking them away, arranging and rearranging its furniture. Floating driftwood lodges on a shoal in mid-channel and before long a towhead—or sandbar—forms, which soon becomes an island. Next year the island is gone. A mudbank caves in and joins the turbid waters, only to settle out in some quiet backwater. Churning eddies swirl against the banks, and the floodwaters dig canyons in the river bottom, carrying the silt until it lodges against a snag or an old boat wreck. The ceaseless waves chew at the shores, tugging at clam shells and setting driftwood afloat to follow the fate of the river.

Always the Mississippi changes its mind. It wanders back and forth across the alluvial deposits, its meanders growing into enormous loops. The two sides of a meander loop draw closer and closer, forming a narrow neck. Suddenly the river slices through, abandoning miles of riverbed. The former bed becomes a landlocked oxbow lake. Man, disregarding the river's decision, says that though the Mississippi acts capriciously, the law does not—boundaries stay where they were. So a Tennessee farmer finds his land on the Arkansas side, but he still votes and pays taxes in Tennessee.

In geologic terms, the Mississippi's delta begins at the junction with the Atchafalaya River, well north of Baton Rouge in Louisiana. Over time the Mississippi has shifted its route to the sea, choosing new distributaries and building new deltaic lobes. In the early 1950s, the U.S. Army Corps of Engineers began a battle to prevent the Mississippi from abandoning its present course and selecting the Atchafalaya as its new exit. If the engineers fail, Baton Rouge and New Orleans will be left without a river. The geologic story of the Mississippi is far from over.

ONE

Sources

Itasca to Bemidji

Quest of the Waters

ON COMING TO the head of these falls, we appear to have reached a vast geological plateau, consisting of horizontal deposits of clay and drift on the nucleus of granitical and metamorphic rocks, which underlie the sources of the Mississippi River. The vast and irregular bodies of water called Leech Lake, Winnipek, and Cass Lakes, together with a thousand lesser lakes of a mile or two in circumference, lie on this great diluvial summit.

HENRY ROWE SCHOOLCRAFT, 1820,
AT POKEGAMA FALLS

*T*HE MISSISSIPPI BEGINS its quest for the Gulf of Mexico from Lake Itasca, a small lake in Minnesota a hundred miles from the Canadian border. The lake is cupped in low hills sprinkled with ponds and marshes. The surrounding country is a plateau that forms a principal continental divide. From here water flows in three directions: north to Hudson Bay, east to the Great Lakes, and south to the Gulf of Mexico.

Long and thin, Lake Itasca has three prongs that reminded the Chippewa of antlers, so they called the lake Omoskos Sogiagon, or Elk Lake. Henry Schoolcraft, the explorer who determined it was the source of the Mississippi, renamed it Lake Itasca by taking three syllables out of *Veritas Caput* [*sic*], Latin for "true head."

The infant river flows out of the northernmost prong. A drop of water that starts its journey at the outlet will reach the ocean in sixty days. Every year thousands of visitors come to the state park at Itasca to see the headwaters. Most cannot resist stepping across the tiny stream, on stones that were placed for the purpose. To cross the mighty Mississippi takes only six paces.

Three centuries passed between the discovery of the mouth of the Mississippi at the gulf and the location of its source in the Minnesota wilderness. A succession of explorers searched for the headwaters, but the source remained a mystery for decades, hidden in northern Minnesota's labyrinth of lakes and marshes. New Orleans and St. Louis were founded and grew into cities while miles to the north the Chippewa hunter still paddled his canoe through unmapped forests.

Lieutenant Zebulon Montgomery Pike, the first to search, was sent by the United States Army to explore the upper Mississippi. More famous today for his explorations in the west, in his day Pike was equally well known for his expedition in search of the Mississippi's headwaters. The trip took place in 1805 right after the Louisiana Purchase and Lewis and Clark's epic voyage up the Missouri River. Pike's orders included mapping the course of the river, procuring mineral and plant specimens, selecting fort sites, and establishing contact with the Indians.

For a journey into territory that was virtually unknown, the expedition was a hastily planned effort. After only a month of preparation, the lieutenant set out by boat from St. Louis with twenty soldiers. It never occurred to Pike to hire an interpreter, and he knew little of the upper Mississippi's rapids or the climate. The exploring party started late in the season, in August, and was heavily laden. Their vessel was a seventy-foot keelboat, loaded with barrels of flour and pork. The heavy boat had to be rowed and dragged laboriously upstream.

ZEBULON
MONTGOMERY
PIKE

By Pike's account they made forty miles a day, a highly unlikely average, but perhaps they were helped upriver by the wind that persistently blows out of the south. Yet the expedition was soon behind schedule. To replenish their supplies Pike often left the boat to hunt game. On one occasion his two favorite hunting dogs disappeared on the prairie, and he left two soldiers behind to search for them, assuming the men would catch up by nightfall. Nearly a week later the two men still had not appeared. A French Canadian fur trapper found them struggling to make their way along the bank; for six days they had lived off raw river mussels and tried to overtake the keelboat. The trapper paddled them upstream to rejoin the others.

Six weeks went by in the grueling trip upriver. At a fur post called Prairie du Chien, Pike abandoned the heavy keelboat for more sensible craft, small flat-bottomed boats called bateaux. When the expedition left the post, it was entering the relatively unknown upper reaches of the river, and Pike was in a race with winter. He was eager to find the headwaters, and his stamina was phenomenal. He pushed himself and his men so hard that his sergeant broke a blood vessel and vomited two quarts of blood. At this point, the expedition stopped to construct a fort to shelter the sergeant and other invalids. Pike ordered the men to build canoes and pushed on with a final assault team.

As they struggled upriver, the snows came, and game was scarce. The river froze. Pike had sleds built and kept going. Hunters sent out to find food became exhausted in the deep snow and suffered from frostbite. But once again trappers familiar with the country came to Pike's rescue, feeding the half-starved expedition and showing them how to make snowshoes.

In the end, Pike wound up at the wrong lake, far from the real source, but his failure is understandable. The runoff of surface waters in northern Minnesota is complicated, and in winter the topography is hidden beneath ice and snow. Certain that he had found the source, Pike moved back to the fort he had built and waited for the spring thaw. By the time the expedition returned to St. Louis, it had been gone nearly nine months.

LAKE ITASCA, 1853

The next to search for the headwaters was Lewis Cass, governor of the territory of Michigan. In 1820 Governor Cass organized a party of forty, which paddled large freighter canoes and penetrated as far as what is today called Cass Lake, a hundred miles below Itasca. Indians told Cass of Elk Lake, Omoskos Sogiagon, but said the water ahead was too shallow for large canoes. The governor contented himself with Cass Lake.

The next to enter the ranks of Mississippi explorers was one of the most flamboyant characters in American history, Giacomo Costantino Beltrami. In 1821 when he was 42, Beltrami was exiled from Venice as a suspected conspirator in the plots for a separate Italian kingdom. He left his estates to become a gentleman traveler. A classicist, he took in the antiquities of Europe, then in 1823 came to the United States. On a whim he decided to take passage on the *Virginia,* the first steamboat to ascend the upper Mississippi.

During the voyage, each time the captain of the *Virginia* stopped to take on wood or negotiate rapids Beltrami had time to go ashore. On one occasion he wandered into the forest on the trail of wild turkeys. He became lost but used his compass to return to the river. By then the steamboat had gone on and was nowhere to be seen. Beltrami rushed along the bank, firing his gun. To his relief, he found the *Virginia* around the first bend, aground on a sandbar.

At the end of May the boat arrived at the Falls of St. Anthony, the present site of Minneapolis. An army post, Fort Snelling, had been established at the falls, and Beltrami stayed at the fort until by chance an American expedition under Major Stephen H. Long arrived. The major was commissioned to survey the border between Canada and the

BELTRAMI

United States. Beltrami attached himself to the expedition, although against the major's better judgment.

On July 7 they started on horseback up the banks of the Minnesota River, a tributary that enters at Minneapolis. As the expedition turned west, the Italian and the major formed a dislike for each other. Beltrami thought Maj. Long stupid and the major thought Beltrami frivolous. The Italian decided to separate from the expedition and go off on his own.

Aware of the Cass and Pike expeditions, Beltrami hit on searching for the headwaters of the Mississippi. Undaunted by the wilderness, he hired an interpreter and two Chippewas to accompany him north up the Red Lake River by canoe. The current of the Red was strong, and there were many rapids. The interpreter soon turned back.

On August 14 the little party was ambushed by Sioux, who fled when they saw a white man. Beltrami's Chippewa guides, one of them wounded, refused to continue. They tried to persuade the Italian to follow them into the woods, taking a land route to avoid the Sioux. The self-styled explorer was reluctant to leave his canoe and provisions, not to mention his musket, ammunition, and sword. He went on by himself.

> But I was totally unacquainted with the almost magical art by which a single person guides a canoe, and particularly a canoe formed of bark, the lightness of which is overpowered by the current. . . . Frequently, instead of proceeding up the river, I descended . . . Renewed efforts made me lose my equilibrium, the canoe upset.

Beltrami retrieved his canoe and gear and proceeded on his way by wading, drawing the canoe behind him with a thong of buffalo hide. In water up to his waist, the Italian found himself enjoying the adventure—the solitude and feeling of independence.

That night his gear and clothing were soaked and he had no flint to light a fire. By morning his clothes were still wet, but it was alright because soon, the intrepid explorer tells us, a storm came up anyway. The rain continued until nightfall. The following day his baggage was becoming moldy from the incessant soakings, so Beltrami unpacked a red silk umbrella and rigged it up to cover the gear. The determined Italian, far from home, waded on.

Luckily, two days later he met with some Chippewa paddling downriver. The Indians were dumbfounded by the vision of a white man walking in the water. The "great red skin" puzzled them. By sign language, Beltrami persuaded one of them to paddle him to Red Lake.

The Indian left him there in the care of a Chippewa family. They obligingly found a half-breed to guide him to the source of the Mississippi. The half-breed mistakenly took Beltrami to a small, heart-shaped lake—not the antler-shaped Elk Lake that would later be called Itasca. Delirious with imagined success, Beltrami named his discovery Lake Julia and hurried downstream, bestowing a name on every pond he encountered. Finally reaching the Mississippi and supposing he had been up the main branch, Beltrami continued his triumphant descent accompanied in his mind by the shades of Marco Polo, Columbus, and Amerigo Vespucci. At Fort Snelling he booked passage on a steamboat to New Orleans and became at any rate the first man to travel virtually the whole length of the Mississippi.

After Pike and Beltrami, the actual discovery of the source was an anticlimax. The mineralogist on the 1820 Cass expedition, Henry Rowe Schoolcraft, had stared longingly at the channel that flowed into Cass Lake, meandering through the cattails and wild rice savannas. He had vowed to return.

Compared to the earlier explorations, the Schoolcraft expedition of 1832 was sedate and serene. Funded by the government for the ostensible purposes of settling intertribal conflicts and vaccinating the Indians against smallpox, the expedition was large and included a military escort. Canoeing from Sault Ste. Marie, the group reached Cass Lake on July 10. At that point a smaller detachment of five canoes, each with one gentleman as passenger and two paddlers, continued the journey. They were guided by a Chippewa chief, Ozawindib, and carried provisions for ten days.

They reached Itasca in three, raised an American flag, fired a volley, named the lake, and paddled back downstream. In their story, the most troublesome problem encountered was finding enough dry ground for a camp, reminding me of times members of our canoe expedition stepped into mud a foot deep or became trapped in stinging nettles. Inconvenient, but undramatic.

During the next fifty years Itasca was seldom visited, the only whites to see it being the occasional surveyor and missionary. In 1881 an adventurer exploring the region found a lake above Itasca he claimed was the true source, and for years a controversy raged. It was finally determined that the lakes in the area are interconnected by underground seepages and springs, and that the ultimate source is the basin as a whole. But the waters do not join to become an infant river until they flow out of Lake Itasca.

HENRY R. SCHOOLCRAFT

Even before the controversy was settled, the shores of the lake began to hear the ring of the ax. First came timber cruisers, those hired to scout the woods for usable timber, then a wagon road was built and "settlers" began to stake out fraudulent homestead claims, which they immediately sold to the lumber companies.

In October of 1888 Jacob V. Brower, a lawyer and historian, was sent by the Minnesota Historical Society to map the headwaters and determine the actual source once and for all. The lake was still remote and wild, a hundred miles from the nearest railroad and thirty from the nearest frontier town. Brower camped at Itasca for five months, surveying and drawing maps. Out of this work grew his idea of preserving the Mississippi's headwaters. The turn of the century would see the emergence of the conservation movement and growing interest in setting aside parks. Lake Itasca lies near an ecological interface, the boundary between the conifer and prairie communities; early promoters of the headwaters park recognized the importance of preserving this ecotone of forest and grassland.

For years Jacob Brower kept the idea alive at his own expense. In 1891 a bill to establish Itasca State Park was introduced to the legislature, but it was opposed by lumber interests who managed to tack on a crippling amendment specifying that the allocation of a salary for a park commissioner would run out in sixty days. The opponents underestimated Brower. He promptly took on the job himself and, when the salary ended, continued to work without pay.

Itasca State Park existed, however, only on paper. Commissioner Brower's first step was to acquire the federal lands that lay within the proposed boundaries. By 1894 the park consisted of 10,879 acres, but that was only one-third its eventual acreage. Brower tried in vain to secure the private holdings of lumbermen such as John Pillsbury, Thomas B. Walker, and Frederick Weyerhaeuser. In 1895 he was replaced by a political appointee, and he was never reimbursed for his four years of service.

HON. J. V. BROWER

Brower devoted the final years of his life to an attempt to halt lumbering in the park. He was opposed by the state's attorney general, who stated publicly that purchase of standing pine in Itasca to preserve it "would be an idle waste of money." This fight Brower lost. Roads were soon constructed to get the pine out, and a logging dam was built just downstream of Itasca, flooding out the timber on the shores of the lake.

In the meantime, the park's new commissioner died, and his daughter, Mary Gibbs, took over as acting superintendent. In one of the most heroic acts of the early days of conservation, Mary attempted to open the gates of the dam to lower the water level and save the timber, while a logging foreman stood by threatening to shoot her. She did raise the gates, but the company later took her to court and obtained an injunction ordering her not to interfere.

The battle to halt the lumbering was over for good once Samuel R. Van Sant was inaugurated as governor of the state. Van Sant was one of the largest shippers of logs in Minnesota, the state's third governor to be directly engaged in the logging business. Free to do as they pleased in Itasca, the lumbermen increased the height of the dam, built sluiceways, and scraped out and straightened the tiny Mississippi. Large-scale logging continued until 1919, when the last cutting was completed. Only then was the private land within the established park boundaries relinquished, the land denuded of trees and piled with slash.

TODAY PARTS OF ITASCA State Park are highly developed. Paved roads lead to a research station, a museum, and an inn. The night we arrived we heard a loon call, but the bird we heard was not breeding. The Common Loon, Minnesota's state bird, has not successfully nested on Lake Itasca in years. Disturbance by fishing boats is probably responsible.

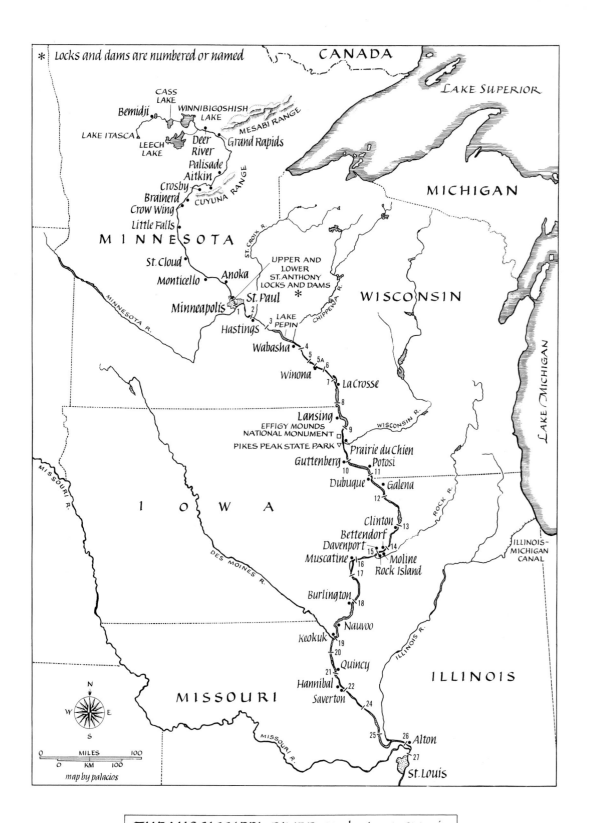

THE MISSISSIPPI RIVER: Headwaters to St. Louis

Still, most of the park remains wild. Young loons do grow to maturity on the lake, and such rare birds as the Arctic three-toed woodpecker nest in the tall pines—the ones that escaped the ax. The towering Norway pines in Preachers Grove, named after a religious convention that camped there, started their lives in 1714. And moose and even timber wolves, though not residents, travel through Itasca. The day before we started downriver, we caught sight of a black bear and watched a bald eagle feeding on a fish. The eagle was perched on a beaver lodge.

When we arrived in early June, the ice had "gone out"—broken up—less than a month before, so the aspen were in their spring green. The new birch leaves were nearly white. Once we portaged around the stepping-stones at the outflow and started down the fledgling Mississippi, we paddled back through time. The stream is hardly changed from Jacob Brower's day.

Even when the water is high, it is a shallow creek. We were forced to wade the first mile, towing the canoes behind us. The stream twisted and turned beneath overhanging alders, its water clear enough to see the sand and pebbles on the bottom. At times the banks closed in to no more than six feet apart, and our big canoes could barely manage the turns.

We had started out at noon. During the course of the afternoon we portaged around a couple of old wooden bridges and four beaver dams. We passed a cabin or two, someone's summer camp, and before long entered an open marsh where the creek meandered so much that you looked across grass to see the heads of the people in the front canoe. The silent heads glided over the grass, seemingly disembodied.

Since we had made a late start, we camped the first night at Wanagan Landing a short distance below Itasca. Along the sixty-mile stretch from the state park to the town of Bemidji are five designated campsites, each a grassy field with a fireplace, a table, an outhouse, and a pump for drinking water. (We carried water containers and a purifying kit but had no need of them until the Mississippi grew into a river.) The campsites are marked on canoeing maps provided by the state. The riverbank at Wanagan Landing was muddy and infested with leeches, but the campsite was crowned by a fairyland knoll of jack pine. That night we had a full moon, and ice crystals formed outside my tent.

In this first stretch, sometimes the valley would narrow so that tamarack and black spruce grew right to the river's edge; other times the floodplain, carved thousands of years ago by a glacial stream, would broaden into sedge marshes. Red-winged blackbirds flitted through the willow thickets and great blue herons flew low over the canoes. Once we floated directly beneath a great horned owl and his mate, who blinked down at us and swiveled their heads as we tried to glide by with silent paddles. Another time we saw a deer standing motionless beside a sod hut built into a hillside. Meanwhile the first tributary of note, La Salle River, entered on the right. All this time we were paddling north. The river takes a hundred miles to decide to head to the Gulf of Mexico.

As we approached the first town, Bemidji, we passed an occasional farm. In the final stretch before town, we entered a swamp where the basswood and ash leaned low over the water, and the current was very swift. Sharp bends concealed fallen trees that blocked the channel. It was as dangerous as any water I have seen in my years of whitewater canoeing. Our canoes would smack into the trees and stay there, pinned.

We took a layover day in Bemidji to reorganize after the sixty-mile shakedown. We shellacked our wood-and-canvas canoes where they were abraded from rocks, restocked our wicker pack baskets with food, and rid ourselves of all excess gear. Our big freighter canoes were then less cramped, though still carrying four or even five people each plus waterproof bags and ammunition boxes for cameras and other delicate items. Even after merciless jettisoning, for the next thousand miles each paddler, kneeling, would be crammed into a space two feet by two feet.

A few months before I had watched our canoes being made in a factory in Canada. The company that constructed ours has been building wood-and-canvas canoes since 1897. In the early days, the Hudson's Bay Company bought all the factory could produce; today it's mostly big freighters that go up north to James Bay and the Arctic. White cedar ribs are steamed in a pressure cooker to make them pliable, then shaped over a wooden form. Cedar planking is nailed to the ribs and covered with a skin of canvas treated with waterproofing. After being painted, the canoes are packed for shipping in hay wrapped with burlap.

They had brought us sixty miles. Now they would carry us another thousand.

Facing page: *Pond, Itasca State Park, Minnesota.*

Fungus, Itasca State Park.

Mossy Stones, Lake Itasca.

Canoe paddle in the headwaters.

The first portage, above Bemidji, Minnesota.

Pond below Grand Rapids.

Reeds in the river, near Bemidji.

Sunrise on the river, near Grand Rapids.

Riverbank below Grand Rapids, Minnesota.

TWO

Childhood's End

Bemidji to the Twin Cities

Dusk at Crow Wing

In the Sky
I am walking,
A Bird
I accompany.

OJIBWE
DREAM
SONG

*T*HE SURFACE GLOWED FAINTLY without color; the peepers and crickets were almost too loud. Reflections of trees along the shore became shadows of shadows. The wind rippled the water in patches, confusing the eyes into imagining shallows ahead. Looking back for the other canoes, I could almost find the almost-seen shapes that inhabit the darkness behind us.

That evening at twilight Alexandra Brown, who had taught us the northwoods paddle stroke, invited me for a stroll. She and I knew little of the place where we were camped except that it was a state park commemorating an Indian village.

We walked away from the woods where our tents were pitched, and turned downstream. We came to a hilly meadow overlooking a long stretch of the Mississippi at its confluence with the Crow Wing River. Tall, bushy spruce fringed the field. Red pines were scattered here and there, showing the long candlesticks of new growth. In the gathering dark we could make out markers indicating where the Ojibwe encampment had stood.

Sunken depressions in the ground outlined the shapes of a fur trading post, a storeroom for furs, and a few cabins. Here had been a schoolhouse, there—a hole partly filled with dirt and overgrown with grass—the settlement's well. Digging there, said Alexandra, who likes old tools, would likely yield generations of pocket knives, lost as their owners whiled away the time. The Mississippi flows swiftly at Crow Wing, and its silence echoed that of the village. Here the past was passing still.

In the dark we walked with later settlers along an ox cart trail that led to a ford across the Mississippi. But then we backtracked to an overlook where we were back with the Ojibwe braves keeping watch through the trees for approaching Sioux. In shallow holes the Ojibwe lay and fired down at the canoes of their enemies.

FAR DIMMER WERE the ancestors of the Ojibwe, the shadowy ones who crept into the forests that were newly emerging as the ice sheet retreated. These Pleistocene hunters stalked the mammoth and great bison, hurling spears tipped with fluted points. Some say the fluted-spear people were the continent's first exploiters, the first to radically change the environment. They are believed to have burned off whole forests to expand the grasslands and improve their hunting. And these Paleo-Indians of the Pleistocene were probably the first to accomplish species extinctions. The mammoth and mastodon could have died out as a result of habitat loss caused by the violent climatic changes at the close of the Ice Age. But it is likely that the Pleistocene hunter helped escort the elephantine mammals to their end.

The generations that came after the big-game hunters found the meat supply dwindling. They hunted deer and small game, and turned to gathering shellfish and wild plants. These people of the "Archaic Period" knew how to shape pottery and employed copper tools. Along the upper Mississippi the Indians of this early period flourished from about seven thousand to three thousand years ago. An Archaic site has been discovered at Itasca. The site is known to be early Archaic because it contains bones of the *Bison occidentalis,* the great bison stalked by the big-game hunters. One of the oldest domesticated-dog skulls in North America was found at the same site.

WITHIN HISTORICAL TIMES, the region now called Minnesota was disputed by the Ojibwe (corrupted into "Chippewa" by Europeans) and the Santee Dakota, or Sioux. Living too far north for significant agriculture, these two tribes were nomadic hunters mainly dependent on the white-tail deer and buffalo, although they also gathered maple sugar and wild rice. The Ojibwe had been among the tribes pressured by the whites into westward migration, and they in turn were fighting the Sioux for living space. The battle at the Ojibwe camp of Crow Wing in 1768 was a decisive defeat for the Santee Sioux.

Crow Wing saw fur trading activity as early as 1771 when a British trader wintered at the mouth of the Crow Wing River. By then, France had been defeated in the French and Indian War, and had ceded its colonial possessions to Britain. Control of the fur trade had passed into British hands. The French traders, or *coureurs de bois,* had cleared no forests and had plowed no soil. But if their impact on the land was light, their effect on its

INDIAN SUGAR CAMP

people and animals was not. They had seduced the Indian into depending on European trade goods—guns, knives, blankets, and whiskey—and had taught him to strip the river of its furbearers rather than to harvest only enough for the immediate need.

The British followed the lead of the French, encouraging the Indians' taste for whiskey to ensure a continuing flow of beaver pelts. One British trader, Duncan McGillivray, was candid about the policies of his employer, the North West Company: "When a Nation becomes addicted to drinking, it affords a strong presumption that they will become excellent hunters—in order to satisfy their craving."

Along the upper Mississippi, British control of the trade lasted only a few decades. Following the American Revolution, the United States took over British possessions east of the Mississippi, and after the Louisiana Purchase, the territory west of the river. One purpose of the Pike expedition in 1805 was to establish American authority over the fur traffic, but it was some time before the North West Company relinquished its trade dominance to the American Fur Company.

Lieutenant Pike visited three British posts, including the headquarters of the North West Company's Fond du Lac Department. In his report Pike noted that the department

HUDSON'S BAY COMPANY EMPLOYEES

employed three accountants, nineteen clerks, two interpreters, and eighty-five canoemen. He also mentioned twenty-nine Indian women and fifty children "belonging to the Establishment." In the report, Pike estimated that the Fond du Lac Department sent out forty canoe-loads of furs a year. The furs were taken up tributaries to the Great Lakes and transferred to freight canoes that carried up to fourteen men and a payload of three tons.

Although the French traders, the *coureurs de bois,* had been replaced by British agents, French Canadian voyageurs still paddled the canoes, their muscle and skill responsible for taking the birchbark craft up foaming rapids and across windy lakes. The voyageurs endured great physical hardships. The company employed small men, about five and a half feet tall, small so as not to take up cargo space. On portages each voyageur often carried two ninety-pound loads, at a dog trot. Not surprisingly, back trouble and hernias were common complaints. The voyageur wore a colorful sash at the waist to give support during portages. He also wore sashes below the knees to stop mosquitoes and ticks from crawling up his legs. During portages these sashes were tied higher to keep the kneecaps from popping out of place.

Pike gave a description of one of the British posts he visited. It was surrounded by a square stockade that contained the agent's residence, the men's quarters, a storehouse, and a combination workshop, store, and clerk's room. Outside the stockade was a four-acre garden where the British grew four hundred bushels of potatoes a year. Potatoes were the only vegetable grown.

Pike found the Indians supplying the British with a varied repertoire of furs: beaver, bear, badger, deer, fox, fisher, lynx, marten, mink, otter, raccoon, and muskrat. In turn the British stocked a wide assortment of trade goods: blankets, cloth, gunpowder and shot, tobacco, beaver traps, axes, guns, knives. An archaeological dig at a fur post on the Snake River, which feeds into the St. Croix and then into the Mississippi, has supplied evidence that the company store also carried kettles, buttons, needles, soap, and jewelry. The Snake River post was a part of the Fond du Lac Department. It was a small post used only one season, during the winter of 1804–1805. It has been faithfully reconstructed by the Minnesota Historical Society.

The North West Company established its farthest upriver posts at Lake Bemidji and Cass Lake—sixty miles and a hundred miles downriver from Itasca. By 1823 the American Fur Company had opened a post near Lake Winnibigoshish, the northernmost point the Mississippi reaches. That same year, it may have established a post at Crow Wing. But within a couple of decades, the fur trade began to decline. By then, the Ojibwe village and fur post at Crow Wing had developed into a town, an outfitting center serving ox cart trains on the Woods-Red River Trail, which crossed the Mississippi at Crow Wing. By the 1860s, the town had a population of six hundred and boasted better than thirty buildings. But in 1871, Crow Wing was bypassed by the railroad, spelling its doom.

It was in the 1860s, while Crow Wing was still thriving, that the long war between the Ojibwe and the Sioux finally came to an end, as both tribes gave way before the flood of white settlement. In 1862 massacres of hundreds of settlers by the Sioux resulted in the Sioux's removal from Minnesota. During the same period the Ojibwe ceded their lands to the government and were concentrated into the Leech Lake Reservation, which takes in two lakes the Mississippi flows through—Cass and Winnibigoshish—as well as Leech Lake. As late as 1898, the Leech Lake Reservation was the site of an uprising, one of the last recorded battles between Indians and United States troops.

Today nearly five thousand Ojibwe—Chippewa—live on the reservation. As it was for their ancestors, wild rice is an important part of their economy. *Zizania aquatica,* abundant in the shallow lakes through which the Mississippi flows, sprouts in late April from seeds that settled into the mud the previous autumn. Beneath the water the leaves bud out in mid-May; the submerged stem develops, and the grass-like plant reaches the surface by early June. Once the wild rice grows a foot or two above the water, spikelets develop that carry the staminate and pistillate. Within three weeks after pollination the seeds develop and, once ripe, detach easily from the stem. If unharvested, they fall to the lake bottom.

The month of August was known as the rice moon, for it was the time of ripening. The kernels mature at different rates, so a stand was picked lightly every day or two over a period of weeks. An Indian and his wife harvested together, the man poling a canoe gently through the tall grass of the rice stand. The woman sat holding a short stick in each

GATHERING WILD RICE

hand. With one stick she bent the stalks, and with the other she knocked the ripe kernels into the canoe.

Today the Indians use the same technique, although sometimes, like one Chippewa couple I met, the woman poles and the man uses the ricing sticks. Alice Hill's pole is a handmade "duckbill" pole that ends in a Y for getting a purchase in the mud. Her brother, Phillip Ellis, uses white cedar sticks with sharpened points, thirty inches long by an inch in diameter, the size being set by law. While Alice keeps the canoe moving slowly, Phillip hits the rice twice, once to loosen the kernels and once to make them fall. The movement is rhythmic, and they stop occasionally to smoke a cigarette and chat.

In the old days, when the canoe was full the couple put ashore and the rice was spread to dry on birchbark mats. Then it was parched in an iron kettle to loosen the husks. In a shallow hole lined with deerskin, an Indian tread on the kernels to remove the hulls. He held two poles tied to a sapling to steady himself. Finally the grain was poured slowly back and forth between birchbark winnowing trays, so the wind would carry off the chaff. The finished rice was stored in woven birchbark bags sewn across the top with basswood cord.

Today some elderly Indians, such as eighty-year-old Jacob Jones of Cass Lake, still cure their rice in the old way. But most sell their harvest to buyers who work out of pickup trucks in town. The buyers pass the rice along to processing plants. There it is cured for a week or two on a large asphalt slab resembling a parking lot. The curing loosens the hulls to prepare them for the parching drum, where the rice is dried at a temperature of 275° F. Conveyor belts move the parched rice to screens for removing such debris as leaves and twigs, and on to machines for hulling, winnowing, and bagging.

Until the early 1960s the price of wild rice fluctuated wildly, according to the harvest. To stabilize the supply, plant geneticists developed a domesticated form that could be grown in paddies. By the mid-1970s Minnesota—the nation's major supplier of wild rice—had seventeen thousand acres of paddy rice, much of it along the Mississippi north of the town of Aitkin. On the Leech Lake Reservation the Chippewa operate a two-hundred-acre paddy. As the production of paddy rice has increased, harvests of lake rice have declined.

The paddy rice is harvested with combines that have large wheels to keep from sinking in the water. Machines are also used to spray the fields; as with other monocultures, paddy rice is plagued by insects and plant diseases. Growers use Malathion (an insecticide), Diathane (a fungicide), and 2,4-D (an herbicide). Tests show no residues, but wild-rice buyers such as Louis Chalich, who is also the sheriff of Cass County, and Cindy Anderson, a buyer for the past five years, believe the public deserves labels on the packaging to distinguish between paddy rice and naturally grown lake rice. One processor, Darrow Gibbs of Deer River, admits, "It's a question the industry has been wrestling with for years."

Some believe paddy rice and lake rice differ not only with regard to pesticides, but also in respect to taste. Jacob Jones, who cures his rice the old way, compares paddy rice to soggy rice crispies and lake rice to old-fashioned oatmeal. Few of us have taste buds sophisticated enough for a blindfold test, yet we can all feel the loss of one of our few remaining wild foods—yet another step on the path away from Crow Wing.

4

From Furs to Pines

A Shanty-man's life is a wearisome one,
Although some say it's free from care.
It's the swinging of an axe from morning till night
In the forests wild and drear.

Or Sleeping in our bunks without cheer
When the cold winter winds do blow,
But as soon as the morning star does appear
To the wild woods we must go.

LOGGER'S SONG

*T*HE FUR TRADE DID NOT FADE for lack of furs. Though it is true that beaver were practically extinct, such valuable furbearers as mink and muskrat remained plentiful. The trade died because its labor force was in a sharp decline and because other extractive industries moved in.

For many Indians the fur trade had brought major changes in lifestyle. Farming tribes that had lived in permanent towns were forced to adjust to hunting, with its nomadic way of life. The new mobility resulted in more intertribal contacts, more competition for furs, more warfare. Wars, together with the ravages of smallpox, wiped out entire tribes. In 1849 a fur trader wrote to his partner: "Furs, my dear child, I have none. It is not with twenty Indians that we can make anything."

Then came whites interested not in furs but in land and pines. The Sauk were one of the first of the Mississippi's tribes to fall victim to the appetite of the settlers and lumbermen. In 1804 the Sauk surrendered their lands east of the Mississippi. By treaty they were to be allowed to remain until the land was actually sold, but when squatters began arriving, most of the Sauk migrated west of the river into Iowa. Black Hawk, an aged war chief of the Sauk, was born near the confluence of the Mississippi and the Rock River, where his tribe had had a village for a century and a half. Fearing that the land west of the river would also be wrested from his people, Black Hawk enlisted the support of the Winnebagos, Potawatomis, and Kickapoos to make a concerted resistance.

The governor of the territory called out the militia, who chased the Indians through northern Illinois and southern Wisconsin until, on August 3, 1832, most of the tribe was slaughtered at the massacre of Bad Axe. The old chief was captured and sent on tour through the cities of the East. He said to the whites, "Rock River was a beautiful country; I loved my towns, my cornfields, and the home of my people. I fought for it."

After the defeat, the Sauk signed away six million acres west of the Mississippi, for which the survivors were to receive an annuity of $20,000 a year for thirty years.

When annuities were negotiated, some fur traders claimed and received a share on the grounds that the Indians had not repaid credit advanced to them during lean years. In effect the government subsidized the traders for helping persuade their "employees" to come to the treaty table. Some agents had the foresight to see that the fur trade was at an end. When investing the stake they had acquired from the treaty money, they were shrewd enough to diversify.

＊＊＊

WHITE PINE, AN EASILY WORKED and therefore valued wood, grew in an unbroken belt from Maine halfway across the continent to the prairies of Minnesota. By the mid-1800s the lumbermen who had cut Maine and Michigan moved into Wisconsin, then edged up the Mississippi to the less accessible woods of northern Minnesota. From 1860 to 1890 it was the pinelands of the upper Mississippi that slaked the nation's lumber thirst.

By the Treaty of 1867, the Ojibwe land in northern Minnesota was purchased for seven cents an acre. Soon after the treaty was signed, government surveyors appeared along the Mississippi, dragging their chains through the woods. Once the land was surveyed and offered up for sale, the lumber companies sent in timber cruisers.

The cruiser was the successor to the *coureurs de bois*. The one ranged the woods looking for furs, the other for pine. The early cruiser went alone or with a couple of Indians to paddle his canoe. In later years he took along a compassman and sometimes a cook. It was a demanding job: the cruiser had to know where he was at all times, which tracts were public land, which trees were sound and which diseased, and which streams would float logs in the spring.

Most of all he had to be accurate. In the early days, estimates of the amount of timber in a tract were crude, but later the cruisers developed more scientific techniques. One approach was to mark off a tenth of an acre and count every tree, then measure their diameters. Next the United States volume table was used to compute the footage of timber in each tree. The cruiser multiplied this total by ten to arrive at the footage per acre. He worked acre by acre until he had covered a 40-acre tract, then moved on to the next 40. A section, 640 acres, might be a three-day job.

One cruiser was so accurate that his estimate on a $1 million tract was only 1.7 percent less than the actual cut, a difference easily accounted for by the year's growth that took place between his cruise and the cutting.

Before the Treaty of 1867, some lumbermen simply helped themselves to timber from the Ojibwe land. But the majority waited for the government's purchase and then acquired their timberland at public sale, paying the legal minimum of $1.25 an acre. Better yet, Civil War veterans could be found who would sell their land warrants for as little as forty cents an acre.

In a single decade more than one million acres of Minnesota pineries passed into the hands of lumbermen. Usually the land was bought outright, although sometimes only the stumpage rights were purchased. Land grants leased from railroads and agricultural colleges were major sources of cheap stumpage. As with the Ojibwe timber, not all the pine was acquired legally. Abuses of the Preemption and Homestead Acts were not uncommon. Employees of lumber companies homesteaded thousands of acres, staking claims and building the required shacks and then, as soon as they had established title, transferring ownership to the companies. Government investigators sometimes found huts in the forest that were only two feet wide and two feet tall.

Some loggers found it more convenient to ignore boundaries. George Henry Warren, a timber cruiser, told how the thieves operated:

> It was a country where the custom had grown among lumbermen to enter a few forties of government land, sufficient at least to make a show of owning a tract of timber on which to conduct a winter's operation of logging and then to cut the timber from adjacent or near-by forty-acre tracts of land yet belonging to the government.

By the 1890s ownership of the pinelands was becoming concentrated in the hands of a few large companies. The largest in the state was that of Frederick Weyerhaeuser. The corporation he founded is still one of the giants of the industry.

Like John Jacob Astor, Weyerhaeuser was a native of Germany. He emigrated in 1852 and in 1860 made his first investment in the lumber industry by purchasing a sawmill at the junction of the Mississippi and the Rock River, where Black Hawk's village had stood. The down payment was $500. Within a few years Weyerhaeuser controlled a second mill in Rock Island. Born with a genius for forming conglomerates, by 1870 he persuaded competing lumbermen to cooperate and form the Mississippi River Logging Company for purchasing timberland on the Chippewa River. The syndicate, which Weyerhaeuser presided over for forty years, came to control much of Wisconsin's pine. Then followed a long succession of companies either founded or bought out by this Carnegie of the lumber business: the Beef Slough Manufacturing, Booming, Log Driving and Transportation Company; the Chippewa River Improvement and Log Driving Company; the Shell Lake Lumber Company; the Eau Claire Lumber Company; the Pine Tree Lumber Company. By 1902 Frederick Weyerhaeuser was president of twenty-one companies and was known as the Lumber King.

He fathered four sons, and all of them ended up in the family business. John, the eldest, went to the Pacific coast to take charge of Weyerhaeuser interests in Washington and Oregon, Rudolph to Cloquet near Lake Superior, Frederick Edward to the Weyerhaeuser forests in Arkansas, and Charles, the number-two son, to Little Falls on the upper Mississippi near Crow Wing.

LUMBERMAN'S CAMP

AT LITTLE FALLS WE FOUND a welcome refuge one rainy day in the plush library of a museum dedicated to Charles A. Weyerhaeuser. Such reminders of Minnesota's lumber days are strewn along the river like logs stranded on a spring drive. They include Paul Bunyan statues and Lumbertown, U.S.A.'s. But for the more discriminating, the Minnesota Historical Society has done another of its fine reconstructions, a turn-of-the-century logging camp. It is called the Forest History Center and is located near the town of Grand Rapids, ten days' paddle from Itasca.

To ensure authenticity the historical society invited former lumberjacks to visit the camp. The oldtimers suggested a few changes. They pointed out, for example, that the bunkhouse always had a skylight above the woodstove. The skylight provided ventilation, a necessity when seventy men hang wool sox over a stove to dry. The society installed a skylight, but nothing could be done about another inauthenticity: the group of buildings is surrounded by second-growth deciduous woods. The original camp would have stood in the midst of a devastation of stumps.

We arrived in Grand Rapids at an inauthentic time of year. During the logging season—in winter—a layer of snow would have covered the tarpaper roofs, and the log walls would have been banked with snow. The first reconstructed building we entered was a barn large enough for two dozen horses. The horses provided the muscle for

LOG HAULING

pulling sleds piled high with newly-cut logs. At night, when the teamsters were done hauling, the ruts in the logging roads were sprinkled with water to freeze. The ice made the huge loads possible. Crewmen called "road monkeys" hauled river water in a tank wagon. At forty below it must have been a cold job. To ensure that the men would not refuse to work when the temperature plunged, the foreman allowed no thermometers in camp.

The camps were relocated every season or two in order that the lumberjacks would never lose time by walking more than a couple of miles to work. Jobs were specialized. The "chopper" notched the tree to make it fall in the direction desired. Two "sawyers" with a crosscut saw stood on each side of the trunk and sawed toward the notch. After the tree was down, the "swamper" cleared off the branches, the sawyers cut the trunk into lengths, and the "barker" stripped the undersides to make them slide. The "skidder" hitched up a team and snaked the logs to the road, where the "rigging gang" piled the sleds with loads ten to twelve feet high.

The road monkeys placed hay on the steeper hills to keep the heavy sleds from pushing forward and crushing the horses. The teamster had to be highly skilled, for a single accident could cripple him for life. Once the logs were unloaded at the riverbank, a "scaler" measured them and computed the number of board feet per log, noting the figures in a book and reporting to the foreman on the cut for the day. As the final step, the "stamper" marked each log with a brand to denote ownership. Thousands of marks were registered with the state surveyor general; one Weyerhaeuser company used a bullseye, another a double X.

In 1900 a foreman was paid an average of sixty-eight dollars a month, a cook received fifty-two, a sawyer thirty, and a road monkey twenty. By then nearly sixteen thousand men worked in the camps of northern Minnesota. Few attempts were made to form labor unions because the union movement was barely underway by the time the pine was gone.

But the loggers could buy a form of health insurance: nuns from Grand Rapids came out to sell tickets to the Catholic hospital. Twenty-five cents a month entitled the woodsman to free board and nursing in case of accident.

The first lumberjacks came from Maine. Later Norwegians, Swedes, and Finns mixed their languages with those of Russians, Bohemians, Serbians, Poles, Greeks. Many of the immigrants logged in order to save enough to homestead; others already owned farms but were after winter incomes. At night they would write letters home, or sharpen their axes, or sit on the deacon's bench and swap stories.

Breakfast consisted of buckwheat pancakes, potatoes, salt pork, beans with blackstrap molasses, fried cakes with brown sugar (similar to doughnuts), and coffee. A pipe completed the meal.

Lunch was brought to the men by the cookee, or assistant cook, who built a bonfire of slash for the loggers to stand around. In the intense cold their beans sometimes froze on the plates. Work was considered done when the moon came up. Hurrying to the dining room, the jacks ate on tin plates at long, oilcloth-covered tables. The company policy that meals were eaten in silence was enforced by the cook, who moved the men efficiently through their apple pie and out of the dining room within fifteen minutes.

An annual grocery list might include eighteen thousand pounds of beef and nine thousand pounds of sugar. All this had to be brought in, plus supplies for the company store, where the men could charge Copenhagen snuff and moosehide moccasins against their earnings. Most of the supplies came up during the summer by shallow-draft steamboat to Grand Rapids, the head of navigation. At Grand Rapids the goods were transferred to freight wagons to be taken to the camps. Each day as many as a hundred teams left town. Drivers strapped themselves in to keep from being jostled out when the wagons bounced over boulders. If the tote roads became impassable, citizens of the town made extra money by packing supplies on their backs.

Because of the cost of bringing provisions from far downriver, lumber companies actively encouraged farmers to settle southern and western Minnesota. In 1850 the territory had a population of 6,000 people. Seven years later, in 1857, the population had skyrocketed to 150,037. Three years after the Homestead Act of 1862, the state numbered 250,099.

Most of western Minnesota's oak and maple and walnut and elm was simply put to the torch in order to clear the way for growing wheat. The Scandinavian farmers who settled the hardwood forests and prairies drove their harvests to Minneapolis to the flour mills powered by the Falls of St. Anthony. They returned with their wagons loaded with lumber to build their barns. Sales at the sawmills rose and fell with the fortunes of wheat—with the blight, the drought, and the grasshoppers.

EACH YEAR IN APRIL or May the hardiest of the lumberjacks exchanged their axes for peavies and their rubber-bottomed pacs for spiked boots. As the spring rains swelled the tiny Mississippi to a torrent, some daredevil would take on the dangerous task of breaking the rollways holding back the logs that had been piled on shore. The mountain of logs accumulated over the winter tumbled and splashed into the water.

A river pig's hours were long and wet. He was soaked most of the time, especially the newcomer, and this from dunkings in a stream whose banks were deep in snow. He had no time to change clothes as the drive had to keep moving to take advantage of high water.

Three crews kept the drive rolling. The advance men, or "driving crew," steered the logs and kept them in the current. The "jam crew" came next and were responsible for breaking up jams that formed at bends or rapids. To do this meant finding the key log, a log jabbed into the riverbed in such a way that it held back the whole mass. A volunteer would yank it loose or chop it loose, and then run for his life. On stubborn jams dynamite was used. One logjam that happened just above Crow Wing was so recalcitrant it blocked the Mississippi for sixteen days.

The job of the rear crew was the least dangerous but the most unpleasant. The rear crew worked from flat-bottomed bateaux miles behind the main drive, wading into muck and ice to round up strays. All three crews started at dawn and kept at it until eight or ten at night. A wanigan—a shanty on a raft—followed the drive and housed the cook and supplies. Meals were often irregular. The wages, five dollars a day, were the highest in the logging industry. If all went well, the drive from Grand Rapids to Minneapolis, 325 river miles, took forty days.

Each year before the log drive started, crews were sent out to cut brush, remove windfalls, and clean out rocks. Where necessary they built dams and dirt walls to keep the logs in line. Sometimes, as was done at Itasca, the loggers stored the winter's cut on the frozen surface of a convenient lake instead of the riverbank. Once the ice thawed, the logs were ready to begin their journey. In recent years we have learned that this practice degraded the water quality. According to a 1971 study by the Environmental Protection Agency, the bark would loosen and sink to the bottom, where in decomposing it depleted the oxygen dissolved in the water. Until recently a papermill in Grand Rapids used the river to store pulpwood. Because of the effect of bark's decomposition, they were required to stop.

The last big log drive on the Mississippi took place in 1916, after most of the white pine had been cut. As the lumber companies resorted to timberland that was more and more remote, the drives became longer and more expensive, causing the price of white pine to rise. Before long, Minnesota's pine could not compete with Douglas fir from the Pacific Northwest and yellow pine from Arkansas, Louisiana, and Mississippi.

After the white pine was gone, the state's legacy was a succession of disasters. As early as 1870, huge forest fires burned across the cutover lands. More than a million acres were consumed by the blazes. The logging operations had left behind mounds of slash—branches and leaves—as deep as forty feet, and when the debris caught fire, the wind fanned the flames into fire storms. One of the worst fires was the holocaust that destroyed the town of Hinckley in eastern Minnesota on a dry September day in 1894. Refugees fled on flaming trains or tried to survive in the shallow water of a nearby gravel pit. Four hundred and eighteen people died.

After each fire, the state legislature took a tentative step toward forest management. The position of forest commissioner was created, then a corps of rangers, and then the

Minnesota Forest Service. But the public as a whole did not support conservation. Minnesotans were convinced that agriculture would follow, once lumbering had eliminated the overstory. They were farmers, and farmers wanted land cleared of trees and ready for planting. The people were willing participants in the destruction of the forests.

To dispose of their cutover lands, the lumbermen formed land companies. Agents were dispatched to Finland, Norway, Sweden, Russia, and Austria to encourage immigration. In Little Falls, Charles Weyerhaeuser formed the Immigration Land Company in 1898 to sell the cutover land of the Pine Tree Lumber Company. Northern Minnesota was to be the new breadbasket of the nation.

Soon after I arrived in Minnesota, I met a seventy-two-year-old lady whose father had worked in a logging camp. He had bought forty acres of cutover land for grazing horses and cows. But the pinelands of northern Minnesota were not the rich prairie and hardwood lands of southwestern Minnesota. The land was either swampy or it was sandy, and unsuited for agriculture. Today the north is dotted with abandoned homesteads.

Little reforestation was done in Minnesota. In 1927 the state passed a law allowing cutover lands to be reclassified as auxiliary forests, which would then qualify for a lower tax rate. It was hoped this would encourage the lumber companies to hold on to their cutover lands and reforest them. Applications for auxiliary status required the approval of the State Forestry Commission and of the board of commissioners in the county involved.

In 1929 a Weyerhaeuser subsidiary in Cloquet, a town in northeastern Minnesota, filed an application to reclassify 172,000 acres of cutover land. The county commissioners denied the application on the grounds that the county could not afford the loss of revenue. The Weyerhaeuser Company decided to abandon the land and pay no further taxes. This was common practice—letting cutover lands become tax delinquent and revert to the state. Twenty years after the law was passed, only 228,000 acres had been reclassified as auxiliary forests.

The executives of Weyerhaeuser were sufficiently farsighted, however, to recognize that the timber on the Pacific coast was the last. Switching to a policy of sustained yield, the corporation began to hang on to its cutover lands and keep the taxes paid up. The company initiated experiments with reforestation, starting with land that had been so badly burned that natural reseeding would be impossibly slow. Weyerhaeuser established America's first tree farm and became, out of enlightened self-interest, one of the more progressive lumber companies in the country.

One of the main reasons the public supported the plunder of the nation's pines was the widely held belief in their inexhaustibility. Timber cruisers, politicians, farmers—all accepted the myth that the nation would never be able to cut all the pine. In 1852 Congressman Ben C. Eastman of Wisconsin expressed the common belief:

> Upon the rivers which are tributary to the Mississippi, and also upon those which empty themselves in Lake Michigan, there are interminable forests of pine, sufficient to supply all the wants of the citizens in the country, . . . for all time to come.

Whether the lumber companies themselves believed the myth is doubtful, for they had seen the white pine of Maine and Michigan fall to the ax. In Minnesota the companies resisted movements to set aside forest preserves, such as Jacob Brower's effort to create Itasca State Park, because they were already fearful of an impending timber famine.

In their fifty-year frenzy in Minnesota's forests, the loggers cut sixty-seven billion board feet. What happened to all that pine? It became barns and fences. It built the cities of the Midwest: Minneapolis, St. Louis, Omaha, Kansas City, Des Moines, St. Joseph, Wichita, Topeka, and Denver. In one year alone, Minneapolis constructed thirteen miles of new buildings, and in 1887 the city laid sixty-seven miles of wooden sidewalks. Six million feet of lumber to make a boardwalk.

5

The Waters Ran Red

The Miners of the Iron Range
Knew that there was something wrong.
They banded all together, yes
In One Big Union strong.
The Steel Trust got the "shivers,"
And the Mine Guards had some fits,
The Miners didn't give a damn
But closed down all the pits.

INDUSTRIAL WORKERS
OF THE WORLD SONG

GRAND RAPIDS LIES ON THE EDGE of the Mesabi Iron Range, one of the greatest iron reserves in the world. The formation, 120 miles long by 3 miles wide, stretches from the banks of the Mississippi northeastward toward Lake Superior. Nearly three billion tons of ore have been gouged from the Mesabi since the first mines were opened in 1892. South of Grand Rapids from Aitkin to Brainerd, the Mississippi flows for miles through a secondary iron range, the Cuyuna. Rich in manganese as well as iron, the Cuyuna supplied 90 percent of the nation's manganese in World War I.

Geologists say that the first iron-rich volcanic rock formed during the Precambrian period two billion years ago. Geologic time took a long step into the early Paleozoic, and Minnesota came to be covered by a sea rich in iron and silica. The minerals settled to the sea bottom and built up beds of a low-grade iron ore called taconite. About 500 million years ago the iron formation underwent upheaval and weathering. Groundwater circulated through cracks in the taconite, dissolving and removing the silica and leaving a

highly concentrated ore called hematite. Hematite is a dark red ore with a 60 percent iron content, compared to 20 percent for the parent material, taconite.

In 1890 two timber cruisers discovered a deposit of soft hematite on the Mesabi. They realized that the ore was so accessible that no underground mining would be needed. It could be shoveled directly into cars and shipped to the steel mills. The two cruisers were brothers, Leonidas and Alfred Merritt. The Merritt brothers formed a mining company, and their discovery touched off a land boom. In the Panic of 1893 the brothers, short of capital, borrowed from the Oliver Iron Mining Company, which had close ties with the Carnegie Steel Corporation, and from the American Steam Barge Company, owned by John D. Rockefeller. A year later the Merritts were forced to sell out to Rockefeller and the Oliver Company to meet their debts. Today the Oliver Company, a division of U.S. Steel, is the giant of the range. The fortunes on the Mesabi were made by large steel corporations, not the Merritt brothers.

Just as the mining companies began moving into Minnesota, the big logging concerns were leaving, except for a few that stayed to profit from both resources. In 1911 Charles Weyerhaeuser's Pine Tree Lumber Company leased iron-ore deposits on the Cuyuna Range. And the state cooperated with those lumber outfits that wanted to expand. For example, the legislature passed a law making it possible for loggers donating cutover lands to the park at Itasca to reserve the mineral rights.

The early mining camps consisted of rough shacks, housing men who had immigrated from Wales and the tin mines of Cornwall. These skilled hardrock miners worked twelve hours a day with picks and shovels, often knee-deep in water. Before long the softer ores began to be worked, and more miners were needed. Boxcars rolled in, filled with laborers: Scandinavians, Slavs, Italians, Austrians, immigrants from forty-three countries. To accommodate the larger labor force, the mining companies built "locations," company towns with rows of identical frame houses. Some had electricity and running water. Where facilities were less modern, weekly baths for the children were scheduled at school.

Often boom towns of the logging era faded into ghost towns once the timber was gone, but because of the Mesabi, Grand Rapids survived. The town was founded in 1872 when Warren Potter built the first "permanent" building, a store with a canvas roof over four log walls. By the end of the first decade, in 1881, the town consisted of eight structures, including a hotel and saloon for lumberjacks. A few years later a one-room school was built, serving two white children and three Chippewa.

Grand Rapids saw its first real growth in the 1890s when it was incorporated as the county seat. The population was 1,546. The town now had a hospital, a public library, a bank, a cigar store, and a tailor. Old photographs show that the stores had high false fronts. By then the Central School had been built; today it serves as a museum, its banisters polished by nearly a century of hands.

In 1899 Grand Rapids boasted that it had two hundred bicycles and its first high school graduate, Miss Bertha Fuller. Two years later it had a telephone company with sixty subscribers, and the Itasca Paper Mill had been built. In 1909, the year the town paved eight blocks on Third Street, nearby mines produced 579,671 tons of iron ore.

It was just about then that the Oliver Iron Mining Company, the company that bought out the Merritt brothers, fired several hundred workers for requesting better wages and shorter working days. Before long, scabs were brought in to break a strike, and hundreds of miners were blacklisted. Less than ten years later, the whole range went out on strike, and violence flared between hired strikebreakers and the Industrial Workers of the World, the Wobblies.

In 1910 the miner worked six days a week and averaged three dollars a day. Out of this he had to pay for his own tools and materials: blasting caps, fuses, powder, candles (later carbide lamps), ax handles, shovels, and shoes that wore out in a few weeks of mine use. Savings had to be laid aside against the possibility of winter layoffs and accidents. Cave-ins made the work risky. Wives and children counted with anxiety as the mine whistle blew four times for an injury, five for a death.

During World War I strip mining replaced underground mines as improvements in earth-moving equipment made removal of the overburden practical. In the meantime the papermill in Grand Rapids changed its name to Blandin Paper Company, and in 1931 the town built a concrete bridge over the Mississippi. In 1942 the mines of the county produced 18,496,395 tons of iron ore.

After World War II the ore began giving out, but the mining days were not over for Grand Rapids. Once the better grade of ore—hematite—was mined out, processing the parent ore became economical. The 1950s saw the development of a technology for extracting taconite. To process the lower-quality ore, huge quantities are blasted from the earth and then crushed and ground to a fine powder, which is passed over magnetic separators to draw out the iron. This taconite concentrate is then formed into pellets for shipping to steel mills. Two-thirds of the taconite is nonmagnetic and is discarded as tailings.

To find out more about Minnesota's mining days, past and present, I took a trip eastward from the Mississippi along the Mesabi Range. I passed through one mining town after another: Coleraine, Taconite, Calumet, Nashwauk, Keewatin, Hibbing, Chisholm. At one time many of these location towns were situated on top of underground mines. After open-pit mining evolved during World War I, the companies relocated entire communities. They even picked up and moved one town that had a population of ten thousand. The location towns are still being shifted around today, as new deposits of taconite are discovered.

The frame houses on the Mesabi are stained red with taconite dust, and the road to the Iron Range Interpretive Center in Chisholm is coated with a fine layer of red powder. The powder is kicked up by trucks along the highway and lands on top of roadside mounds of tailings.

I passed one red canyon after another. To produce taconite takes a huge quantity of the crude ore, so the pits are larger than the cuts made for hematite. Mining taconite also takes a great deal of energy, because the lower-quality ore requires more processing.

Minnesota once produced 25 percent of the world's iron. Taconite from the Mesabi still contributes nearly 6 percent. To encourage investment in the Iron Range, in 1964 the state passed an amendment to its constitution limiting taxes on taconite operations for twenty-five years. Less than two decades after the amendment, Minnesota's legislators began considering comprehensive regulations to control metallic mining from initial siting through until the time when a mine is deactivated. The new rules will require reclamation of mines and revegetation of tailings to curb erosion, as well as the resulting air pollution from dust and water pollution from leaching of toxic materials.

On the east end of the Mesabi, the city of Duluth discovered in 1973 that its drinking water contains asbestiform fibers. When ingested, the particles can cause kidney cancer. The city takes its water from Lake Superior, not far from where Reserve Mining Company was found to be dumping sixty-seven thousand tons a day of taconite tailings. Litigation ensued and, in a famous settlement, Reserve agreed to switch to on-land disposal. The tailings will have to be contained in a reservoir in order to prevent their blowing about—asbestos has its greatest carcinogenic effect when it is inhaled.

———————————◆——◆———————————

BACK ALONG THE MISSISSIPPI near the town of Crosby, I visited the last active mine of the Cuyuna Range. Operated by a small outfit called Pittsburg Pacific, the mine is worked for a low grade of hematite. The operation is economical only because of the ore's high manganese content, manganese being a scarce mineral vital to the manufacture of steel. The company takes out five hundred thousand tons a year and expects to work the mine for another five or six years.

The final days of each major extractive industry are repetitively similar. In fur trading a few agents hung on, obtaining muskrat pelts from settlers who trapped as a winter sideline. In lumbering, and in hematite mining, the large operators got out as soon as profits diminished, leaving the cleanup of scraps to small-time entrepreneurs.

An official of Pittsburg Pacific fitted me with a hardhat and we drove out to the mine. We parked on a dirt road overlooking the pit and I gingerly climbed out on the crumbling edge. Far below, straight down, were a couple of matchbox trucks. In the Mesabi Range the ore is found in horizontal layers; in the Cuyuna it is vertical. As a result the Cuyuna mines are narrow and deep. Water must be pumped out continually. Pittsburg removes three thousand gallons a minute to a series of settling ponds. The ponds empty into Black Bear Lake and from there the water flows into Miller Lake and the Black Bear River and then into the Mississippi. The company takes samples at the outflow. In the old days, red water at times overflowed from the pits into lowland lakes and streams.

Even today, surface runoff is loaded with material eroded from abandoned open-pit mines and from barren piles of taconite tailings. The runoff contaminates nearby streams with sediment and heavy metals. Iron and manganese are often found in high concentrations near inactive mines. At Grand Rapids the Mississippi takes on a reddish color, apparently caused by mine drainage into a tributary, the Prairie River.

Originally the Cuyuna Range had more than forty mines. Once they were deactivated, the pits filled with water. The state has stocked some of these new lakes with trout. Pittsburg Pacific pointed out that developers have been selling lakeshore cottage lots, but this would seem a coals-to-Newcastle atonement in Minnesota, the "land of ten thousand lakes."

The Pittsburg mine is scarred by deep gullies caused by the previous owner, who took no measures to control erosion. Minnesota's new mining regulations will require surface overburden at the edge of the pit to be sloped back more gradually than was done in the past. Pittsburg has faced its own cuts with rock and dirt. Shrubs and small trees have taken root over perhaps half the surface. The company is seeking a variance from the new regulation requiring a more gradual slope. To lessen the angle of their cuts would mean removing so much overburden that the operation would no longer be economical. Pittsburg Pacific maintains that the new rule, besides putting them out of business, would mean a much larger scar and that the greater devastation is not justified in the case of a narrow ore body.

The state Department of Natural Resources disagrees. It maintains that as the deep pits fill with water, wave action will cause erosion. Over geologic time, undercutting and slumping will flatten the slope into a natural lake configuration, but for the next few millenia the pits will have steep, barren, unstable slopes, hardly the sort of beach for a lakeshore cottage.

In the future Minnesota's mineral cornucopia will yield other resources, such as copper and nickel. Exploration for uranium is being conducted near the village of Palisade, at the north end of the Cuyuna Range. The primary effects of uranium mining on the river corridor would come from seepage of radium-contaminated mine effluents and emission of radon gas from tailings, which can double the cancer risk for generations to come.

6

Of a Wild and Scenic River

Dans le cours du voyage,
Exposé aux orages;
Préoccupés du temps,
Battu de tous les vents.
Ah! je vous dis, mes frèr's,
Personne, sur la terr',
Endure tant de misèr'.

VOYAGEUR SONG

*B*Y THE TIME WE HAD PADDLED past Grand Rapids and put in at Crow Wing, the Mississippi had come close to making an enormous circle. For 350 miles we had followed its twists and turns, but by air we were only 70 miles from Lake Itasca. At Crow Wing the river began to turn southeast. When it reached Minneapolis, after another 140 miles, it had bent itself into the shape of a gigantic question mark.

In that first month of canoeing, we had seen the Mississippi change. From a stream so narrow that a paddler's outstretched arms could touch both banks, it had become a true river, averaging four hundred feet wide by the time it neared the Twin Cities. From a shallow twelve inches it had deepened to an impressive fifty feet. Its clear waters had seemed black as the depth increased and had turned brown as we passed peat bogs. Along its banks, evidence of glaciation had become overlain with more mature floodplain sediments.

During its first miles the young river had flowed in and out of several large lakes— Lake Bemidji, Cass Lake, and, the largest of all, Lake Winnibigoshish. On Winnibigoshish we had kept close to shore, for the waves can become dangerous as they build up across thirteen miles of open water. Our work was easier once we left the lakes and entered the slow water of marshes, filled with phragmites and reed canary grass. Great blue herons waded through the shallows, lifting their long legs as they poised for a strike. Although the great blues are declining in most parts of the United States, we were treated to the sights and sounds of a couple of heron rookeries. The first time we took the noise to be a gathering of hundreds of frogs. At the second rookery I counted eight nests perched atop a group of white pines, and from the commotion I judged there were many more back in the trees.

Much of this time the river was flowing through the Leech Lake Indian Reservation and also through the Chippewa National Forest, which ranks among the top two breeding areas for bald eagles in the contiguous United States. At the forest headquarters John Mathisen, a nationally known expert on eagles, told me that nesting success in Chippewa has increased in the past five years.

By the time we reached the haunting beauty of Crow Wing, the northern coniferous forest had given way to deciduous woods. North of Crow Wing the white pines that once stood supreme have been replaced by a mixture of pine, spruce, fir, birch, and aspen. To the south the hardwood forests were cut in the late 1800s to make way for farms, but the trees along the riverbanks were spared. Except for an occasional pasture at river's edge, the shores still remain wooded, and the stream flows lazily beneath a green canopy. After miles of trees, to come upon a cow at the edge of the water was more of an attraction than an intrusion.

Today, instead of the ax or the plow, the riverbanks of the upper Mississippi face a typically modern stress: resorts and summer cottages. In the final seventy miles above Minneapolis, the pressures of residential development are becoming intense. At Anoka, thirteen miles above the city, suburban homes line the shores. River traffic—pleasure boats and waterskiers—is heavy.

Yet even this close to the Twin Cities, aerial photographs show that seventy percent of the shorelines are still wooded. In the early 1970s those who love the Mississippi worked to preserve this stretch under the Minnesota Wild and Scenic Rivers Act. In July of 1976 a fifty-mile section from St. Cloud to Anoka was designated as part of the Minnesota system, which is one of the best of the state wild and scenic river systems. Zoning regulations along this section now require minimum lot sizes, building setbacks, and restrictions on cutting the vegetative screen. Scenic easements were purchased, as well as land acquired outright to protect the river corridor from uses incompatible with wild-and-scenic status, such as strip mines, factories, and trash dumps.

Some of the same citizens who worked for the state designation were instrumental in nominating the entire upper stretch from Itasca to the Twin Cities—489 miles—for inclusion in the National Wild and Scenic Rivers System. Under the system's enabling act of 1968, rivers or sections of rivers are classified as wild, scenic, or recreational depending on the extent of human tampering. Sixty-one rivers have received protection to date, including the Lower St. Croix, which drains into the Mississippi below St. Paul. The Upper Iowa and the Wisconsin are other direct tributaries that are candidates for inclusion.

The upper Mississippi was selected for study status in 1975. It had received the support of Walter Mondale when he was a senator from Minnesota, as well as President Carter's recommendation. The upper Mississippi is the largest continuous river segment that has ever been considered.

The study, completed in 1977, recommended that the lower fifty miles continue to be administered by the state and that three hundred miles of the upper reaches be included in the national system. Most of the stretch from Itasca to Bemidji would be classified as wild, and the rest either as scenic or recreational. The study suggested that the most compelling reason for inclusion, apart from natural beauty, is the river's importance to our national heritage. As one local environmentalist said, "Of all the rivers in the U.S., the grand old river ought to be the first to be protected."

When the study was presented to Congress, it was remanded to the National Park Service for further planning and public reaction. Local landowners had expressed reservations about what they saw as a federal takeover. Among those who were upset were the townsfolk of Palisade, at the north end of the Cuyuna Range.

Platted in 1910, Palisade had a population of three hundred by 1932, but today the village has dwindled to half that. Many of the storefronts are vacant. The only restaurant is a bar and grill with wooden booths. It is located in a converted bank building, the bank having folded in 1929. Beneath the original stamped-tin ceiling, a jukebox stands next to the old vault.

While our group fed in coins, I was next door in the post office with Eugene Howe, postmaster and mayor, who was telling me that Palisaders are dedicated to preserving the river as it is. Not only do they oppose the wild and scenic river proposal, but they are also against the Great River Road, a scenic parkway being built from Lake Itasca to the Gulf of Mexico. As part of the Great River Road project, the town's riverfront park would be modernized with picnic shelters, tennis courts, and trailer hookups. Even though this would bring badly needed tourist dollars, Palisade is not interested.

I left the post office and talked with others along the street. The minister's wife disagreed with the mayor. She said that many people, especially the younger generation, support development of the town's park. But down at the feed coop, the farmers took the mayor's side. They see the Great River Road and the wild and scenic river proposal as "just more federal land grabs."

The townspeople are Finns. When walking up from the river, I had noticed that even the trash in a junkyard was neatly stacked. Most of the farms outside town are small, just a couple of dozen cows, and the Finnish farmers want their land to remain in their families. When Mayor Howe wanted to build a cottage beside the river, even he was unable to persuade them to sell a lot. The farmers want things to stay the way they are.

Landowners along the river, fearing encroachment by the federal government, proposed their own plan at the county level. In the spring of 1980 several of the counties that border the river formed the Mississippi Headwaters Board (MHB). In September 1980, the board issued a scheme for protecting the river at the same time the National Park Service published its new master plan. The park service decided to shelve its plan for the time being and to enter into negotiations with the MHB.

Environmentalists are apprehensive about this move. They would like to see the federal plan revived, because the county plan provides only short-term protection through zoning. Zoning regulations are always subject to the granting of variances.

Environmentalists are concerned not only about residential growth but also about signs of incipient industrialization. Two sections of river are already disqualified by a couple of power plants. One, a coal-fired generating plant in Cohasset, owned by Minnesota Power and Light Company, supplies power to Grand Rapids. The Cohasset plant emits the worst air pollution north of the Twin Cities and contributes to the problem of acid rain. The other plant is a nuclear facility owned by Northern States Power Company. Located a short distance above Anoka, the Monticello nuclear plant is plunked down in the midst of a thick forest. The only warning of its presence is the aerial dispersion tower.

One of the leaders of our expedition, Steve Andersen, served as nuclear policy chairman of the environmental advisory committee to the Federal Energy Administration. As we paddled past Monticello, Steve gave a short lecture on the impacts of nuclear plants on rivers. Nuclear facilities are invariably located on riverbanks or along a coast, since large quantities of water are required for cooling. The liquid wastes discharged do not significantly raise the level of radioactivity in river water. But inevitably some isotopes *are* ingested by aquatic organisms, to be concentrated as they pass up through the food chain from prey to predator.

Steve went on to say that a more significant impact is produced by the dispersion tower, which emits gases that are highly radioactive. Thousands of curies of krypton and other radioactive elements with half-lives ranging from a few minutes to 9.4 years, routinely pour out of the stacks. Because Monticello's reactor containment is enclosed in a square building, it lacks the distinctive and ominous shape associated with a nuclear plant. Even so, when we passed we paddled quickly, thinking of those escaping gases.

Also in the upper Mississippi but unable to qualify for wild-and-scenic status are seventy-two miles of slackwater above a handful of turn-of-the-century dams. Where an impoundment exists, the section below the dam or above the slackwater pool can still be designated as wild so long as the flow remains sufficient to preserve the qualities for which the river was selected. Officially the reservoirs were constructed for flood control, and to augment flow below the Twin Cities for improving navigation. The unofficial reason, I was told by the Corps of Engineers, was to keep water flowing to the lumber and grain mills of Minneapolis. The Weyerhaeusers and Pillsburys had powerful lobbies in those days.

Today, according to the Corps, the reservoirs provide recreation and wild rice habitat (this, again, amid the "land of ten thousand lakes"). Being low, the dams are unable to produce electricity. One of them, the Coon Rapids Dam just above the Twin Cities, did at one time have a hydroelectric generating plant, but the company that owned the dam found it uneconomical to operate. That same dam was rated by the Corps, which has the responsibility for inspection, as unsafe. Its spillway is too small to handle a big flood.

Before the dams were built, the upper Mississippi had what must have been exciting whitewater: Knife Rapids, Little Falls, and Pokegama Falls, which, with its twenty-foot drop, would have been unrunnable. Today the only rapids left are mild ones at St. Cloud—Sauk Rapids.

Usage of the upper river is surprisingly light, according to the Bureau of Outdoor Recreation. Besides fishermen and hunters, an estimated two hundred canoeists a year float from Itasca to some long-distance destination, whether it is Grand Rapids, the Twin Cities, St. Louis, or New Orleans. Admittedly, recreational use will expand if the Mississippi is designated as a wild and scenic river. Some soil compaction and loss of natural groundcover would then be unavoidable, but access can be controlled and use restricted before the river's capacity is approached.

Inclusion of the upper Mississippi in the federal system would curtail residential development, protect water quality, and prohibit such new dams as the one that was proposed for Days High Landing, where an archaeological dig would be flooded out. Inclusion would save a number of other historical sites as well: trading posts, missions, trail crossings, and steamboat landings. Most of all, it would ensure protection of our "grand old river's" beautiful and fragile headwaters reach.

THREE

Old Times and New Times

Twin Cities to St. Louis

The Biological Time Capsule

FROM TIME TO TIME we meet monstrous fish [an alligator gar or a catfish], one of which struck so violently against our canoe, that I took it for a large tree about to knock us to pieces. . . . On casting our nets, we have taken sturgeon and a very extraordinary kind of fish [a paddlefish]; it resembles a trout with this difference, that it has a larger mouth, but smaller eyes and snout. Near the latter is a large bone, like a woman's busk, three fingers wide, and a cubit long; the end is circular and as wide as the hand. In leaping out of the water the weight of this often throws it back.

FATHER JAMES MARQUETTE, 1673

BY THE TIME THE MISSISSIPPI has completed its question mark at Minneapolis and meandered on down to the Iowa border, a single state has claimed nearly a third of the river's entire length. The quality of water Minnesota sends downstream is therefore critical. Many river towns, including St. Louis and New Orleans, obtain their drinking water from the Mississippi.

North of the Twin Cities, the water is fairly clean despite eleven municipal and industrial dischargers of some size. Sewage treatment plants on the upper stretch are being upgraded, although more slowly than was intended by the Federal Water Pollution Control Act and Clean Water Act. For example, as late as 1978, the town of Bemidji was discharging phosphorus into the Mississippi below the outlet of Lake Bemidji. The inadequately treated sewage was causing unnaturally high levels of fertility in the vegetation of Cass Lake and Lake Winnibigoshish. Residents living downstream raised a protest and succeeded in forcing Bemidji to begin upgrading its treatment plant. In the meantime the town is required to pour its effluent into its own segment of the river, Lake Bemidji.

At about the same time in Grand Rapids, the federal Department of the Interior found that mercury discharged from Blandin Paper Company was lodging in sediments downriver and contaminating fish. A new sewage treatment plant was built, but it is not yet operating satisfactorily. Polluters such as the Grand Rapids papermill and the Bemidji treatment plant are called "point" sources of pollution, sources where the entering pollution can literally be pinpointed. "Nonpoint" sources, such as runoff from feedlots, farms, mine tailings, and urban streets, are more dispersed and therefore more difficult to control. The worst example we saw was a feedlot right on the riverbank, two days' paddle below Palisade. But this is only one of many nonpoint sources. Each and every rainfall, hundreds of farms pollute the river's upper reaches with organic wastes and pesticides.

AT MINNEAPOLIS THE RIVER flows through a gorge. From water level, much of the city is hidden behind wooded bluffs. At the base of the bluffs are small sand beaches, where occasionally families are still seen swimming. A few miles downstream, at St. Paul, the riverfront is lined with industries and barge terminals. At the very end is the Metropolitan Wastewater Treatment Plant, appropriately located on Pig's Eye Island. Named for one of the original settlers, a whiskey peddler, Pig's Eye is the worst single source of pollution on the Mississippi above St. Louis.

One reason for the impact of Pig's Eye is the fact that the Mississippi at Minneapolis is still a small river. Its ability to dilute the wastes of a major city here is much less than at St. Louis or New Orleans. The ratio of population to stream flow at Minneapolis is twelve times the ratio at St. Louis, eighty-five times that at New Orleans. Especially during seasons of low flow, the Twin Cities overload the Mississippi's capacity.

Since 1967 the Twin Cities have been attempting to upgrade the Pig's Eye plant's sewage processing from primary to secondary treatment. In primary treatment, the solids are settled out; in secondary, biological decomposition is added to the treatment cycle. An initial attempt ran into difficulties. Under the new system the excess sludge, which for years had simply been dumped into the river, was instead incinerated. The smoke and smell proved much worse than anticipated, leading to fines for air-quality violations. Satisfactory secondary treatment is expected to be achieved in the early 1980s, but by the mid-1980s population growth will render the new facility inadequate.

A fisheries and wildlife consultant had warned us, "Canoeing the stretch below the Twin Cities is unhealthy." We paddled through it but, on his advice, after passing Pig's Eye we waited a number of miles before swimming again.

The numerous sand beaches between Minneapolis and St. Louis do attract large numbers of swimmers. Yet by the time we were halfway through Iowa, a doctor cautioned us to stay out of the water as much as possible. In his practice he finds numerous cases of shigellosis—dysentery—among those who water-ski on the Mississippi. Though we stopped swimming, at our mid-morning and mid-afternoon nut snacks we had no way to wash hands that had been splashed while paddling. The coleader of the expedition, historian Bob Weyeneth, spent the final days of the trip in a hospital with an intestinal infection caused by *Staphylococci aureus*. Contaminated food might have been the culprit, but contaminated water was a strong possibility.

Railroad bridge, Pallisade, Minnesota.

Towboat at Lock and Dam #8 seen through a glass brick near the Minnesota–Iowa border.

Facing page: *Clearing mist over the river, central Minnesota.*

Highway bridge, Brainerd, Minnesota.

Bridge, Sauk Rapids, Minnesota.

Perrot State Park, Wisconsin.

Porch and window reflections, Villa Louis, Prairie du Chien, Wisconsin.

Facing page: *The Mississippi from Perrot State Park, two and a half miles above Lock and Dam #6.*

Morning on the river, central Minnesota.

In 1975 residents downstream from the Twin Cities learned that, in addition to sewage, the city sends down one of the more sinister of modern poisons, polychlorinated biphenyls. PCBs are an industrial chemical used as an insulating fluid in electrical transformers and capacitors. Manufactured since 1929 by Monsanto Company of St. Louis, PCBs are also used in paints, lubricants, plastics, insecticides, and adhesives.

Besides being suspected of causing cancer, polychlorinated biphenyls have been linked to ailments of the skin, liver, and reproductive system, as well as nervous disorders and birth defects. When we paddled through downtown Minneapolis, I noted a sign on the riverbank: "Frequent eating of fish not recommended. Women of childbearing age and children under 6 should not eat any fish from these waters."

When objects containing PCBs are discarded in landfills or burned in incinerators, the PCBs are released into the atmosphere and find their way into the soil and water. Their manufacture was banned in 1979, but by then 1.5 billion pounds had infiltrated every ecosystem on the planet. After a half century of widespread use, it may take years for the release of PCBs and their chemical by-products even to peak.

Once ingested, PCBs are stored in an organism's fatty tissues. Being bioaccumulative, PCBs occur in greater and greater concentrations as they work up the food chain from microscopic organisms to fish, birds, animals, and humans. It is estimated that forty percent of the American population have concentrations of 1 ppm (part per million) in their fatty tissues. The United States Food and Drug Administration has halted the sale of fish that contain 2 ppm PCBs.

Because PCBs are almost insoluble, when found in water they are usually attached to a suspended solid such as silt. If the river slows down, the silt and the PCBs settle to the bottom. Below the Twin Cities the current moves steadily until it reaches Lake Pepin, a widening of the river twenty miles long.

On the Wisconsin side, Lake Pepin is lined with four-hundred-foot bluffs. The bluffs, cream colored when lit by the setting sun, have rock outcroppings that look like crumbling medieval battlements. Pepin has long been famous for its storms and for waterskiing, boating, and fishing. The day we paddled the lake, I counted thirty sailboats.

In May of 1975 a study determined that the bottom sediments of Pepin are highly contaminated with PCBs. That same month the Food and Drug Administration required a commercial fisherman to bury twenty thousand pounds of carp taken from Pepin. Before the month was over, the landowners around Lake Pepin held a general meeting. Called together by their neighbors Dorothy and Ed Hill, they formed the Citizens for a Clean Mississippi. The Hills had long been concerned about Pepin. They had seen it filling with sediment and seen the algal blooms caused by overfertilization by phosphates. Ed, a retiree from the Soil Conservation Service, died not long after the founding of the Citizens for a Clean Mississippi, but Dorothy carried on as president of the group.

Covering years in minutes, Dorothy told me of the growth of the CCM from that initial meeting when seventy people attended to the present twenty-six hundred members. With the help of her neighbors, she persuaded county boards to provide financial assistance. She initiated a letter-writing campaign and lined up support from chambers of commerce, sportsmen's clubs, women's clubs, fraternal organizations, farmers' unions, businessmen, and city governments.

Facing page: *A six barge tow enters Lock and Dam #7 near La Crosse, Wisconsin.*

MAIDEN'S ROCK, LAKE PEPIN

"The commercial fishing on Lake Pepin," Dorothy went on with her dynamic, rapid-fire history, "is almost done in. They used to take two million pounds of carp a season in Lake Pepin. PCBs have put a hundred people out of work." In 1975 the Food and Drug Administration banned the interstate shipment of fish from Pepin. Recreational fishing is destroyed too. "We used to see forty or fifty boats at a time sport fishing. Now you just see sailboats, mostly owned by people from the Twin Cities."

Dorothy realized, as she researched the problem, that it was not just PCBs. "We've got everything—mercury, lead, cadmium, all the heavy metals." Most are industrial wastes. At that time Pig's Eye was putting three hundred tons of sludge into the Mississippi every day. By 1977 the CCM had contacted lawyers to see about a suit. At the same time, Dorothy was pressing for a dialogue with the Minnesota Pollution Control Agency and the Metropolitan Waste Control Commission.

Finally permit hearings were held. They dragged on for seven weeks. In the end, Pig's Eye was granted a new permit to continue discharging. The CCM felt the decision was too lenient, so an attorney was assigned to intervene and a compromise was worked out. The CCM won two points: Pig's Eye would no longer be allowed to put its excess sludge into the Mississippi, and the Metropolitan Council, which holds the purse strings in the Twin Cities, would now take equal responsibility with the Metropolitan Waste Control Commission for the operation of Pig's Eye. The CCM had also wanted a moratorium on extending sewer lines to new subdivisions until the treatment plant was in compliance with its discharge permit. Until Pig's Eye could handle what it already had, the CCM wanted further growth deferred. To effect the compromise, this ban on expansion was conceded for the time being.

As the months went on, to the consternation of subdivision developers, the CCM renewed its opposition to sewer extensions. "I can see," Dorothy said, "if I had a youngster ready to move into a house, I could be sympathetic. But nothing is going to happen until the people of the Twin Cities get upset."

In January of 1980 things began to happen. The U.S. Environmental Protection Agency initiated legal proceedings against the Metropolitan Waste Control Commission and the Metropolitan Council, for failure to bring Pig's Eye into compliance with its discharge permit. In the meantime, under pressure from contractors and developers, the state granted forty sewer extensions and decided to continue granting extensions for one year.

The CCM's achievement of a ban on river disposal of sludge and a switch to incineration may not greatly reduce Lake Pepin's PCB pollution, since a substantial percentage of the chemical is thought to reach the river through atmospheric deposition. Incineration not only increases this PCB fallout, it also requires five million gallons of oil a year. Ed McGaa, an Oglala Sioux, has proposed an alternative. Ed, a lawyer and currently manager of secondary airports in the Twin Cities, owns six thousand acres of remote land on the Pine Ridge Indian Reservation in South Dakota. He and the tribal leaders, though aware the sludge contains PCBs and heavy metals, are eager to use it to revitalize their barren

ST. PAUL, FROM DAYTON'S BLUFF, 1872

land, with the hope that grass can then be grown. The Metropolitan Waste Control Commission has conducted a pilot project in which 125 tons of sludge was transported to South Dakota. The state university is monitoring the test plots.

Even if a way were found to dispose of the sludge without contaminating Indian land or the Mississippi, the PCBs already in Pepin will remain for many years to come, continually stirred up by the passage of barges and recirculated in the water. And, even once point sources like the sludge are cleaned up, more will keep entering from nonpoint sources.

One major nonpoint source for polychlorinated biphenyls is urban runoff. The PCBs settle from the air onto city streets where they lie dormant, along with asbestos, pesticides, and such traffic-originated heavy metals as lead. The first hard rains sends the whole pharmacopoeia of pollutants into the sewer system.

Like most cities, Minneapolis and St. Paul have a number of combined sanitary and storm sewers. In a heavy rain the sewage-treatment plant, unable to handle the extra load, discharges the overflow. The PCBs pour into the river along with the storm water and untreated sewage. St. Paul is built on a limestone ledge, which would make rebuilding its sewer system extremely expensive. The solution to urban runoff currently suggested by the Environmental Protection Agency is to improve city housekeeping: better street sweeping, trash removal, and especially catch-basin cleaning. The need is urgent, because urban runoff of toxic pollutants increases as population and industry grow.

We have progressed from producing organic sewage, which is biodegradable and differs only in degree from the pollution manufactured by nature itself, to producing substances that are much more insidious. Even low concentrations of toxic chemicals can affect aquatic ecosystems, particularly those receiving a variety of pollutants. Most grim is the possibility of a synergistic reaction, in which several poisons combine to create an effect worse than the sum of their effects individually.

Since the PCB scare in 1975, the prohibition against commercial fishing has been gradually extended downriver. At Winona, forty miles downstream from Pepin, Bud Ramer has been fishing the river for years, but now his carp cannot meet the 2 ppm limit. At Lansing, sixty miles farther down, one of the two largest fish companies in the area finds its catch tests at 1.7 to 1.8 ppm.

Although the commercial take on most of the upper river has remained fairly constant for years, the variety of species has declined. Today few fish except carp survive in the twenty-five-mile stretch between St. Paul and Hastings.

Early explorers and settlers had been impressed by the fish in the Mississippi. In 1869 Oliver Gibbs, Jr. wrote in *Lake Pepin Fish Chowder* of catching in one day "three or four kinds of bass, two of pickerel, two of pike-perch, the mascalonge and a dozen kinds of other curious and gamey, handsome fish. . . ." Thomas Jefferson wrote in 1781:

> The Mississippi will be one of the principal channels of future commerce for the
> country westward of the Alleghaney. . . . This river yields turtle of a peculiar kind,
> perch, trout, gar, pike, mullets, herrings, carp [carpsuckers], spatula fish of 50lb.
> weight, cat-fish of 100lb.-weight, buffalo fish and sturgeon.

Carp, a hardy fish introduced to the United States in the 1880s, has dominated the commercial fishery of the Mississippi since the early 1900s. All others have declined, including buffalo, catfish, freshwater drum, lake sturgeon, and bullhead. Walleye, sauger, yellow perch, and white bass have disappeared entirely from the commercial catch. The total poundage of fish caught has remained stable; the relative abundance of various species is what has changed.

Thirty-four Mississippi River fish are included on state lists of threatened and endangered species. The paddlefish and alligator gar, two of the Mississippi's most distinctive fish, are on one or more lists in Minnesota, Wisconsin, Illinois, and Missouri. Both are fish with long geological histories.

The paddlefish, *Polyodon spathula,* made its appearance during the Paleozoic. Today this living fossil is found only in the Mississippi. Like sharks, another ancient fish, the paddlefish has a cartilaginous skeleton. It has a broad, flat snout and swims with its mouth gaping wide to strain plankton and crustaceans from the water. Paddlefish used to be found measuring six feet in length and weighing more than a hundred pounds, rivaling the other monsters of the Mississippi—the blue catfish and alligator gar.

The Mississippi River holds more ancient species than any other body of water in the United States. The continued existence of the paddlefish, alligator gar, sturgeon, and alligator snapping turtle is most likely a result of the stable environment provided by the river. Its deep canyons and sluggish water do not change quickly, and such a "time capsule" environment impedes evolution. Swamps and the depths of the ocean are other prehistoric habitats that harbor living fossils.

The sole known relative of the paddlefish lives in the Yangtze River in China. Other than the eastern United States and East Asia, few continental masses survive that have retained large freshwater drainage systems for hundreds of millions of years. As a result, the two continents have a number of floral and faunal similarities. Habitats resistant to change, such as the ancient and extremely deep pools of the Mississippi, are rare. They depend for their survival upon relative isolation from external forces. Yet the river depths, slow to flush, accumulate toxic pollutants. The continued introduction of even slight concentrations could render these exotic environments uninhabitable, and eliminate forever an entire segment of the biotic spectrum.

8

They Came To Stay

SCATTERED EVERYWHERE through the groves and brush lands were remnants of the prairie which the forest growth had not yet captured. Along the borderland, between the prairie and the encroaching brush, were wild plum and crab apple patches in great abundance, with less frequent clusters of red, black, and choke cherry and patches of red raspberry and grape vines. Before the coming of rusts and blights, the fruit of these wild trees was excellent and abundant.

ELLISON ORR,
"REMINISCENCES OF A PIONEER BOY"
IN *ANNALS OF IOWA*

DOWNRIVER FROM THE TWIN CITIES, the upper Mississippi offers one excursion after another into the past, starting twenty-five centuries ago at the end of the Archaic period, when the enigmatic "mound builders" appeared in northeastern Iowa and southern Wisconsin. These early Indians built low-relief earthen mounds, apparently used for burial purposes. Each mound was constructed during a period of years. The women were the ones who moved the dirt, carrying thousands of cubic yards in handwoven baskets.

As the mound culture matured, the mounds were constructed to represent various animals. Bear, bird, panther, and turtle are the shapes most commonly identified by archaeologists. Thousands once existed. Today many have been destroyed by erosion and the plow, but several dozen of those that remain are preserved at Effigy Mounds National Monument.

The national monument is located in Iowa across the river from the town of Prairie du Chien. We left our canoes and climbed the monument's Fire Point Trail, which ascends through woods to a glade with a low hill. The perimeter of the hill forms the outline of a walking bear: Little Bear Mound. The trail continues past other mounds—probably not effigies—and then leads to an overlook three hundred feet above the river. A ranger accompanied us and provided background on the mound builders.

Their culture developed in a region that included three habitats: prairie, riverine, and forest. The tallgrass prairie and grassland openings within the forest were grazed by elk and bison; the swamps and sloughs were home to waterfowl and fish; the woods teemed with deer and small mammals. The three biomes existed in close proximity within a geographically narrow area, fading into one another to form a rich and productive mosaic.

Such diversity was attractive to prehistoric hunters. In autumn when game became scarce the bands would break up into family units, coming together again in summer when food was abundant. Besides hunting, the Indians gathered acorns, walnuts, maple sugar, and edible wild plants such as arrowhead and yellow lotus.

A region so rich in food but small in size might have stimulated continual feuds unless, as one hypothesis suggests, the effigy mounds served as territorial demarcators as well as graves. The bear and other shapes, denoting different clans, probably indicated the boundaries of hunting territories. Such markers would have mitigated any conflict inherent in diverse hunting and gathering groups exploiting a limited geographical area. The mounds were a cultural response to an environment. The land shaped the forms of society, and the societal forms shaped the land.

The effigy mound culture lasted until the twelfth century, at which time it was supplanted by a people identifiable with the Iowa, a tribe in existence within historic times. Later, pressed by eastern tribes who had been displaced by the whites, the Iowa moved farther west.

We crossed the river from the national monument to Prairie du Chien, skipping several hundred centuries from the mound builders to the fur trade. "Prairie of the Dog," named after an old chief of the Fox tribe, was a fur post as early as 1673 and became in time the major rendezvous north of St. Louis. The Mississippi River served as Prairie du Chien's highway for bringing in furs trapped in the far north.

A fur trader named Hercules Louis Dousman arrived at Prairie du Chien in 1826 as the confidential agent for John Jacob Astor, founder of the American Fur Company. Within a few years, in 1843, Dousman had built a red brick house on top of an Indian mound at the town's riverbank. He called the Georgian mansion "The House on the Mound." He and his wife filled the dwelling with fine furniture and art objects, and the Dousman home became a center for culture in what was otherwise still a wilderness. Later the house was razed by their son, who erected the cream-colored brick residence that stands today, called Villa Louis.

Dousman, like other traders, saw the approaching demise of the fur trade and put his money into lumber and steamboats. He also speculated in land. All three proved to be shrewd investments. The 1840s were boom days for the new steamboat lines. On upriver

BRIDGES ON THE MISSISSIPPI, AT DUBUQUE

trips the steamers brought immigrants from Europe—settlers hungry for land. On return trips the boats transported the resources of the newly opened upper valley: hides, grain, lumber, and lead.

Among the earliest settlers in this area were miners to work the lead mines of Wisconsin, Iowa, and Illinois. Where the three states come together, three river towns grew—Potosi, Galena, and Dubuque—forming the center of the lead industry of the upper Mississippi. Forty miles from Prairie du Chien we stopped at Potosi, today a sleepy village, to visit St. John Mine. It is representative of ten thousand mines that once operated in Grant County, which was one of five counties that constituted the lead region.

St. John Mine, owned by a man named Willis St. John, was opened in 1827. When the miners first arrived, Black Hawk and the Sauk were still a threat. No permanent buildings could be erected because the Indians would burn them out. So the miners slept in "badger huts," holes dug in the hillside. Each hut was barely larger than a coffin. From a distance they resembled badger burrows, and since the miners were Wisconsin's first settlers, the state became known as the "Badger State."

The ore, containing a high-grade lead and sulfur mineral called "galena," was used to make lead shot. Being an easily reducible metal, lead could be smelted using primitive techniques. A smelting furnace straddled Potosi Creek, which runs through the village and down to the Mississippi. Once melted, the lead and sulfur would separate and fall into the stream, sinking to the bottom to cool. Later the bottom would be scraped for the lead, the sulfur being left. Only the fish, if any survived, know how much lead was missed.

The pigs of lead were shipped downriver to Dubuque, where again they were melted down. The liquid was poured into holes at the top of a "shot tower," a wooden structure between sixty and seventy feet high. On its way to the bottom, the lead cooled and solidified into pellets. The shot tower still stands at Dubuque.

Potosi had a population of nine thousand at the time of the lead boom, which lasted from 1838 to 1848. The miners came from the south: Kentucky, Tennessee, and southern Illinois. In 1848 many were drawn by the California gold rush, so many that Potosi dwindled to three thousand in only two years. During its one decade of prosperity, the town shipped thousands of pounds of lead. St. John Mine alone produced 250,000 pounds.

The next wave of settlers came, like the miners, from Kentucky and Tennessee. They were woodland farmers, pioneers who were accustomed to viewing trees as obstacles to be eliminated and land as raw material to be used until worn out, and then abandoned. They were less interested in fields than in animal husbandry—raising horses, cows, mules—and in hunting. When the game gave out and the soil was no longer productive, they moved on.

They were followed by immigrants from Europe, who traveled upriver by steamboat as deck passengers. Crowded together, they shared the space with their wagons and livestock. Cabin fare was one cent a mile, but deck passage was much less. They slept on bales or the deck itself, and cooked their meals on a sheet-iron stove. Guidebooks, such as *The Emigrant's Directory to the Western States of North America,* provided advice for the newcomer to the Mississippi:

> The greatest inconvenience to strangers . . . arises from the immense swarms of mus-
> quitos, which prey upon him, and give him a fever of vexation: it is impossible to travel
> with any comfort in the summer, without being prepared with musquito-curtains, as a
> protection by night.

Land-starved, these Europeans were the settlers who stayed on the "Middle Border," who learned to maintain the soil fertility, who built houses and barns, and fenced in their fields. They were the hardworking, frugal, "excessively industrious" pioneers that the great naturalist John Muir pictured in his autobiography about his boyhood in Wisconsin.

In 1849 the elder Muir brought John and two of his siblings from Scotland to the frontier. The mother and other children remained behind until a home was established. After a six-week sea voyage, the family traveled inland. They were laden, like most pioneers, with too many possessions. They carried a cast-iron stove, provisions, and a four-hundred-pound box containing beam scales, iron wedges, and carpenter's tools. Muir's father settled on a quarter-section "oak opening" on Wisconsin's prairie. He built a shanty with bur-oak logs. Then began the labor of making a farm.

"I was put to the plough at the age of twelve, when my head reached but little above the handles. . . ." It fell to John, the eldest, to do the heaviest work. He put in long, sweaty days plowing, sowing, hoeing, harvesting, chopping stovewood, feeding the animals, building fences, and grubbing out stumps. Even when sick with mumps, he worked.

One year he hand-dug a well, cutting ninety feet deep through fine-grained sandstone:

I had to sit cramped in a space about three feet in diameter, and wearily chip, chip, with heavy hammer and chisels from early morning until dark, day after day, for weeks and months. In the morning, father and David lowered me in a wooden bucket by a windlass, hauled up what chips were left from the night before, then went away to the farm work and left me until noon, when they hoisted me out for dinner. After dinner I was promptly lowered again, the forenoon's accumulation of chips hoisted out of the way, and I was left until night.

The Muir fields were put into wheat, corn, and potatoes until, in only four years, the soil was exhausted. But soon the farmers of Wisconsin learned to grow English clover on the worn-out fields, plowing it under to restore them. From then on, the Muir corn was rotated with clover. Not all the farming practices of the Wisconsin pioneers were as ecologically sound. Aldo Leopold tells how the early settlers cut hay off the marshes, and later drained them for fields. Subsequently the organic soil dried out; peat fires burned uncontrollably and, to drown them, the marshes had to be reflooded. The crane population was devastated by the succession of disturbances.

Only three or four years after the Muirs began, every quarter-section within a radius of four miles was taken up, mostly by immigrants from Great Britain. Frame houses were built, wells dug, orchards planted, fields drained, and towns established. "In a very short time," Muir tells us, "the new country began to look like an old one."

It took only twenty years—the twenty preceding the Civil War—to settle the tallgrass prairie: Illinois and southern Wisconsin, the eastern half of Iowa, and the northern part of Missouri. Unlike the European pattern of small farms grouped around villages, the farms of the Midwest were large and spaced far apart. Mercantile services were supplied by a few good-sized towns. Of these, the river towns had the advantage of location, a window on the world. The economic base of the river town was built around supplying the settler with manufactured goods such as tools, brought upriver by steamboat. For a return cargo, the river town collected the products of the Mississippi Valley.

Lumber more than anything else was responsible for the growth of the upper Mississippi's river towns. Each one had its sawmill, and some had several: Winona in southern Minnesota; La Crosse in Wisconsin; Dubuque, Clinton, Davenport, Muscatine, Burlington, and Keokuk in Iowa; Quincy in Illinois; and Hannibal in Missouri. A resident of Winona told me that when the town rebuilt a downtown street, the road workers tried to dig down to hardpan but hit nothing but sawdust and old logs.

Lumber sawed at the mills was floated down to market in rafts. A crew of twenty or so steered the raft, manning thirty-foot oars along each edge, while a pilot shouted orders. In the center were huts for the oarsmen, plus a shed for the cook and his helper. At first the rafts were constructed of lumber. But when in 1843 a boom holding a winter's cut of logs broke, scattering the logs before they could be taken to a sawmill, an enterprising lumberman gathered the runaways and had them made up into a raft. He employed Stephen B. Hanks, a cousin of Abe Lincoln, to pilot it to St. Louis for sale of the logs. By 1857 log rafts outnumbered lumber rafts three to one.

The largest log raft ever to go down the Mississippi was 270 feet wide by 1,550 feet long, much longer than an ocean liner. The largest lumber raft, containing even more

wood, covered six acres. Though the rafts were long, they were flexible enough to twist into C's and even S's at tight bends. That kind of huge mass was hard to stop. When a crew was forced to tie up because of fog or a head wind, the men would pass a thick hawser around a tree on shore. The momentum was so difficult to check that the tree was often uprooted.

A pilot, responsible for a valuable cargo, was a highly paid and respected member of the river community. He tended to be something of a dandy. The usual outfit consisted of French calf boots, black trousers, a red shirt, a wide-brimmed hat, gloves, and a black silk cravat tied in a square knot with flowing ends. The crew members were much lower on the social scale. Because of the raftsmen's reputation for drunkenness and fighting, church-going townspeople hated to see a raft coming.

As early as 1851, steamboats were used to push the rafts across Lake Pepin. By the 1860s steamboats were in regular use for rafting on the whole upper river. Some were owned by steamboat companies and some by logging companies. On the maiden voyage of the *J. W. Van Sant,* the first riverboat designed just for rafting, Frederick Weyerhaeuser went along as a guest to see how the new vessel performed. By 1873, sixteen to eighteen rafts a day were passing the town of Davenport.

The *Ottumwa Belle* ran the last raft down the Mississippi in 1915. Stephen Hanks rode as an honored guest. An old man by then, he had not only piloted the first log raft, he had ridden on one of the first lumber rafts. The whole era had passed in one man's lifetime. The raft boats were sold and converted to general towing or excursion work.

ONE MORNING ON THE RIVER below Minneapolis, the *Delta Queen* appeared to us out of the fog, an apparition from the past. As she glided slowly by, against the current, we radioed her pilothouse. Her calliope began to serenade us, hauntingly. People on the top deck jogged in slow motion to the music. She blew her foghorn once; the long, soulful note disappeared with her into the mist.

Minneapolis is the boundary between the wilderness river and the river of history. Upstream from the metropolis, it is the marshes and the eagles that upstage the towns. Below the Twin Cities, the shores are still wooded, but it is the old settlements and traffic of the river that constitute its soul. The Mississippi of Mark Twain still lives in its towns, and the towns still long for their riverboats.

People gather when they hear a steamboat is due. As we left the town of Wabasha, we paddled past families on houseboats and threaded our way through dozens of swimmers, all greeting the *Mississippi Queen*. Both *Queens* are excursion boats that ply the Ohio and Mississippi. A few days later we arrived at another town just as the *Mississippi Queen* was departing. The calliope played "Dixie" and "You Are My Sunshine" and "Cruising Down the River," as she moved sedately from shore with smoke pouring from her stacks, the crowd waving, flags flying, and a flotilla of small boats to escort her. As she turned to go downstream she filled the channel, like a Currier and Ives print against the beautiful hills of the Mississippi.

One river town that especially evokes the steamboat era is Nauvoo, Illinois, 196 miles upriver from St. Louis. Nauvoo was founded in 1839 by Mormons fleeing persecution. In a mere seven years the Mormon settlers transformed a swamp into a city of brick houses, in its heyday the largest in Illinois.

One of our expedition's coleaders, economist Steve Andersen, was born in Utah to a Mormon family. He brought along a diary in which his great-great-grandfather, Perrigrine Sessions, chronicled the travels of the family between 1832 and 1856. In 1835 Steve's ancestor had met Brigham Young, disciple of the prophet Joseph Smith, the founder of the Church of Latter-day Saints. After Perrigrine Sessions converted, he sold his farm in Maine and took his family to Kirtland, Ohio, to be near Joseph Smith. Before long, the headquarters of the church was moved to western Missouri, and a number of families like the Sessionses went along. Perrigrine bought land, fenced in a hundred acres, and planted corn and potatoes.

The Mormon settlers were not kindly received by the Missourians, who feared the large influx of newcomers would drive up land prices. They also feared the Mormons would vote in a block and gain political control. Most of all, their animosity was directed toward the Mormons' claim to have received new divine revelations.

Open hostility soon flared up. Mormon houses were burned and their stock stolen. In the winter of 1838 the harassment escalated to bloodshed; seventeen Mormons were shot when they took refuge in a log building. The mob fired at the hapless victims through chinks in the walls.

The Mormons abandoned their homes in midwinter and fled to Illinois. Perrigrine tells of their trials:

> When we arrived at the Mississippi River, there were some two hundred families camped on the bank who could not get across because the ice ran so thick and the weather was so cold that boats could not pass over. Many of them could not get much more than parched corn to eat. There was three inches of snow on the ground.
>
> This brought sickness, and on one night two of the brethren died for the want of the comforts of life. Women gave birth to their children on the road, in tents. Some of them never saw the inside of a house until their babies were three weeks old. My wife and mother were taken with chills and fever during the eleven days we were there. At last we crossed the river and bid old Missouri farewell.

Once in Illinois, the Mormons were ready to make a new start and build a town. For the site, the prophet Joseph Smith selected a swampy river bottom sloping up to a wooded bluff. It was the only land available at a reasonable price. A land broker named Isaac Galland offered the church twenty thousand acres for two dollars an acre. Like many speculators in those days, Galland appears to have sold lands for which he did not own clear title, and to have sold them more than once. The future site of Nauvoo already had a small village, Commerce City, one of the many "paper towns" of the Mississippi.

All along the frontier, hopeful promoters platted townsites and had maps engraved showing streets, stores, and churches, none of which existed except in the speculator's mind. The pamphlets, circulated in New York and Boston, attracted droves of buyers with the lure of lots at bargain prices in towns with "promising" futures. What the unwary Easterner really bought was prairie and river bottom. By the time he traveled by steamboat up the Mississippi, the land shark had disappeared, leaving the luckless owner to search for his lot amid the sloughs and marshes.

Often the unhappy merchant or craftsman had no choice but to stay and make the best of his mistake. The paper town would then take on a semblance of reality in the form of three or four miserable log cabins. Usually, like Commerce City before the Mormons came, it never succeeded in growing into a real town.

But in the case of Commerce City, Joseph Smith selected it for the new Mormon refuge because, in his words, "no more eligible place" presented itself. Commerce was chosen even though the area was so wet that it was difficult for a person on foot to negotiate, much less a team. For the future metropolis of Nauvoo, Smith laid out a gridiron of 150 squares of four acres, each divided into four lots. Each parcel had room for a garden, an orchard, and domestic animals. The residents would have their farms outside the city. To overcome America's increasing segregation of town and farm, Smith envisioned a new society of urban agriculturists.

Within a year Nauvoo had a population of nearly three thousand. As with the paper town of Commerce City, the houses of Nauvoo at this point were still log cabins, and many, like the one the Sessionses inhabited with two other families, had no floor or chimney. For the first few months Perrigrine and his wife were sick with fever. They

were fortunate to survive, for many of their neighbors died from malaria during the summer of 1839 and the following summer, before the swamp was drained.

In 1840 the Illinois legislature was persuaded to grant the town a charter that made Nauvoo a quasi-sovereign state with its own militia. The existence of the legion was later to contribute to a new wave of anti-Mormon fear.

By late 1842 the population had grown to ten thousand. Perrigrine and others were sent on missions in America and abroad to make converts and bring them to Nauvoo. Brigham Young and the Council of the Twelve Apostles went to Great Britain, where they converted about five thousand persons and smoothed the journey to the New World. Vessels were charted to reduce costs, and provisions were bought wholesale. The Mormons even built a steamboat, *Maid of Iowa,* to bring immigrants up from New Orleans.

The economy of Nauvoo was based on agriculture, but with so many converts pouring in, the town desperately needed industry. The Des Moines Rapids on the Mississippi River had sufficient fall to provide a head of water to drive machinery. But harnessing the Mississippi was a big undertaking. The Mormons considered various proposals and actually began raising funds, but nothing ever came of the project; the economy remained mostly preindustrial with cottage and light industries. Nauvoo had a gristmill, several sawmills, a match factory, a leather "manufactory," a tanyard, a rope and cord maker, a lime kiln, several brickyards, a glove and strawbonnet shop, a brewery, a bakery, a pottery, a tool factory, a cabinet maker, a blacksmith, a spinning-wheel maker, a printing office, several tailors, cobblers, and wagoners.

Before long, Brigham Young and others were replacing their log cabins with small brick homes. Perrigrine Sessions built a house on Hotchkiss Street, next door to Lyon's pharmacy. The Mormons began constructing a temple of solid limestone with a tower 165 feet tall. It crowned the bluff and commanded a sweeping view of the river in both directions. A system of schools was organized, a newspaper printed, and plans formulated for a university. By 1844 the population was nearly twenty thousand, and Nauvoo had become the largest city in Illinois. Once again, neighboring towns were growing apprehensive about this Mormon enclave in their midst.

In the election of 1844, the Mormons became alienated from both political parties—Whigs and Democrats. They decided to run Joseph Smith for president. Elders were sent on campaigning missions to every state in the Union. It was in January of that year that a toast was drunk in the city: "May Nauvoo become the empire seat of government!"

In June, dissenters who had left the church published a newspaper advocating the repeal of Nauvoo's charter and accusing Smith of practising polygamy. Smith had their press destroyed and the apostates fled. He then called out the Nauvoo militia, prompting the dissenters to swear out a warrant for his arrest on a charge of treason. Pledged protection by the governor of Illinois, Smith surrendered. He and his brother Hyrum were incarcerated at the nearby county seat. On June 27, 1844, an anti-Mormon mob attacked the jail and killed both brothers.

Within a few months open civil war broke out. Dozens of outlying farms were burned, and many were killed on both sides. By the winter of 1845, after only seven years in Nauvoo, the stunned Mormons decided once more to abandon their hard-earned holdings and seek a homeland in an isolated wilderness where they could worship in their own way. During the years in Nauvoo, the Mormon faith had come to include a belief in plural marriages. Polygamy, at first a closely guarded secret confined to the church leaders, was later to become a primary source of contention between the federal government and the Mormon church in Utah.

Perrigrine Sessions, whose wife died early in 1845, remarried a year and a day after Joseph Smith's death, marrying Lucina Call and, on the same day, her sister, Mary. When the decision was made to leave Nauvoo, Perrigrine and his wives went into the wagon-building business. The church advised a family of five to provision itself with "one good wagon, three yoke of cattle, two cows, two beef cattle, three sheep, one thousand pounds of flour, twenty pounds of sugar, one rifle and ammunition and a tent and tent poles." Total cost was $250.

On February 4, 1846, a vanguard of Mormons ferried their wagons and teams across the Mississippi on a fleet of flatboats. During the first week four hundred teams and 1,350 Mormons crossed to Iowa. The exodus, under the leadership of Brigham Young, was spread over four months. By summer nearly 15,000 had begun the long trek to Utah.

Following the departure of the Mormons, a traveler who happened through Nauvoo noted that no more than one house in ten was occupied. Windows were broken, fences were down, gardens were choked with weeds, and front doors were open and sagging. As for the temple on the hill, it was gutted by fire in 1848 and later destroyed by a tornado.

In 1849 a group of French socialists called Icarians moved into the abandoned city to experiment with a utopian community. At their peak the Icarians at Nauvoo numbered between twelve hundred and eighteen hundred, but within a decade the community disbanded. Today Nauvoo is a quiet river town with a population of eleven hundred. The chief industries are wine and cheese making, but tourism is growing. In 1961 the Mormon church purchased several hundred acres and began the restoration of Nauvoo. Sixteen homes and several shops have been rebuilt on their original sites and meticulously decorated with furnishings of the period. Lyon's pharmacy is among the restorations, so Steve Andersen was able to locate the exact site of his ancestral home.

———————————————◆———————————————

BUILDINGS THAT HAVE REMAINED in continuous use produce a feeling for history that cannot be duplicated by a re-creation or even a restoration like Nauvoo. In Hannibal we found a cigar shop that has been operating without interruption for a hundred years. The proprietors, eighty-five-year-old Clarence Schaffer and his wife, are only the third owners. The glass counter, filled with cigars, pipe tobacco, and chewing tobacco, looks exactly the same as it does in old photographs that the Schaffers keep beneath the counter. A card game is usually being played in the back room, where a light hangs above the playing table and a spittoon stands beside each chair. In 1902 Sam Clemens, visiting Hannibal to deliver the commencement address at the high school, stopped in to play a few hands of rummy.

Living history like the cigar shop and restorations like Nauvoo are what makes this piece of the Mississippi special. The old river towns, far off the interstate system, are quiet pockets of the past. They are there to stay. Their worn sidewalks and decaying sawmills have an air of peaceful waiting, waiting for what one riverman remembered as the steamboats' "forlorn whistles in the dark."

The opportunity to time travel in the river towns is luring more and more people to this part of the river. The Army Corps of Engineers estimates that from Iowa to Missouri more than fifteen million people spend some of their leisure on the Mississippi. They go fishing in the sheltered sloughs, sailing and waterskiing on the open expanses of water above the dams, swimming off the sandy beaches, camping on houseboats, duck hunting in the fall, ice fishing in the winter, and birdwatching or sightseeing at any season. The energy situation will no doubt reduce the rate of growth in the area's recreational use, but at the same time the number of people seeking recreation is expanding. The population of the counties bordering the upper river is expected to grow at a rate significantly faster than for the United States as a whole. River use is projected to have the greatest increase near the Twin Cities, the Quad Cities (Davenport and Bettendorf in Iowa; Rock Island and Moline in Illinois), and St. Louis.

The potential use is so great that the Department of the Interior in 1972 submitted a proposal to establish an Upper Mississippi River National Recreation Area. It would stretch along 660 miles from Minneapolis to near St. Louis, consist of 623,300 acres, and provide information centers, boat ramps, campsites, marinas, supervised beaches, canoe trails, hiking trails, and bridle paths. Although much of the upper river meets the criteria for designation as a recreational river under the National Wild and Scenic Rivers Act of 1968, a national recreation area was believed able to provide better protection for the river corridor and fewer conflicts with commercial traffic.

On the upper Mississippi, recreational users and commercial traffic—the towboats—sometimes clash. Towboats are a misnomer, because the barges they move are pushed rather than towed. A string of barges lashed together makes up a "tow," and a tow is sometimes as long as a quarter of a mile. Like the lumber rafts, barge tows develop so much momentum that they cannot come to a halt in less than a half mile to a mile. They present a hazard to small boats crossing in front of them.

Barge traffic and associated modifications to the river have created additional hazards for the recreational user, such hazards as submerged "stump fields"—the remains of trees that died after dams were built to raise the water level and deepen the channel for barges. We had one close call in a stump field near Potosi and another near accident connected with navigational aids for barge traffic near Wabasha on Lake Pepin. A trick current caught one of our canoes and swept it into a buoy marking the deep channel. Striking amidships, the canoe rode up on the buoy and the upstream gunwale shipped water. The buoy popped up, lifting the canoe and dumping occupants and gear into the water.

I was a passenger in the canoe. I had a disabled shoulder and my arm was in a sling beneath my life jacket. When thrown overboard, the best I could do was kick my legs and thrash with one arm. One of the students, Tina Greene, grabbed the collar of my preserver and towed me to the upturned canoe. I hung on while she swam away to gather floating water bottles and suntan lotion. Just as Steve Andersen's canoe came to the rescue, I lost my grip on the keel. A wave engulfed me. My head went through the armhole of my life vest, and the preserver held me under. When I managed to surface I yelled, "Hey Steve, I think you're losing me." The canoe made another pass and he yanked me aboard.

The whole rescue was a model of group coordination. The canoe and all hands were saved, and almost no gear lost. But, though we were experienced canoeists and had taken every precaution from life preservers to a VHF radio and a full set of charts, we had two serious scrapes with navigational improvements in only sixty-seven days.

As recreational and commercial use on the upper Mississippi increases, accidents and conflicts will also increase. The Corps of Engineers is proceeding with a project that may greatly expand commercial traffic and industrial growth along the upper river. It is likely that recreational boating will eventually be sacrificed, as it has been on the lower Mississippi. If so, the canoes and the steamboats will vanish for good.

9

Too Thick to Drink
Too Thin to Plow

IN THE DIVISION of the Mississippi which we had passed from La Prairie des Chiens, the shores are more than three-quarters prairie on both sides, or, more properly speaking, bald hills, which instead of running parallel with the river, form a continual succession of high perpendicular cliffs and low valleys; they appear to head the river and to traverse the country in an angular direction. . . . In some places the Mississippi is uncommonly wide, and divided into many distant rivers, winding in parallel course through the same immense valley.

ZEBULON PIKE, 1805

FROM THE TWIN CITIES TO ST. LOUIS, the Mississippi wanders across a wide floodplain bordered by rolling hills and bluffs as high as six hundred feet. At times the hills follow the shore, then dip down into side valleys. The valleys beckon to river travelers but pass like country roads unexplored.

Down in the floodplain the river is braided by islands into a labyrinth of sloughs, merging into marshes and ponds. From an airplane the main channel would be difficult to discriminate, were it not for an occasional towboat pushing a string of barges. Back in the sloughs, fishermen in skiffs try their luck beneath circling clouds of ducks. Beavers cross the water, their wakes widening V's behind them.

During the late 1920s the beaver was successfully reintroduced to the wildlife refuges that stretch along most of the upper Mississippi. These backwaters are one of the most productive habitats in nature. The water is shallow, allowing the sun to penetrate to submerged vegetation nourished by organic nutrients washed down from upstream. Fish spawn in the quiet pools, birds feed on the aquatic plants, and muskrats make the mud-banks their home. In autumn bald eagles are lured to the sloughs in search of wounded waterfowl. By December the eagles move to the channel, finding pools where the water is free of ice so they can feed on fish. Between five hundred and seven hundred eagles congregate along the upper Mississippi, their Midwestern wintering grounds.

These fertile backwaters are dying. Dams built in the 1930s to deepen the main channel are choking the floodplain lakes and sloughs with silt. The dams have so accelerated the natural process of sedimentation that a fourth of the sloughs have been converted to marshland in only forty years. If nothing is done, within the next generation or two the upper Mississippi will be transformed from a natural river into an artificial canal bordered by mud flats.

The destruction has been accomplished in the name of inexpensive transportation. It has happened in increments, each innocent in itself, starting in 1824 when the federal government authorized the removal of hazards to commercial traffic. That was the year after Beltrami—the explorer with the red umbrella—had taken passage on the first steamboat to probe up the Mississippi to the Falls of St. Anthony. The river that Beltrami saw was shallow and difficult to navigate because of rapids and snags. After 1824 government boats patrolled the river taking out boulders and removing "planters" and "sawyers"—trees that fall in the river when a bank caves in. A planter is a tree that then plants itself in the riverbed, ready to tear the hull from a boat, and a sawyer is one that saws up and down in the current. A sawyer is twice as dangerous as a planter because it is frequently underwater and invisible.

With the snags gone and the river safer for navigation, small steamboats with shallow drafts soon plied the upper Mississippi and many of its tributaries. By the 1860s the raft boats had been introduced to push long strings of logs. Then in 1878, to accommodate riverboats with a greater draft, Congress directed the Corps of Engineers to deepen the navigable channel to 4.5 feet.

To constrict the river's flow and increase its velocity so it would scour the channel, the engineers built hundreds of "wing dams" (called wing "dikes" on the lower Mississippi) out of brush and rock. Wing dams are jetties that jut out from shore. To build them, willows were cut from along the riverbanks and dolomite quarried from the bluffs. Sunk at right angles to shore, the wing dams help confine the water to midstream, where it digs a deeper channel. Sandbars tend to form behind the dikes and gradually narrow the river. To further deepen the water, the Corps constructed "closing dams" across many of the side channels where the river flowed around islands. Closing dams keep the flow out of these sloughs and in the main channel.

To discourage erosion, the shore opposite a wing dam was in most places fortified with rocks. The rock protection was called "riprap." Without it, the current deflected from the wing dam with increased velocity would chew away at the opposite bank and begin to form a loop, intensifying the river's natural tendency to meander. Together, riprap and wing dams were intended to tame the river into a narrow, deep, straight canal that would be easy to navigate.

By themselves, however, riprap and wing dams did not achieve the 4.5-foot depth. The Corps of Engineers had to initiate the expensive, endless process of dredging—

digging out the sandbars that build up between the river's deep pools. In the 1800s, the bars were a constant hazard to steamboats. The pilot who was unwary or misjudged the water would find his sternwheeler running aground, and it would sometimes take days to work free, even with the passengers pitching in to help.

In 1907 Congress decided to authorize a six-foot channel in order to accommodate more powerful vessels carrying heavier payloads. This was a last-ditch attempt to save the steamboat in its death struggle with the railroad, by helping water transport compete economically. The Corps went ahead with dredging to six feet, but the steamboat was doomed. River traffic continued to decline.

During World War I the government, in need of an expanded transportation system for carrying war materials, sponsored the Federal Barge Line. River traffic experienced a rebirth. After the war, barges were used for transporting coal and grain, and by 1930 the six-foot channel was considered obsolete. The public had raised no objection to the earlier modifications, but this time, when a nine-foot channel was proposed, the Izaak Walton League stepped forward to fight the project on environmental grounds.

In addition to deeper dredging, the Corps proposed to construct a series of dams on the upper Mississippi to achieve additional depth by raising the water level. The sportsmen's league was sufficiently farsighted to suspect that the reservoirs would fill with silt. Other opponents of the project, such as the U.S. Bureau of Fisheries, expressed misgivings on the grounds that too little was known about the biological effects.

This was the second time the Izaak Walton League had fought for the Mississippi River. In the early 1920s the newly-formed league had successfully campaigned against a project to drain the river bottoms for agriculture. The sportsmen had proposed an alternative: a wildlife refuge to protect the rich bottomlands. On June 7, 1924, Congress established the Upper Mississippi Wild Life and Fish Refuge.

It has been said that the Mississippi was to the Izaak Walton League what Yosemite was to the Sierra Club. Today the upper Mississippi refuge contains 194,000 acres of wetlands extending from the foot of Lake Pepin to Rock Island in Illinois. It is a maze of sloughs, lakes, marshes, and islands. Environmentalists believe large portions qualify for wilderness designation. With a visitation of 3.5 million people a year, it is the most heavily used wildlife refuge in the United States.

In the case of the nine-foot channel, however, the voice of the barge industry was louder than that of the Izaak Walton League. Congress approved the upper Mississippi project, and the engineers went to work on the massive task of building twenty-nine dams. The system constitutes what the Corps calls a "stairway of water," a series of slackwater pools each a step or two lower than the one upstream. Each dam has one or more locks to take river traffic to the next pool. Near the dams the current is hardly noticeable even in times of high water. Only during floods, when the gates are all the way open, does the Mississippi once again flow free.

The locks and dams were completed during the 1930s except for Lock and Dam 19 at Keokuk, Iowa, which was an older dam built in 1914 to produce hydroelectric power. It is the only one on the Mississippi that generates electricity. It produces 135 megawatts, whereas the Corps estimates the potential of the system at 2,400 megawatts. The dams were built with navigation in mind and no other purpose.

Much of the floodplain was submerged under the reservoirs created by the dams, making the Mississippi wider at La Crosse in Wisconsin than it is at New Orleans. With the water level raised, new wetlands were formed and old ones expanded. Each pool has three distinct ecological habitats. The tailwater area just downstream from each dam most resembles the preimpoundment condition of the river: sloughs and islands. The middle area, once islands and hay meadows, is now marshes and shallow water. At the lower end is an open-water pool. It is the open water that contains submerged stump fields. The total water surface has been greatly increased at the expense of bottomland forests and meadows. Aquatic habitat has expanded and terrestrial declined.

The increase in water surface initially caused an explosive growth in wildlife populations that favor pooled conditions. Fish that inhabit slow-moving water have benefited, but sturgeon, paddlefish, and others that prefer a fast current are reduced to feeding in the tailwaters downstream of the dams. The Corps claims that even these species are helped by the stabilization of water levels. Prior to the dams' construction, backwaters filled with fish were cut off from the main channel each year when the high water receded. The stranded ponds dried up by late summer. During the 1870s the U.S. Bureau of Fisheries instituted a rescue program for returning landlocked fish to the river. This work was made unnecessary by the nine-foot channel, because the backwaters began retaining water throughout the year.

The reservoirs also provide an ideal habitat for one of the major food sources for fish, the mayfly nymph, also known as the willow bug or Mormon fly. Hordes of mayflies hatch in June and July, appreciated by the fish but constituting a real nuisance to communities along the river. One evening in Prairie du Chien the head of the Chamber of Commerce drove us around on a sightseeing tour. Each time the car passed a streetlamp we were pelted by a rainstorm of mayflies attracted to the light. A hatch lives only a matter of hours, and the dead insects pile up on boat decks and bridges. Some river towns use snowplows to clean up the mess; at Prairie du Chien the bridge is unlit so the town can avoid having to plow off the slippery corpses.

Raising the water level has also benefited migrating waterfowl and such marsh birds as egrets and herons. Although little data exists, biologists agree that usage of the river corridor by migrating flocks increased after 1930. A major migratory route, the Mississippi had always attracted a great variety of waterfowl, but apparently they stayed only a short time because food sources were limited. The pooled river has increased usage by providing better habitat than the river of 1930, although some biologists suspect that it does not compare with the Mississippi as it was prior to the first navigation project back in 1824.

Whatever the initial condition of the river habitat, the nine-foot channel did benefit fish and wildlife at first, but everyone, including the Corps, agrees that these benefits peaked a few years ago and we are beginning to see a decline. The ecological boom was temporary because now the backwaters are disappearing, choked with sand and silt. Two of these rich wildernesses—Question Slough and Weaver Bottoms—are near the home of Dr. Calvin Fremling, an aquatic entomologist at Winona State University, forty miles downstream from Lake Pepin. Located in one of the mid-pool zones, Question Slough at one time was a shallow backwater and Weaver Bottoms a meadow where farmers cut hay in the summer and hauled it out in the winter. After the water levels were raised, both became highly productive wetlands—until the decline began. Question Slough winds beneath dense canopies of black willows and cottonwoods, and flows into sunlit marshes filled with duckweed and pool lilies. Weaver Bottoms is the temporary home, during spring and fall migrations, of the largest concentration of whistling swans in the United States. Dr. Fremling, who has lived on the Mississippi all his life and would live nowhere else, has studied Question Slough and Weaver Bottoms for years, watching these rare environments deteriorate.

Some of the backwaters of the Mississippi are threatened by silt and others by sand. In the case of Weaver Bottoms, the culprit is sand. Sluggish water can carry fine silt in suspension, but only fast water has the energy to transport coarse, heavy particles of sand and gravel. Before the dams were built, high riverbanks protected Weaver Bottoms from frequent flooding. Now that the water level has been raised, the banks separating river and marsh are often overtopped. Floodwaters pour in, blanketing Weaver Bottoms with sand. Much of it is dredge spoil, which the Corps of Engineers removes from a nearby sandbar that forms in the channel.

For the past fifty years, the Corps has dredged 1.5 million cubic yards a year between Minneapolis and Guttenberg, Iowa. Until 1974 disposal sites were chosen according to economic considerations without regard to environmental effects. Dredging is expensive, so costs were held down by selecting the most convenient locations. The sand was dumped wherever the dredge boat was working.

The dredge *William A. Thompson* happened to be at Weaver Bottoms the day we passed. It is a functional-looking boat with two decks and a pilothouse on top. A cutter in front was grinding up the river bottom, and a giant vacuum cleaner was sucking the mixture of sand and water into a long pipe supported on pontoons. The spoil was being pumped onto shore rather than directly into the backwaters as was usually done in the past.

We frequently camped on the monuments of sand left by the dredge boats. One day the botanist in our group, Barbara Gudmundson, conducted an ecological tour. Dredge spoil, with its temperature extremes, is a hostile environment. Walking back from the river, Barbara pointed out a sandbar willow seedling—a pioneer—surviving in the barren sand. A pea plant, a nitrogen fixer, was growing in a sheltered depression. Farther back we found sweet clover and milkweed. These first plants produce duff that will encourage later, less hardy species. Winged pigweed, a major colonizer of dredge spoil, helps hold organic matter and prevent the sand from blowing. As we reached the fringe of woods, Barbara identified northern red oak and pin oak, elm and willow. The dredged sand is soft and difficult to walk on, unlike the natural beaches of the lower Mississippi where the sand is packed.

On the upper river it is not unheard of now for a wildlife refuge sign to be nearly buried in soft spoil. Of the waterfowl and other wildlife that depend on the upper Mississippi refuge, dredging has hit the canvasback duck the hardest. As more and more wetlands are drained in other parts of the country, the canvasbacks have congregated along the upper river. At the Keokuk pool nearly one million ducks were counted in a single day in 1969. At any one time a third of the world's population of canvasbacks may be feeding at pools 7 and 8. (The dams and reservoirs are numbered, starting at Minneapolis.) The ducks come down from the north and fly to Chesapeake Bay or the Gulf of Mexico, relying on food along the Mississippi for the energy to finish their migration.

Today the canvasback population has dropped to half the 1969 level. Dredging of the river bottom has decimated the fingernail clam, one of the canvasback's prime food sources.

The clam, or freshwater mussel, beds of the upper Mississippi were at one time the densest in the world. They have declined since the construction of the nine-foot channel. In 1976 two species—the Higgins eye *(Lampsilis higginsi)* and fat pocketbook *(Proptera capax)*—were listed as endangered. Dredging, pollution, and overharvesting are responsible.

In the late 1800s commercial clamming enjoyed a whirlwind couple of decades on the upper Mississippi, until the supply of mussels was exhausted. One bed yielded five hundred tons of shells in a single year. Species with shells suitable for pearl buttons were harvested; the industry ended once plastic buttons were developed to replace the diminishing natural resource. In the 1960s, however, mussels became commercially valuable again when clammers began shipping shells to Japan, where they are used in making cultured pearls.

Although overharvesting and pollution are partly responsible for the decline of the Mississippi mussel, the most dramatic impact on river mollusks has been from the dredging. In July of 1976, for example, the Corps' dredge boat ground up a hundred thousand yards of sand at Prairie du Chien that contained more than 1,700 clams of 33 species, including 60 of the rare Higgins eye.

Where Weaver Bottoms suffers from the effects of dredge spoil, Question Slough suffers from the more insidious problem of silt. Not only does the plow cause erosion, farmers in the surrounding countryside tend not to fence off their pastures. And when a sixteen-hundred-pound animal wanders down to a feeder stream and tramples the vegetation, the bank is torn up and silt loaded with agricultural nutrients eventually washes down to the backwaters like Question Slough.

The eroded soil smothers the slough's submerged plants. With the silt come nitrates and phosphates that stimulate algal blooms and mats of aquatic weeds. The algae and weeds consume oxygen as they decay, and the slough eutrophicates—its water becomes stagnant and excessively fertile. The slough fills in with silt and decaying vegetation.

The process is natural. For thousands of years the river has flooded, leaving behind silt as it recedes, so with every spring some sloughs become shallower. The growth of vegetation speeds up the process by trapping additional sediment, and eventually what were once backwaters fill in and age into marshes. The seasons pass and floodwaters inundate the marshes until they too silt in. A slough is gone, a wet meadow has emerged.

The dams, by slowing the current, have greatly accelerated the normal process of sedimentation. It has changed from a phenomenon that takes centuries to one that flashes by in a matter of decades.

Everyone on the river from housewives to biologists to fishermen will tell of a favorite backwater that has filled, within memory. Dr. Fremling has documented that Gibbs Slough, now ankle deep, contained 11.5 feet of water just after the dams were built. Harold Berdon, manager of a fishing company, remembers a stretch of open water that two decades ago was 16 feet deep. Today it grows willows.

Most estimates give the backwaters that are left fifty years or less. The change could happen even faster. In the past, sedimentation took place underwater where it was invisible. But now as the silt reaches the surface and plants speed up the accretion, the rate of sedimentation may become exponential.

As the backwaters silt in, the marshes creep downstream. The marshlands of the middle region become meadows—terrestrial habitat that is biologically less productive—and the open pools turn into marshes. In most cases what is already lost cannot be retrieved. At the same time, few new backwaters are coming into existence.

In the past when the Mississippi flooded, its raging waters would sometimes cut through one of the meander loops that form as the river wanders across its floodplain. The stranded former channel became an oxbow lake, a new backwater. In time it too underwent siltation and formed a marsh. Year after year the spring floods came and the cycle repeated itself. Old wetlands dried up, new ones formed. A river system has a dynamic equilibrium, continually replacing its lost backwaters by meandering.

Hydrologists believe that rivers meander because the most probable path of a randomly moving particle is not a straight line, but a sine-generated curve—a meander. Watch water trickle down a shower stall. When the discharge is just right, it will meander. What is true of water in a shower is true of a river in its natural state. But when rock riprap is used to control bank erosion, the normal pattern of meandering is disturbed. Hydraulics experts with the Corps of Engineers will not go so far as to say they have achieved a stable channel, but along most of the upper Mississippi no oxbows have formed in the past ten years. The lost wetlands are not being replaced.

We could reverse this process, but a hydraulics engineer would be reluctant to do so. Releasing the river from constraints and allowing it to reestablish meandering channels would reduce the Mississippi's value for navigation. And as the wetlands silt in, the water stored in them has to go somewhere. To accommodate the increased volume, the main channel will either increase its width or, if it is confined by bluffs, increase its depth and velocity. Without the wetlands the channel will become deeper and faster: a stable, trained, hydraulically-efficient waterway, ideal for navigation. Or, as others see it, a dull gray canal between mud flats.

ONE MAN FELT THERE HAD to be a way not to destroy thousands of acres of wetlands. Keith Larson, who holds a doctorate in wildlife ecology, canoed with us for a couple of days, although he had to leave when the pace aggravated his coronary condition. In the early seventies, as chief ecologist for the Corps' St. Paul District, Keith became aware of the damage caused by dredging. He felt it his duty to inform the public. He left the Corps and became a public affairs officer and research advisor for the U.S. Fish and Wildlife Service.

To spread the concern he felt, Keith began an intensive campaign. He put together a slide show, "The Great River," which won third place in the International Film Festival in Chicago. He produced pamphlets and television programs, and he conducted tours of dredge sites for army generals, scientists, and environmentalists.

In 1973, with awareness of the impact of dredging on wetlands and wildlife growing, the state of Wisconsin initiated a lawsuit against the Corps. The engineers had never prepared an environmental impact statement for the operation and maintenance of the nine-foot channel. In March of 1974 a federal district court granted Wisconsin an injunction against dredging. The Corps, the state, and the Fish and Wildlife Service agreed that it was time to talk.

In authorizing both the dams and the wildlife refuge, Congress had created the problem by mandating two uses of the upper Mississippi that are inherently contradictory. Late in 1974 it was decided that an interagency study program was needed to resolve the conflicting demands on the river. At the first meeting Keith Larson was the one to think of an acronym for the task force: GREAT, or Great River Environmental Action Team.

A cooperative effort was begun that is to continue for ten years, until 1983. Keith is not among those seeing it through to the end because, after two coronary operations, in 1977 he was forced to retire. His illness, the government acknowledges, was caused by job stress. Keith describes himself with a smile as "a casualty of the environmental wars."

GREAT was carved into three divisions for different stretches of the river. GREAT I, from the Twin Cities to Guttenberg, Iowa, completed its study in 1980. GREAT II, Guttenberg to Saverton, Missouri, and GREAT III, Saverton to the confluence of the Ohio, got a later start. Work groups were made responsible for determining what research was needed and contracting with universities and private firms to conduct it. The major emphasis is dredging and its impact on wildlife, but attention is also paid to other demands on the river, such as recreation.

GREAT has laid the groundwork for interagency cooperation, helped focus public attention on the plight of the Mississippi, and stimulated needed research. A start has been made at dealing with the problem of channel maintenance. Inspection teams composed of representatives from the Corps, the interested states, and the Fish and Wildlife Service are now sent out to locate environmentally preferable sites for spoil disposal. But careful siting is still difficult in emergencies when dredging is necessary to free a grounded towboat.   .

GREAT has also instituted pilot programs to test new ways of handling dredge spoil: open-water disposal where the river itself is used to transport the sand closer to acceptable sites; booster pumps to raise the spoil up inclines and across backwaters out of the floodplain; permanent pipelines for chronic troublespots; and dredge stockpiles near population centers so the public can use the spoil for landfills, road sanding, and concrete aggregate.

One of GREAT's major recommendations was that the depth of maintenance dredging be reduced. In the past the Corps dredged eleven or even thirteen feet in order to accommodate vessels with a nine-foot draft, having interpreted the nine-foot mandate of Congress to mean draft, not channel. Reducing the depth would save millions in tax dollars and alleviate the disposal problem. Then during times of low flow when the water's depth is most critical, in order to ride safely in the river, barges would carry lighter loads. This curtailing of operations would be an acknowledgment of the inherent limitations on water transportation imposed by nature.

Dredging to a reduced depth was tried in 1977 in the GREAT I district. In that year the amount of spoil dredged decreased from a former average of 1.5 million cubic yards a year to 202,000 cubic yards. The decrease was partly due to the reduced depth dredging, but 1975 through 1977 were drought years, when the river did not have sufficient flow to transport the coarse particles that form sandbars. In 1978 and 1979 the rains were heavier, the river moved more sand, and dredging once again increased.

Other studies for GREAT investigated the effect of side-channel alterations. For the Question Slough area, measures were recommended to restore some of the flowage patterns that existed before the locks and dams were built. Gated aeration culverts were installed to bring in oxygenated water, along with a partial closing dam to reduce the influx of sediment. But Question Slough is only one of many wetlands. Each is unique and must be studied individually to determine the best method for slowing its deterioration. Much of what we need to know about the Mississippi will require long-term monitoring and research.

Numerous problems of the river are no closer to solution today than they were in 1974. Dredge spoil is not yet sold to the public. There are legal issues that revolve around the government being in competition with private sand and gravel companies. Nor is riverine disposal used; GREAT did not have the funds to investigate the impact of dumping sand into the main channel to be carried downstream. Sending down clouds of sand may prove to be a poor idea: one study showed that even ordinary dredging resuspends fecal coliforms. At the same time, reduction in the depth of dredging is being vigorously opposed by the barge industry. And the overriding question remains: How can fish and wildlife survive the stresses imposed by barge traffic in the very midst of their spawning and feeding grounds?

Various alternatives exist. One is to pronounce the wetlands dead. Let them silt in. But if they do, we will see a deterioration of water quality, because the backwaters function as biological cleansers. In the slow water of the sloughs, pollutants settle out along with sediment. Dr. Fremling compares the impoundments to sewage treatment lagoons. They have helped keep the Mississippi's water quality, at least below Lake Pepin, tolerable. But as the water surface decreases—as everything but a central canal silts in—the fecal coliforms, the PCBs, the lead, the mercury, the cadmium, the pesticides will all show up at the water intakes of dozens of towns and cities that depend on the Mississippi for drinking water.

If the river bottoms are allowed to deteriorate, those towns will also face more destructive flooding. Wetlands serve to temporarily store excess water, releasing it slowly so that downstream the floodwaters gather over a longer period and have a lower crest. Backwaters moderate the extremes of a flooding river.

The Mississippi's backwaters are considered to be the most important aquatic resource left in the United States. If they become terrestrial habitat, they will be farmed and eventually industrialized. Dr. Thomas Claflin, an aquatic ecologist at the University of Wisconsin at La Crosse, argues in an unsentimental, hard-nosed way that we should save the Mississippi's wetlands because to keep what we have is cheaper than to spend millions developing new wetlands. The Corps of Engineers has already built experimental marshes, but they are expensive—and small. What makes the Mississippi's backwaters so valuable to wildlife and recreationists is that they are an integral unit. A Washington official defended the Mississippi with an apt comparison: "You can't duplicate the Grand Canyon with dozens of little canyons."

If we decide not to write off these places of beauty, some-say the only thing to do is to rip out the dams. Eliminate commercial navigation on the upper Mississippi. One biologist who leans toward this radical solution suggests that bulk commodities such as coal and grain currently transported by barge could instead be moved by unit train. Those who shrink at such a drastic and possibly unrealistic step can only suggest admittedly stopgap measures, to help the wetland resource last a little longer.

As we mold the river to our needs, we make it more vulnerable to such threats as pollution and excess silt. Taking away the Mississippi's ability to meander, to adjust its channel, has made it less able to cope with external changes. It is less resilient and more dependent on artificial management to maintain its natural resources. Managing the channel to prolong the life of the backwaters will be expensive—like any life-support system. The Mississippi highway will not be a cheap road, as it has been in the past. Seven or eight years ago, to move dredge spoil cost the Corps fifty-nine cents a cubic yard. Today it runs three dollars. As costs rise, river transportation will be less and less competitive. Society will have to pay the increasing price of maintaining an unstable system—a river channelized for navigation.

Lining the Mississippi and tributaries like the Chippewa River with riprap reduces streambank erosion, the major source of sand. But a river that does not expend energy eroding its banks will scour its bed, and the sand thus taken up will be deposited in bars that require dredging. As long as the Mississippi is used for commercial navigation, dredge spoil will be a headache demanding more and more expensive remedies—unless the wetlands are allowed to fill and the river attains the hydraulic efficiency of a canal. In that event we will have to spend a great deal more on sewage treatment and flood control.

In the case of silt, once it is in the river it is there to stay. The best solution is to treat the underlying cause—poor soil conservation practices. The fiery red sunsets beloved by river dwellers are the product of dust from Missouri and Iowa farms. In Iowa, erosion is so severe that in many counties two bushels of topsoil are required to grow each bushel of corn.

Davenport, an Iowa river town, is surrounded by the rich farmland of Scott County. Scott County's erosion rate is two and a half times the national average. Nationwide we lose 4.8 tons per acre per year; Scott County loses 13.2 tons. One cause is the increasing cultivation of hilly land, prone to erosion. As prime agricultural acreage is lost to urban sprawl—as farms on the fringes of Davenport are turned into subdivisions and shopping centers—steep pastures end up sown in row crops.

In addition, an ironic positive-feedback loop has developed. The army engineers improve the river for navigation, thereby encouraging the Scott County farmer to take advantage of the cheap transportation by increasing food production, which today requires cultivating steeper and steeper land. Bumper harvests result, like the one in 1979; and because the farmers have no room to store their grain, they press for more grain barges. The expansion of barge traffic completes the loop by requiring an increase in river maintenance.

AN IOWA TRIBUTARY OF THE MISSISSIPPI

The greatest threat to the upper Mississippi may well be agribusiness. The sole goal of corporate-owned farms is to maximize profit. Often policy is to plow up every inch of ground, including hedgerows and windbreaks. Oversized tractors are used that are too big to manage the tight curves required by contour plowing.

The soil conservation practices learned in the 1930s were forgotten as food prices rose in the 1960s. And as long as prices go up, the Midwest will gladly be the breadbasket of the nation, just as the North African desert was once the granary of the Roman Empire. As a French philosopher has said, the forests came before civilization, the deserts after. Iowa topsoil was once fourteen to sixteen inches deep. Today six to eight inches remain. When that is gone, the world will have another desert.

Heavier application of fertilizer has masked the loss of soil. Today Lonnie Miller, Scott County's young District Soil Conservationist, is hopeful that the rising cost of fertilizers will help turn farmers back to old practices such as terracing, stripcropping, and crop rotation. Lonnie is especially optimistic about the new technique of no-till farming, which he is encouraging in his county. With no-till the seed is planted through the residue of last year's crop. The soil is not disturbed by plowing. At all times it is protected from that minute explosion that occurs when a raindrop beats against bare ground.

No-till cuts growing costs in half by reducing the number of times the tractor must go over the field. The farmer need not plow or disc. He needs fewer machines, and the ones he has can be smaller, since less horsepower is needed if the soil is not to be turned upside down. The farmer comes out ahead in equipment, labor, and fuel. The bad news is that to control weeds he must continue spraying with herbicides and in fact may even need to increase their use slightly, unless he finds the techniques of organic farming feasible.

In 1979 Lonnie Miller persuaded Scott County farmers to put fifteen hundred acres into no-till, up from two hundred acres in 1978. Studies for GREAT I determined that most of the sediment in the river washes off of nine million acres out of the watershed's fifty-one million acres. The cost of reducing upland erosion by one-third would be $243 million initially and $44 million in yearly expenditures for maintenance.

Whatever happens in the cornfield, mud will continue to come down the Mississippi just as it always has. The only way to protect the wetlands completely would be to let the river play things its own way: in other words, eliminate commercial navigation. If that is not to be, some compromise must be found, some means of considerate coexistence. Jerry Schotzko of the Upper Mississippi Wild Life and Fish Refuge suggests the only realistic approach is to limit future expansion, both by commercial and recreational interests. Growth by either one imperils the wildlands. When it comes to resolving conflicts, he says, those pressing for the other interests—navigation and recreation—always look toward gains. Fish and wildlife are just trying to hold their own. Every time we compromise when it comes to wilderness, we increase the earth's losses, but all that happens to the other interests is that they reduce their future gains. They operate on earnings; the earth, approaching bankruptcy, operates on capital.

10

The Crossroads

COMPANY PR MEN have developed a kind of Tugboat Annie rugged individualism image for the industry. In fact, many of the towing companies are subsidiaries of some of the largest and most powerful corporations in the nation, among them U.S. Steel, Phillips Petroleum, Cargill, Peabody Coal, Consolidation Coal, Wyandotte Chemicals, Atlantic Richfield, DuPont, Exxon, Tenneco, and Union Carbide.

JONATHAN ELA, TESTIMONY BEFORE
SENATE SUBCOMMITTEE, 1977

*B*Y THE MIDDLE OF AUGUST the fading of summer had forced our expedition to end the canoe phase of the journey at Hannibal. Three of us continued in an old motorboat, gear crammed in every inch of the aging hull.

In a day or two we reached the next-to-last lock: Locks and Dam 26 at Alton, Illinois, just above St. Louis. For three or four miles above the dam, the shores were lined with towboats parked end to end. At the gates of the lock, the water was filled with maneuvering barges. We threaded our way between the *Hornet,* the *American Beauty,* and the *National Progress,* feeling as vulnerable in our open boat as a moped among semitrailers. We were the only little boat in sight.

We slipped between a barge and the lock's guidewall, gingerly working our way to the chain that rings a bell to let the lockmaster know a recreational boat waits below. Our borrowed two-way radio had been returned, so we could not announce our arrival as we had at upstream locks—from a safe distance. Once we reached the bell, we could not hear it ring, and we were too low in the water to see over the wall, so we had no way to tell whether our arrival was noted. Uncomfortable about rocking in the waves shoulder to shoulder with a steel barge and a concrete wall, we backtracked upstream and tied to a "dolphin," a timber pile filled with dirt. Weeds poked out the top. Lack of waiting areas for pleasure boats is one of the issues being addressed by GREAT. In the canoes we had sometimes drifted into a side channel and held class while waiting in the hot sun. But here we could see no haven, only barges.

Before long, deckhands on a neighboring towboat yelled for us to move as they were about to adjust the tension on steel cables mooring them to our dolphin. For lack of an alternative we went down to the lock, approached a tow, and called to a deckhand to find out what was happening. He asked his captain to radio the lockmaster. The word was that we would be put through the auxiliary lock as soon as it emptied. The deckhand added ominously that we should wait somewhere else, or we might be crushed between his boat and the barges that would emerge.

At five in the afternoon, after three hours waiting, we were locked through. Traffic, we found out, had been backed up for days. Lockmaster James Fogilphol, a civilian employee of the Corps for thirty years, explained the situation. A barge heavily loaded with scrap iron had bent in the middle and sunk while locking through. Salvage operations had caused a massive traffic jam. According to the lockmaster, this kind of shutdown is rare, something that happens perhaps once in a decade.

Short delays, however, do occur regularly at the Alton lock, which rivermen consider a bottleneck. It is located strategically at the crossroads of the Mississippi system, right below the confluence with the Illinois River and right above the Missouri. Traffic coming up from the Gulf of Mexico splits at Alton. A little more than half heads up the Illinois to the Great Lakes, and the remainder goes to destinations on the upper Mississippi.

Locks and Dam 26 is turning out to have a strategic place in history as well. In 1968 the Corps of Engineers decided that the 600-foot lock and its 360-foot auxiliary facility were obsolete and recommended that they be replaced by two 1,200-foot locks. The replacements would be located two miles downstream, along with a new dam, and the old structures would be removed.

The enlargement was bitterly opposed by Midwestern environmentalists, who maintained that the resulting increase in traffic could set the Mississippi onto a path of irreversible decline. What transpired in the following six years was a showdown over the future of our biggest river and the role of the waterways in our national transportation system.

———————————◆━━◆———————————

IN 1974 THE ARMY ENGINEERS completed planning for the new locks and published an environmental impact statement as required by law. At that point, the Izaak Walton League and the Sierra Club became alarmed; they feared the Corps was taking the first step toward a twelve-foot channel.

Many felt the actions were a repetition of what had happened on the Ohio. There the army had replaced a 600-foot "obsolete" lock with a 1,200-foot facility, and then built another, and another, all without Congressional permission. When enough new locks were in place, the Corps went to Congress and asked for authorization of a twelve-foot channel. The rationale was that a deepened channel was needed to accommodate the increased traffic utilizing the modernized locks. By then the most expensive components

Facing page: *Arrowhead and backwater from an island in Illinois.*

Card players, Hannibal, Missouri.

Mayflies in Prairie du Chien.

A backwater at Quincy, Illinois.

The Union Electric hydroelectric power plant in Keokuk, Iowa.

A governing device for one of the turbines in the Keokuk hydroelectric plant.

Facing page: *A backwater in Illinois.*

Farm machinery, Stonefield Village, Wisconsin.

The Mississippi Queen near Lake Pepin, Minnesota.

Reflections, Hannibal, Missouri.

of a twelve-foot channel—the locks—had been constructed, and Congress was easily persuaded that the benefits of a deeper channel far outweighed its by-then-minimal costs. Environmentalists on the Mississippi feared a similar domino ploy.

The issue went to court. As attorneys prepared the case, it became apparent that an association of twenty-one Midwestern railroads was considering a parallel suit. Their position was that the government should not subsidize the growth of water transport, draining traffic from other modes. For several months the environmentalists and the railroads sniffed each other over, with a modicum of trust on either side. But to file separate actions would have been pointless. Thus was born one of the more improbable partnerships in the history of the environmental movement.

On September 6, 1974, the U.S. District Court in Washington issued a temporary injunction against further activity on the project. The plaintiffs had won the first round. Judge Charles Richey concurred that the Corps had neglected to obtain Congressional authorization and he found it likely that the Corps would be ruled in violation of the National Environmental Policy Act in failing to analyze the ecological impact of expansion on the river system as a whole.

What the Corps was proposing could quadruple traffic on the upper Mississippi. In 1974 the engineers had rated the existing Alton locks as capable of handling 46 million tons of cargo annually. The new structures would have a capacity of 190 million tons. Judge Richey found "unworthy of belief" the Corps' defense that it would simply build a replacement for a deteriorating structure and that this had no relation to expansion.

To handle a four-fold increase, the other locks and dams on the upper Mississippi also would have to be replaced. Yet the total price tag for remaking the system—close to ten billion dollars by the time such a massive project could be completed—had not been included in the cost-benefit analysis. The army was proposing what has been called "the largest construction project in the history of the Midwest," and it was proceeding without a go-ahead from Congress, without an adequate economic analysis, and without an environmental impact statement examining the systemic impact.

Following the court's decision, the Corps of Engineers produced in record time a supplemental environmental statement and a revised economic analysis. Both were subject to intense public criticism, so in an attempt to avoid further delay the Corps decided to phase the project down. It would build one 1,200-foot lock rather than two.

Environmentalists refused to back down, because even one oversized lock would result in a considerable increase in traffic. Large tows can go through a 1,200-foot lock in a single operation taking a half hour. With a 600-foot lock, however, the barges must be uncoupled and taken through in two shifts; this uncoupling and "double locking" takes an hour and a half. The barge companies are increasing their use of large tows. The small locks, even two small locks together, cannot carry the volume of one large facility, and the proposed 1200-foot lock would have to increase traffic.

In 1977 hearings were held in the House and Senate. When the issue cleared committee and reached the floor, pressure was intense for a compromise. On October 21, 1978, the single 1,200-foot lock was authorized. But included in the package was a "user fee" in the form of an excise tax on the fuel used by commercial vessels, as a concession to those who oppose subsidizing the growth of a private industry at taxpayers' expense. The user fees are to force barge companies to contribute to the cost of operating their highway, just as truckers are taxed to help maintain the interstate system and rail companies are responsible for repairing trackage at their own expense.

The tax that was passed, however, is regarded as a token, since it is insufficient to cover the cost of new construction as its proponents had urged. The tax will be phased in over several years until it reaches a maximum of $.10 a gallon. The funds collected will pay six percent of the $5.7 billion the Corps will spend on the inland waterway system over the next five years.

Congress also placed a freeze on additional expansion (a second 1,200-foot lock) until a master plan can be developed to guide future use of the Mississippi. An existing agency, the Upper Mississippi River Basin Commission, was charged with creating the plan by 1982. Besides continuing the dredging studies started by GREAT, the commission is to evaluate the direct effects of commercial navigation on the river ecosystem.

It was these direct effects that environmentalists stressed in the trial, which began on September 10, 1979. Although the Corps now had Congressional authorization, it still had not produced an environmental impact statement that addressed the cumulative impacts of expansion. The army engineers had adopted a build now, study later approach. But what is known of the ecological effects of navigation on a river is slight. The information needed would take at least three years of field studies to accumulate, because the data must be gathered under a variety of river conditions, including floods and low water, and a variety of traffic levels. The quickie analysis published by the Corps in 1975 had shrugged off our lack of knowledge, claiming that the increase in traffic caused by one lock would be "minor" and thus the environmental impacts would be "insignificant." Environmentalists replied that, since we lack data, no one knows the impact of even the present level of traffic.

During the trial, questions were raised that require long-term investigation. For example, what are the effects of the murky brown plumes that aerial photographs show trailing behind tows as they churn along the river? The plumes consist of silt and sand picked up from the river bottom. This resuspended sediment extends as far as 2.5 miles behind the tows. The sand sinks quickly, but the silt drifts downstream to be carried wherever the current takes it. Some silt drifts laterally, entering the side channels that flow into the backwaters, where it compounds the problems caused by dredging.

Pleasure craft have drafts too shallow to create plumes. But barges carrying heavy loads virtually scrape bottom when they cross sandbars. One evening in camp we watched a grounded tow work for several hours to free itself. In the narrow space normally left between the hull and the river bottom, turbulent water kicks up sediment. The powerful propellers help: on the upper Mississippi some towboats have engines with 5000 horsepower.

The Corps' own studies determined that resuspended sediments move laterally into the backwaters. Tom Claflin, the scientist who argued that to save the wetlands we have is cheaper than to build new ones, estimates on the basis of field tests done by the River Studies Center at La Crosse that a single tow passage moves twenty-seven hundred

BALTIMORE ORIOLES

pounds of sediment into the marshes. The center found that the resulting turbidity, as much as 400 percent higher than background levels, lasts for more than two hours.

Invertebrates are buried by this muddy fallout, and fish gills cannot cope with the high concentrations of silt. Fish have evolved to withstand turbid water for brief periods during spring floods but to live in clear water when spawning and growing to maturity. With the tows, the turbidity in the backwater nurseries remains elevated during this biologically sensitive season.

Dr. Richard Sparks, an aquatic biologist with the state of Illinois, testified at the trial that tows on the Illinois River cause the turbidity to rise to a level that prevents the spawning of largemouth bass. The Corps, in the second environmental impact statement, admitted that if high turbidity is maintained continuously, little plant life and bottom fauna can survive.

The Illinois River, which seventy years ago was comparable to the upper Mississippi, today has declined so much that even the Corps calls it "bleak." Polluted, deserted by the flocks of waterfowl that used to follow it north, its once-thriving fishery gone, and its wetlands drained for agriculture or spoiled by dredging and resuspended sediment, the Illinois may well exemplify how the Mississippi will look to our grandchildren.

So many tows pass on the Illinois that the turbidity never returns to natural levels. On the Mississippi, for the water to recover takes two hours, so long that Dr. Claflin believes traffic may have already reached the river's saturation point. At La Crosse, where eleven tows a day pass, turbidity rarely subsides. At Alton, thirty-two a day pass. No one can say what carrying capacity the river has, but it does have a limit. At the trial, the plaintiffs argued that we may have already exceeded that line, and any increase may push the fisheries to ecological collapse.

In addition to the biological effects of turbidity, other questions were raised at the trial to indicate the inadequacy of the Corps' environmental impact statement. It was pointed out that a study is needed to determine the impact of traffic noise on canvasbacks feeding in the channel. Another study is needed to investigate the extent of riverbank erosion caused by wakes. On the lower Mississippi barge companies use towboats with 10,000 horsepower. Riding the wake of one of these boats in a small craft is a challenge, particularly when the back action of waves crashing against the banks meets the original crests. The narrower the channel, the more the surface is churned up. On the lower river, to ride out the wake of one tow can take nearly a half hour.

Riverbank erosion will also worsen on the upper Mississippi as the 1,200-foot lock at Alton encourages barge companies to use more of the big tows. Historically, the average number of barges per tow and their average cargo have both increased, as well as the horsepower of the towboats. A large tow is cheaper to operate on the open river, saving enough to compensate for the extra costs and delay of uncoupling at 600-foot locks. A 1200-foot lock will make large tows even more economical, and hence increase erosion.

The demand for an expanded waterway system itself was created by technological advances. The Alton bottleneck developed in the first place because the barge industry's technology outgrew Locks and Dam 26, which was designed for 600-foot tows. If a new system is constructed to prevent the line-up of these larger tows, its greater capacity will no doubt lead to further technological innovation. According to the American Waterways Operators, the trade association of the water carrier industry, "A major overhaul in vessel design concepts will attend the eventual establishment of a 12-foot channel, in place of the present limiting depth of 9 feet, over much of the Mississippi River System."

The bottleneck at Alton also has been caused by the peaks and valleys characteristic of shipping demands, especially with agricultural products. Farmers understandably hold their grain until the market is right. As soon as the price goes up a couple cents on the bushel, they all want to ship at once. The supply of barges and railroad cars runs out and much of the crop sits in the grain elevators. What does get moved ends up stalled in a bottleneck.

Once the new lock is built, the bottleneck will be passed upstream. The queues that previously formed at Alton will form at 600-foot locks upriver, both on the upper Mississippi and the Illinois. As one after another fills to capacity and is replaced with a larger lock, the traffic jam will keep shifting unless the whole system is rebuilt.

Nor will construction stop with the upper Mississippi. The Corps is already considering a proposal to deepen the river below Baton Rouge to alleviate the latest bottleneck. In 1981 hundreds of barges were parked on the lower river, as they waited for their cargoes to be unloaded and transferred to ships for transport overseas. A deeper channel would allow the freighters to carry larger loads, thereby reducing congestion. But each time one bottleneck is removed, another will appear unless the taxpayer foots the bill to transform every mile of the Mississippi into a superhighway for the barge industry.

No one knows how much the traffic will increase. The Corps' predictions have been notoriously inaccurate. Even outside experts disagree among themselves on the outlook for the major commodities carried on the river. Most expect the transport of industrial chemicals to increase greatly. Transport of grain is expected to go up, of petroleum to decrease.

What will happen with coal is open to debate. In the past, eighty percent of the coal moving through Locks and Dam 26 went to utility plants on the upper river. It originated mostly in the mines of southern Illinois. Peabody Coal, which has a sign six stories high directly across the river from the famous St. Louis Arch, has underground and strip mines thirty-five miles from the city. But today Illinois coal is being replaced by western coal carried on hundred-car unit trains. The coal arrives on the upper river at Clinton and Burlington, bypassing Locks and Dam 26.

Whatever happens with individual commodities, overall traffic is expected to grow. Environmentalists suggest coping with this growth by restricting tow sizes to eliminate double locking, using small, maneuverable switchboats to speed uncoupling when it cannot be avoided, scheduling traffic to reduce the number of empties, and diverting excess traffic to alternate modes of transportation. But we should not, they argue, encourage growth by even a "minor" increase in lock capacity until we understand the environmental effects of the present traffic.

During the trial the plaintiffs contended that the increase would in fact not be minor. In the past, estimates of capacity have shown a surprising inconsistency. Back in 1956 the Corps rated Locks and Dam 26 as having a capacity of only 26 million tons. When actual traffic far outstripped that estimate, the Corps progressively raised their estimation until by 1978 they were saying that the Alton locks could handle 73 million tons.

The new lock, they said, will have a capacity of 86 million tons, an eighteen percent increase over the capacity of the present facility. The Corps decided eighteen percent was a "minor" increase. Now, and at the time that judgment was made, the lock actually handles only 60 million tons. Thus, with the new lock, traffic would actually jump forty-three percent from the current 60 million tons to 86 million tons. The Corps had ignored the increment from 60 to 73 in order to arrive at a smaller increase in capacity and hence a lesser environmental impact.

The estimate of 86 million tons as the capacity of one 1,200-foot lock was arrived at using 1972 tow sizes. With figures based on 1976 tow configurations the Corps reanalyzed the estimate, upping it to between 96 and 101 million tons. Other experts place it even higher, at 138 million tons. So the Corps was now talking about an increase of from 60 million tons to at least 96 million tons. Environmentalists questioned whether this could be considered "minor" and "insignificant."

In 1972 the Corps did a study to determine the feasibility of a twelve-foot channel. The conclusion was that a deeper channel would be economical from Cairo to Alton—the middle Mississippi—and up the Illinois to Chicago, but that current traffic projections would not justify it on the upper Mississippi. The Environmental Protection Agency criticized the study on the grounds that deepening the channel on the middle Mississippi would create the increased traffic that would favor reconsideration of a deeper channel on the upper river.

Inexorably intertwined with the twelve-foot channel study is an on-going study of the possibility of year-round navigation. Being able to run barges in the winter would contribute to quadrupling traffic. At present, Locks and Dam 26 is the river's northernmost point that is usually free of ice. The Corps believes it is economically feasible to use ice-breaking equipment, extending the navigation season to a full twelve months as far north as Burlington, Iowa. Environmentalists question this proposal on the grounds that year-round traffic would place additional stress on fish and wildlife—especially fish, since they winter in the main channel in a near-dormant state, vulnerable to waves and oil spills.

Environmentalists do not, however, blindly oppose commercial navigation. They recognize that barges are an energy-efficient way of transporting bulk commodities for long distances. But they urge that the nation develop an overall transportation policy for the Mississippi Valley before investing in one mode to the detriment of another.

A recent study comparing the energy efficiency of waterway and rail transport revealed that, because rivers twist and turn, barge routes are 1.38 times longer than competing rail routes. Moreover, when cargo originates at a location not on the river or goes to an off-river destination, energy-inefficient trucks are often used to transport it to and from the watercourse.

Too often studies comparing barges and trains average the fuel consumed by all rail traffic, including lines that cross the continental divide. The lines that actually compete with barges follow the relatively flat terrain of the Mississippi, not mountains, and so are more competitive than cross-country rail figures indicate.

What most alarms environmentalists about an expansion of river traffic is the impact on the shoreline. We will see more "fleeting areas"—sections of the river where barges are parked until tows are assembled—and more "terminals"—grain elevators and other places where barges are loaded and unloaded. A resident of Dubuque, Iowa, complained about a fleeting area near his home:

> Last summer they stored twelve to fifteen barges there all summer, did night work, torches, and barging. They were rusty and looked like a junk yard. During the month of August, one barge filled with coal burned for approximately three weeks while two other barges burned for approximately one week.

Barge companies have recently requested permits for dozens of new fleeting areas. One permit application is for a parking area for ninety barges at the foot of Pike's Peak State Park in Iowa, a site currently under consideration for designation as critical habitat for the endangered Higgins eye mussel.

Expansion of water transportation will also encourage more industries, such as chemical plants, to locate on the shores of the Mississippi. New industry will create pressure for new power plants. During periods of low flow, these utilities will compete for water with both navigation and wildlife. It is feared the wetlands will be unable to withstand the pressure of increased industrialization, especially development that is unplanned and piecemeal.

According to the Upper Mississippi River Basin Commission, the trend is for such major urban areas as St. Louis and the Quad Cities to situate industrial belts along the river. The commission also found medium-sized towns like La Crosse and Dubuque and smaller ones like Ste. Genevieve considering new riverfront industrial parks.

St. Louis, the largest metropolitan area on the river, has grown so much I hardly recognize the outskirts of the city where I grew up. Mostly it has sprawled westward, away from the riverfront. But now St. Louisans are contemplating major expansion north and south along the river. Through much of its history St. Louis competed with Chicago and New Orleans, attempting to outdo them as a transportation center. Today the city fathers fear being bypassed by Memphis. To keep pace they are planning an immense expansion of the Port of St. Louis. New fleeting areas and terminals will be provided to service a series of new riverside industrial parks. The port will become a riparian megalopolis, spreading along two hundred miles of riverfront on the Missouri and Mississippi.

TO THE SURPRISE OF THOSE who followed the trial, the environmentalists lost the lawsuit. At 2:00 P.M. on Friday, April 25, 1980, the Corps of Engineers drove the first pilings for the new lock.

11

Forgotten River

As to the river front, the report calls attention to the present deplorable condition. . . .
But new plans are timely. . . . It is proposed that the property lying between the Eads
Bridge and the proposed bridge at Poplar Street and extending back from the levee to
Second Street be purchased by the city, the bluffs for the whole width excavated to a
level with the levee and a broad esplanade constructed the entire distance on a level with
Third Street.

"THE CITY PLAN REPORT OF ST. LOUIS,"
ARCHITECTURAL RECORD, 1908

*E*ACH SUCCESSIVE CITY DOWN THE Mississippi offers a hint of the river's penulti-
mate destiny—factories, iron works, docks, generating plants, switching yards. But
at each metropolis the blank eyes of plants and warehouses persist for only ten or twenty
miles. Always the river flows again between distant pencil lines of green, in union with a
sky that arches over the continent's heart.

In recent years each city along the Mississippi has begun battling a century of grime
and neglect to identify the uniqueness and beauty of its own slice of river. The pressures
are intense, the demands on limited river frontage many. But despite the importance of
the river for industry and metropolitan prosperity, each city is finding room for a river
greenbelt. Urban dwellers are rediscovering the Mississippi.

In St. Louis, the city perhaps most identified with the Mississippi, this rediscovery
took the form of a riverfront park and an enormous arch commemorating St. Louis's role
as the "Gateway to the West." One of the students on our expedition had described the
experience of entering a city by boat as "feeling as though we were sneaking into town
unseen, looking at the city from the inside out." For me, viewing the Gateway Arch from
the water provided just such a new-found urban perspective.

I happened to move away from the city when the Arch was still under construction
down on the riverfront, its two mammoth legs inching up day by day from the skyline.

Even before the legs joined to form an arch, the monument was visible for miles, towering above the city's tallest skyscrapers. I could make it out from Forest Park near where I lived and even from the hill at Washington University, my alma mater, seven miles from the levee. On the kind of clear day that is rare in St. Louis, it is said to be possible to see it from Lambert Airport, thirteen miles out.

People in those days used to scoff. As the legs began to curve together, the standard joke envisioned them ending up off line and passing each other. But today anyone who sees the Gateway Arch in all its stainless steel simplicity and purity of form has to lay doubts to rest. To stand between the legs and gaze overhead at the thin line of its apex 630 feet in the air—higher than the Washington Monument—is to feel a reluctant lump of hometown pride and to glimpse what was in the mind of its renowned architect, Eero Saarinen. At night it is also, as Joe Holmes noticed, a unique chance for us earthbound mortals to observe the rotation of the earth. As our planet spins through the universe, the stars blink out, behind the far-off stainless steel zenith, to reappear on schedule a moment later. The ancients would have marveled.

Our tallest national monument is an inverted catenary curve, the shape assumed by a chain hanging freely between two points of support. Turn that form upside down and it is the strongest of all arches, since the weight passes down the length of the legs to be absorbed in the foundations rather than in a configuration that forces the legs apart. In this case the foundations are sunk fifty feet into bedrock.

Bob Weyeneth, the historian on our expedition, expresses misgivings about the Arch. In his view the "Gateway to the West," a monument to westward expansion, is a tribute to the rape of a continent. To commemorate our nation's conquest of the West is

CITY OF ST. LOUIS, 1872

to be insensitive to the environmental damage and human cost caused by that westward surge. Yet Bob recognizes that one can commemorate continental expansion as a social and technological achievement, and that St. Louis was indeed the funnel of that expansion, making the "Gateway to the West" at least an accurate symbol of the city's history.

Whatever skepticism may exist today about the suitability of the memorial, St. Louisans worked hard for a park as far back as the 1930s. My one-time neighbor Mayor Bernard F. Dickmann spearheaded the movement, together with St. Louis attorney Luther Ely Smith. They led in the formation of a citizens group called the Jefferson National Expansion Memorial Association.

Mayor Dickmann traveled to Washington to seek federal aid. In 1934 President Roosevelt signed a resolution authorizing a memorial to the territorial expansion of the United States, especially Jefferson's Louisiana Purchase and the Lewis and Clark Expedition. In 1939, $9 million was allocated, $2.25 million to come from the city and the rest from the government. Demolition was begun the same year and 82.6 acres cleared. At that point two wars and a string of lawsuits delayed the project. Construction finally began in 1962, too late for Saarinen to view his achievement. The Finnish-American architect died in 1961.

The Arch took three years to build and a degree of engineering precision nearly as mysterious as that of the pyramid builders. A deviation of a fraction of an inch—1/64th of an inch—at the base or during construction would have ruined closure at the top. The engineers, serious men at any time, must have found the sidewalk superintendents unfunny.

A panoramic view of the city is the reward for the visitor who is on sufficiently friendly terms with heights to take the ride to the observation deck inside the apex of the Arch. On one side is the Mississippi, looking narrower than I have remembered it, and on the other the streets of St. Louis, disappearing in the haze somewhere out around Washington University. Straight down, dizzyingly so, are the Old Courthouse and the Old Cathedral, both dating from the 1830s. Dwarfed by skyscrapers, they are almost the lone remnants of St. Louis's past.

Nothing remains of the French village that first claimed the steep rise where the Arch now stands. St. Louis—along with La Crosse, Prairie du Chien, Ste. Genevieve, and New Orleans—is Gallic in its origins. The location for the village was chosen by Pierre Laclède Liguest, junior partner in a fur-trading company in New Orleans. Having received a monopoly to trade with Indians along the Missouri River, Laclède sent his fourteen-year-old nephew, Auguste Chouteau, with a party of men to clear land near the confluence of the Mississippi and Missouri. Laclède joined Chouteau—destined to become one of the city's leading citizens—in 1764.

The houses of colonial St. Louis had steep hip roofs, thatched with long grass cut from the prairie. The roof, steep so the thatch would shed water, ended with a *galerie* or porch, essential in the muggy climate. A few examples of French colonial architecture still stand in Missouri and Illinois, notably the Bolduc House farther down the river at Ste. Genevieve. The Bolduc House, like those that were built in the villages of St. Louis and New Orleans, is surrounded by a log palisade.

FRENCH HOUSE AMONG THE ILLINOIS

With each house lot enclosed, only the ends of the streets had to be barricaded in order to form a continuous fence around the village, protection against Indian attack. Within each enclosure were the outbuildings that served the family's needs: barn, outside kitchen, hen house, storehouse, and stable. Often the compound included a garden and an orchard, and slave quarters.

St. Louis grew slowly at first. By 1800, thirty-six years after its founding, the village had a population of only 925, including 268 slaves. The fur traffic of the founding family, the Chouteaus, dominated the economic scene. In 1809 Pierre Chouteau, younger brother of Auguste, established the Missouri Fur Company, and in 1822 Pierre's son, nephew of the town founder, became John Jacob Astor's partner in the American Fur Company. Later, as the trade began to decline, the family went into other interests, including banking and dry goods.

St. Louis followed the lead of the Chouteau family and turned from furs to supplying wholesale goods to the frontier. With its advantageous location, St. Louis became the crossroads of river commerce and westward expansion. Exploring parties, army detachments, and wagon trains made the Missouri river town their outfitting point, purchasing goods that had been brought up by steamboat. "The business streets," one observer wrote, "are almost blockaded with boxes, barrels, bales and packages. . . ."

No longer a village, St. Louis had undergone a metamorphosis. The streets had developed from dirt to gravel and finally to cobblestone. In one decade alone the town's population leaped from seventeen thousand to seventy-seven thousand. Residential sections retreated inland, leaving the waterfront for hotels, warehouses, saloons, and roominghouses. The 1830s saw a brick construction boom begin with the erection of the "Old Courthouse," for which Auguste Chouteau donated a lot at Fourth and Market. Built of brick and Missouri limestone, the Courthouse was the scene of the famous Dred Scott trial on the slavery issue. Its dome, 190 feet tall, dominated St. Louis's young skyline and was a forerunner of the dome on the nation's Capitol.

In 1832, cholera struck the city and, in 1849, fire. On May 17, 1849, a mattress set out to air on the levee was ignited by a spark from a passing steamer. Spread by high winds, the Great Fire consumed twenty-three steamboats and devastated fifteen square blocks on shore. Within three years St. Louisans had rebuilt. In the district known as Laclede's Landing, just to the north of where the Arch stands today, the buildings constructed after the fire had cast-iron facades, as well as iron structural members and ornamental details, all manufactured in St. Louis foundries. The use of iron was an important innovation, setting the stage for the development of the skyscraper.

The few square blocks called Laclede's Landing are the only streets that still follow Chouteau's original plat. The landing has survived as it was in the 1850s, because the city turned away from the river. With the completion of Eads Bridge in 1874, permitting trains from the East to cross, St. Louis relinquished its faith in the steamboat in favor of a more up-to-date reliance on rail. The revolution in technology spelled the doom of the riverfront. A description of St. Louis by a traveler in the 1890s, Willard Glazier, gives a glimpse of the movement away from the river:

> Front, Second, and Main streets are the principal wholesale avenues, and are lined with immense warehouses. Fourth street contains the most fashionable retail stores, and is the favorite promenade. The longest street is Grand avenue, running for twelve miles parallel with the river. Thirty years ago Carondelet was a separate suburb on the river bank, to the southward, but is now included in the city, the entire intervening space having been built upon.

The idea of reviving the waterfront appeared as early as the 1890s when one of the Chouteaus suggested a reconstruction of the original French village. As pointed out by Bob Weyeneth in a history of urban parks, the more industrialized a city becomes, the more the citizens feel a yen to recreate the natural world. The Chouteau family member who proposed rebuilding the French village was no doubt nostalgic for a way of life closer to nature.

In the 1930s, when the plan for a national monument materialized, the Old Courthouse at the base of the Arch was donated to the National Park Service to serve as a museum and park headquarters. Oddly enough, the Chouteaus then sued to regain possession on the grounds that they had given the land to be used for a courthouse only. Theirs was one of the lawsuits that delayed construction of the memorial.

Now that the Arch towers above a modern skyline, the city is taking a hard look at the rest of the riverfront. Laclede's Landing is the next area slated for renovation. The landing was originally a manufacturing district. Everything from stoves to paints and machinery came out of the iron-faced buildings. Today most are empty derelicts with broken panes of glass overlooking the water. But by the mid-eighties they will house specialty shops, galleries, offices, and apartments. A few restaurants have already opened, and in the streets, the asphalt has been taken up to expose the blocks of granite that were the original pavement.

But St. Louis's riverfront has a long way to go. The city took a backward step by permitting a floating version of a well-known fast-food restaurant to anchor beneath the Arch. In an attempt to make it tasteful, it was disguised as a steamboat and the familiar double arch eliminated, presumably in deference to Saarinen's Arch.

Apart from the fast-food steamboat, the riverfront has potential. It has interesting buildings, such as Union Electric's Ashley power plant, built to supply power for the 1904 St. Louis world's fair—the Louisiana Purchase Exposition—the first fair to have electricity and the fair that introduced the ice cream cone and the hot dog. A half dozen blocks from the river is Anheuser-Busch's Victorian Gothic brewery, six stories high and topped with grinning gargoyles. Next door is the stable for the beer company's famous Clydesdales, furnished with stained glass windows and a chandelier for the comfort of its equestrian residents.

Downstream from the brewery are miles of commercial docks and barge terminals, with glimpses behind the wharves of the old neighborhoods of South St. Louis. Finally the city gives way to bluffs, topped by an occasional home.

―――――――――◆――◆―――――――――

ST. LOUIS IS ONLY ONE of a number of cities and towns along the Mississippi that have already built river parks or are in the process of revitalizing their riverfronts. Included are Winona and Prairie du Chien on the upper river, and Memphis and New Orleans on the lower river. Minneapolis has the most ambitious and far-reaching project, a river park that will take advantage of the city's unique natural scenery—waterfalls, islands, woods, and bluffs. Stretching along fifteen miles of the river, the park will include footpaths for snowshoeing and cross-country skiing, grassy openings in the woods for secluded picnicking and sunbathing, and access points for fishing and canoeing in the river. Nature trails at the foot of the bluffs will lead the hiker across out-of-the-way streams, and a "waterscape" will feature a restored cataract and a moss-covered wood sluiceway that is still standing from Minneapolis's mill days. Just downriver, at St. Paul, environmentalists are hoping to create a wildlife park to protect a rookery that has survived within sight of the downtown. Ornithologists have counted 226 great blue herons, 1,700 black-crowned night herons, and 320 egrets on the same peninsula that houses the notorious Pig's Eye sewage plant.

The river towns, like the cities, show a flourishing renewal of interest in our most romantic and geographically longest national symbol. A number of them are restoring their riverfronts to re-create a nineteenth-century ambience, and building museums to tell the story of the Mississippi—its geologic formation, ecosystems, and human history.

Credit for the rebirth of interest in the Mississippi River must go, at least in part, to the Great River Road. The notion of a scenic road from the headwaters to the gulf was born in 1938 in the same period that the Blue Ridge Parkway and the Natchez Trace were conceived. The idea lay dormant during World War II. After the war, all highway funds went into the interstate system. When the idea of a Great River Road was finally revived, it had undergone fundamental revisions. As initially conceived, it was to be similar to the Blue Ridge Parkway, but today it is referred to, in the bureaucratic tongue, as a "parkway-like facility." Unlike a true scenic parkway, stretches of the Great River Road will be open to commercial traffic.

The Federal Highway Administration estimates the river-length thoroughfare will cost $1.2 billion, of which a tenth is already spent. Existing highways will be utilized where feasible, merely upgraded for safety. Many of the millions slated to be spent on the Great River Road will buy scenic easements to protect the river from clearcutting, tract housing, billboards, and unsightly junkyards. Funds will be spent on a bikeway along the parkway's shoulder and on historical markers, boat-launching facilities, and wildlife observation towers.

Yet despite the good that the road will do, especially in advertising the Mississippi's beauty and thus interesting people in its preservation, government planners showed a lack of imagination in building another road to encourage pleasure driving, when railroad tracks already follow the riverbanks and suggest the energy-efficient alternative of excursion trains. On an excursion train vacationers could take in a segment of the river or ride the whole way. A family on vacation could ask to have their tickets punched, allowing them to get off and spend a day on the water or wander one of the river towns, catching the next train in the evening. They could disembark to see places as diverse as Crow Wing State Park in Minnesota, the Gateway to the West in Missouri, Natchez-Under-the-Hill in Mississippi—once an infamous hangout for river pirates—and the new Jean Lafitte National Historical Park and Preserve—soon to be Louisiana's first national park. For those who wished to canoe for awhile, the craft could be loaded in a freight car and the train serve as a shuttle. Pullman cars could provide accommodations, and period trains could be used, in keeping with the heyday of the Mississippi. The slow engines of yesterday would be reminiscent of the pace of life enjoyed by rivermen in our great-grandparents' day.

The Mississippi is readily accessible to millions who live in the ten states that border it. No great amounts of fuel are necessary for many to reach its banks. To city dwellers it offers recreation at their doorsteps, whether that be boating for a day or visiting a new riverfront park. To everyone it offers our nation's longest natural corridor, an opportunity to travel through hundreds of miles of woods and marshes replete with wildlife. With coordinated leadership from the federal government, those ten states—as diverse in history as they are far apart geographically—are being brought together in offering our nation's longest recreational experience, one unified by the geographic feature that evokes our history more than does any other—more than the Appalachians, the Great Lakes, the Rockies, or even the Great Plains.

FOUR

This Tideless Spell

St. Louis to Baton Rouge

12

The Resurrection of Chucalissa

THEY WERE PAINTED with ochre, wearing great bunches of white and other plumes of many colors, having feathered shields in their hands, with which they sheltered the oarsmen on either side, the warriors standing erect from bow to stern, holding bows and arrows. The barge in which the cacique came had an awning at the poop, under which he sate; and the like had the barges of the other chiefs; and there, from under the canopy, where the chief man was, the course was directed and orders issued to the rest.

THE NARRATIVE OF THE
EXPEDITION OF HERNANDO DE SOTO,
BY THE GENTLEMAN OF ELVAS,
PUBLISHED 1557

AT THE HUT'S ENTRANCE it is necessary to crouch, and inside, the light is dim. The air smells moldy from the packed earth floor and thatched roof. Scattered around the floor are pedestals of dirt the size of coffins, and on each pedestal lies a human skeleton. The empty eyeholes of skulls gaze down at rib cages. Next to the pelvic girdles are pieces of pottery and conch shell necklaces.

The skeletons have lain there a thousand years. A millenium ago their village overlooked the Mississippi just downstream from the present site of Memphis. They raised their crops in the river bottoms below the village, and knew the peace of guiding a dugout through the early morning mists of the great river. They fished at the water's edge and, back among the vine-hung trees, searched for hickory nuts in the sweet-smelling leaf mold. Nurtured by the black soil of the Mississippi Valley, the people of Chucalissa flourished.

They belonged to a civilization surprisingly reminiscent of the sophisticated empires of Mesoamerica. The "Mississippian" culture, so named because archaeologists first discovered it along the Mississippi between St. Louis and Memphis, spread with vigor over much of the Southeast. Villages and towns flowered along the fertile river valleys.

The Mississippian culture developed gradually. As the Indians learned to cultivate the earth, their numbers grew and settlements became permanent. Archaeological evidence indicates that their social organization began to show the complexities of class structure. They had a division of labor with artists, metal workers, traders, and hereditary leaders. The trade network brought grizzly bear teeth and obsidian from the Rockies, conch shells from the Gulf of Mexico, mica from the Appalachians, and copper from the upper Mississippi Valley.

The Mississippian culture had fully emerged by 900 A.D. Rooted in the mound-building societies of the past, it was characterized by towns that each had a central mound devoted to ceremonial activities rather than burials. The mound served as a platform for a temple; the Mississippians were sun worshippers. Grouped around the temple were houses that had conical roofs thatched with grass that hung nearly to the ground.

The Mississippians' largest city was at Cahokia, across the river from St. Louis. Farming villages surrounded the city, which itself covered six square miles and housed tens of thousands. It was the largest metropolitan area north of Mexico. Originally Cahokia had more than one hundred mounds, and it is estimated that nearly fifty million cubic feet of earth was moved in their construction. The crown of the city, Monks Mound, is the largest prehistoric earthen construction in the Americas. It covers fourteen acres and rises one hundred feet. A massive temple once stood on its flat summit.

Like Cahokia, the village of Chucalissa contained a central mound with a temple. The ceremonies conducted in the temple centered on the sun and the changing seasons, important to an agricultural way of life. Using stone axes, the people of Chucalissa cleared their fields with a form of slash-and-burn agriculture. They cut the brush and girdled the trees, set them afire, and then planted between the stumps. Unlike tribes in South America who practice true slash-and-burn agriculture, the Mississippians apparently did not abandon their fields after a season or two. Instead, worn-out earth was left untilled until it regained its fertility. In any one year nearly two-thirds of the fields lay fallow. Villages were dispersed to provide sufficient acreage, and competition for land was apparently responsible for endemic warfare. Parts of the floodplain that were frequently inundated were avoided, but maize could stand brief flooding, so bottomlands were used as much as possible. Most Mississippian sites, however, are found on the low sandy ridges just above the floodplain.

Seeds were planted in holes poked with a sharpened stick, and the soil was cultivated with hoes made from the shoulder blades of deer. In Chucalissa corn, beans, and squash were the three staple crops, but gourds, pumpkins, and tobacco were also planted. Carbonized corn remains are much more plentiful at Mississippian excavations than at earlier sites, which suggests that increasing use of maize may have been responsible for the growth of the culture.

The skeletons in the hut at Chucalissa are almost all of people who had not passed forty. The oldest is a fifty-year-old male. Many, such as a male whose leg had been

THE MISSISSIPPI RIVER: St. Louis to the Gulf of Mexico

amputated at the hip, must have died in warfare. Twenty percent died in infancy, 10 percent in childhood, 60 percent between the ages of twenty and forty. Only 10 percent lived past forty.

IN 1539 HERNANDO DE SOTO landed six hundred miles to the east, on the coast of Florida, with a force of six hundred men and two hundred horses. The Spanish conquistadors marched north into the Carolinas, following tales of riches. Word of their coming preceded them. Many Indian villages resisted, but the Spaniards were formidable with their crossbows and breastplates.

DE SOTO

De Soto apparently believed that a campaign of terror would minimize resistance. Indians who were defeated were killed, or enslaved, chained together and forced to serve as porters. If they rebelled, their hands were cut off and they were turned loose in the forest to starve. Others were crucified, head down. Indian children were thrown into the air and shot down with arrows.

Villages that tried to appease the conquistadors were shown no mercy. Fields and granaries were pillaged, and whole towns were left without corn for the winter. The looted villages were burned, the fields left in ruins. The army moved on, lured by visions of treasure invented by informants anxious to rid their lands of the Spanish locusts.

But on their side the invaders had not escaped losses. As the months passed and the army turned west through Tennessee to Alabama, the conquistadors grew poorer rather than richer. They suffered major defeats as the Indians began offering more effective opposition. By May of 1541, after two years of wandering through the Southeast, half the expedition was dead. The survivors were dressed in rags, their fine armor gone and their swords rusted. They were exhausted from fighting battle after battle, weak from running short of rations, weary from spending entire days wading chest-deep through swamps. Disheartened and disappointed, the expedition had found no gold.

Still searching, they turned northwest and reached the banks of the Mississippi on Sunday, May 8, 1541. De Soto is thought to have come upon the river somewhere near the bluffs on which Memphis stands today, perhaps not far from the village of Chucalissa. The two-mile wide river evidently failed to impress the Spaniards. Their eyes hardly saw the Mississippi, for they were fixed on the shining inner vision of cities of gold still to be found to the west. They saw the great river simply as one more barrier to be crossed.

De Soto is credited by history books as the discoverer of the Mississippi, but in fact he probably knew of the existence of a huge inland river before he ever landed in Florida. An earlier expedition, that of Panfilo de Narváez, had sailed in 1527 along the coast past the river's delta. As early as 1513 the Mississippi appeared on a Spanish map, probably based on information gained from Indians. No doubt de Soto expected to find a river about where he found it.

The Spaniards spent thirty days in an Indian village cutting trees and building barges in which to cross to the far shore. Their first act upon arriving had been to seize the village of Quizquiz, but the town contained little food, so the explorers moved to another village half a league from the river, one not identified in the journals of the expedition. Indians on the far bank sent out two hundred dugouts led by a cacique—a chief—and filled with

DE SOTO IN FLORIDA, 1539

archers who harassed de Soto's men the entire time they were building. One morning before dawn, the weary Spaniards made the crossing in secret.

The soldiers spent more exhausting months tramping through Arkansas and Louisiana, until at last they were forced to give up the search for Eldorado. They retreated to the Mississippi, where, on May 21, 1542, Hernando de Soto died from fever. His men tried to conceal the death. The Indians had thought de Soto a god, and the Spaniards had capitalized on their awe. The body was buried at night, then disinterred two nights later and dumped quietly into the murky waters of the Mississippi. The river had claimed the first would-be conqueror of North America.

The remnants of the expedition built rough ships and set out for the gulf, pursued by hundreds of Indians. A few managed to reach a Spanish fort in Mexico. So ended in total defeat one of the most disgraceful of the bloody Spanish entradas. De Soto, as one of Pizarro's lieutenants in Peru, had learned his trade well and had come equipped with shackles. He and his proud hidalgos had murdered, raped, tortured, kidnapped, committed theft and sacrilege. Twenty years after the Spanish scourge had killed its way across the Southeast, towns were still ruined and fields abandoned. De Soto's route was engraved on the land and in the memories of starving, bitter Indians, who met the next Europeans with bows drawn.

The expedition had brought with it the first ecological exotic to be introduced to North America. Live hogs were herded along as an ambulatory and self-reproducing food supply. Twenty years later they were reported as established in Florida. The long-legged range hog of Extremadura, Spain, had become the South's razorback.

BURIAL OF DE SOTO

The whites had also brought another, more sinister gift—virulent plagues of tuberculosis, smallpox, measles, and cholera. Many of the bones at Chucalissa reveal deformities caused by tuberculosis. The decline of the Mississippian culture is thought to have begun a century or more before the appearance of the Europeans. It is suspected that a climatic change led to a series of crop failures, or that warfare and the depletion of such natural resources as wood for fuel and buildings decimated the Mississippian populations. The town of Chucalissa may in fact have been abandoned sometime early in the 1500s, well before the arrival of de Soto.

Yet that would leave the tubercular bones unexplained. Only massive epidemics brought by the Spaniards could account for the total disappearance, in a little more than a century after de Soto, of populations that once numbered in the tens of thousands. The diseases that spread with deadly speed even as the Spanish strode across the continent were the terminal illness of a once-promising civilization.

BY THE TIME COLONIZATION of the Mississippi Valley began, the only surviving temple-mound culture was that of the Natchez Indians. In the late seventeenth century the Natchez numbered four thousand. They were ruled by a line of despots bearing the title Great Sun, who were carried about on litters. When a ruler died, it was the custom for his wife and closest survivors to be strangled so they could serve him in the hereafter.

The French began colonizing the lower Mississippi in the early 1700s. When the Natchez sacked a French post in 1729, the settlers retaliated and nearly exterminated the entire tribe. The survivors fled for sanctuary to various of the "Five Civilized Tribes," the tribes who dominated the Southeast in historic times. The last temple-mound civilization was gone.

Those five tribes—the Choctaws, Chickasaws, Creeks, Cherokees, and Seminoles—were farmers, like their Mississippian ancestors. They cultivated the three staples—corn, beans, and squash—and some grew secondary crops, such as pumpkins, tobacco, and sunflowers. They tilled fields cleared by the mound builders, like them maintaining fertility through fallow periods. When American settlers began to pour down the Ohio, they found not a forest primeval but a land altered by human use. On the outskirts of the towns of the Five Civilized Tribes were plants that thrive on human disturbance, plants such as those still seen along roadsides and in old fields.

In the decades following the dispersal of the Natchez, the five tribes increasingly assimilated the way of life of the whites. They cultivated larger farms, raised livestock, built European-style homes, and even owned Negro slaves. The Cherokees developed a written language, a newspaper, and a constitution. None of this, however, prevailed once the emerging nation began to covet their land.

In the 1830s the Five Civilized Tribes were forcibly relocated west of the Mississippi, except for a few Seminoles and Cherokees who resisted and were not captured. A fourth died during the removal, which required an arduous overland march and, for some, a trip by steamboat down the Mississippi and up the Arkansas and Red rivers. The Cherokee remember the journey as the Trail of Tears. Settlers took over the Indian farms, and found the orchards the whites cultivated benefited from the fruit trees selected by their predecessors.

Within historic times whole tribes lived along the Mississippi whose names today are almost forgotten: the Chitimacha and Tunica, the Bayogoula and Quinipissa, the Houma, Taensa, Quapaw, the Illini and Osage, Kaskaskia and Kickapoo, the Menominee, Winnebago, Potawatomi, and Sauk. And before them were the Mississippians, the people of Chucalissa, whose true names we do not even know. All we have of them are the mounds, some pottery, and skeletons.

13

A'venturing on the Mississippi

I TOOK A WALK with my Gun this afternoon to see the Passage of Millions of Golden Plovers Coming from the North Est and going nearly South—the distruction of these innocent fugitives from a Winter Storm above us was really astonishing—the Sportsmen are here more numerous and at the same time more expert at shooting on the Wing than any where in the U. States . . . as a flock came Near every man Called in a Masterly astonishing Manner, the Birds immediately Lowered and Wheeled and coming about 40 or 50 yards run the Gantlet every Gun goes off in Rotation, and so well aimed that I saw several times a flock of 100 or More Plovers destroyed at the exception of 5 or 6 . . . this continued all day. When I Left One of these Lines of Sharp Shooters then the Sun Setting, they appeared as Intent on Killing More as when I arrived at the spot at 4 o'clock—a Man Near where I was seated had Killed 63 dozens—from the firing before and behind us I would suppose that 400 Gunners were out. Supposing each Man to have Killed 30 Dozen that day 144,000 must have been destroyed.

JOHN JAMES AUDUBON, 1821

AFTER DE SOTO, 130 YEARS passed before Europeans ventured again to the Mississippi. By the seventeenth century the three big powers—England, France, and Spain—were engaged in a struggle for control of the New World, vying to establish colonies. They were also searching the continent for a profitable water route to the Orient. France sent a fur trader, Louis Jolliet, to explore the Mississippi and so determine whether it might discharge into the Pacific. Accompanying Jolliet was a Jesuit missionary, Père Jacques Marquette, who went not out of greed for gold but out of greed for souls.

Though Marquette and Jolliet's motives differed, they had the same courage. Taking only a small party of five voyageurs, they set out on May 15, 1673 in birchbark canoes.

Friendly Miamis tried to dissuade the priest and merchant from undertaking such a hazardous journey. They would surely be killed by warlike Indians or by river monsters or at least by the ferocious heat. Anyone who has lived along the Mississippi knows that the Miamis did not exaggerate the third danger.

The voyageurs and the gentle, black-garbed priest set out from Quebec for the Wisconsin River, which they followed to the Mississippi. Reaching the main river on June 17, the small band paddled downstream between the bluffs without at first seeing a sign of humans. At night, to be safe, they slept in the canoes. Eight days after entering the Mississippi, they spied footprints in the sand. They examined the prints and found a path apparently leading to an Indian village.

Leaving the voyageurs to guard the canoes, the Father and the trader strode forth alone and unafraid. They followed the path in silence. After more than six miles they came to a village. Their approach was unobserved and they walked so near that they could hear the Indians talking. "We then deemed it time to announce ourselves," the explorers' journal relates. They gave a shout. At this the Indians "rushed out of their cabins," but "having no reason to distrust us, seeing we were but two, and had made known our coming, they deputed four old men to come and speak with us."

Having survived their first encounter with the natives, Marquette and Jolliet proceeded downriver farther into the unmapped wilderness. They began to meet tribes who were hostile, Indians who had reason to dislike Europeans. By the time the two wanderers reached the Arkansas River, they could see their lives were in increasing danger. By then they were satisfied that the Mississippi emptied into the gulf and was not a highway to the East, so they turned around for the arduous trip home, paddling upstream against the current.

Marquette and Jolliet's twenty-five-hundred mile exploration helped establish France's claim to the interior of the continent. Within a couple of decades she began sending colonists to populate this vast new territory called Louisiana. Even before the mouth of the river was settled, military posts were established at key points on the major tributaries up the valley. By the middle of the century France's claim to ownership was supported by a series of fur trading posts. Ste. Genevieve, Missouri, the first permanent settlement west of the Mississippi, was founded as a trading post in 1735, and St. Louis in 1764.

St. Louis came into existence only a year after the Treaty of Paris. By this agreement France, defeated in the French and Indian War, relinquished its holdings west of the Mississippi to Spain and its lands east of the river to England. Within another two decades the British claim was in turn ceded away. Ownership of the territory from the Appalachians to the Mississippi River passed to Britain's former colony. American settlers poured into the Mississippi Valley.

Even as the settlers arrived, naturalists were eagerly exploring the river, attracted to the rich flora and fauna. One of the first was John James Audubon. By the time Audubon traveled the Mississippi, the Spanish had returned control of the territory of Louisiana to the French, and France in turn had sold it to the United States, in 1803. The Americans now controlled the entire Mississippi Valley.

AUDUBON

In 1810 Audubon and a business partner, Ferdinand Rozier, floated a raft with 300 barrels of whiskey from Henderson in western Kentucky up the Mississippi to Ste. Genevieve in Missouri. Within a few years, Audubon, unsuccessful as a businessman, decided to commit his fate to his great dream, painting the birds of America lifesize and in their natural surroundings.

In October of 1820 Audubon took passage on a flatboat to New Orleans. The Mississippi "flyway," at that time considered the primary migratory route of the continent's interior, would offer new and strange species for Audubon's portfolio: cranes and cormorants, curlews and golden plovers.

The immigrant Frenchman stayed for a time in New Orleans, painting birds and supporting himself by drawing portraits and teaching music. He was soon offered a position upriver at Oakley plantation in West Feliciana Parish, the next parish north of Baton Rouge. In the mornings he tutored Miss Eliza Pirrie, daughter of James Pirrie, in drawing, dancing, French, and mathematics. His salary was sixty dollars a month plus room and board. Afternoons he was free to wander the swamps and pine woods in search of birds. From his four months at Oakley date 32 of the 435 elephant folio plates, including 9 warblers.

Oakley, built in 1799, is a tall and airy colonial house with jalousied galleries that reveal a West Indies influence. The ground floor contains a dining room and overseer's office, the kitchen being in a separate building. The second floor has a morning room, parlor, library, and what was Audubon's bedroom—a small room with a French campaign cot. The third floor contains the family's bedrooms. The house has been restored with furnishings of the Federal Period (1790–1830) and is surrounded by a lush forest of live oaks and magnolias, cherry laurel, dogwood, and wild hydrangea. The grounds are part of the hundred-acre Audubon State Commemorative Area near St. Francisville.

MAGNOLIA SWAMP

ABOUT THE TIME STEAMBOATS were becoming well established and Arkansas was admitted as a state, another sort of artistic adventurer traveled the Mississippi. John Banvard, while working on a showboat, conceived the extravagant idea of executing the
largest painting in the world. It would be a panorama of the Mississippi River. His
aspiration was to paint, not a great picture, but a big one, one that would do justice to the
scenery of the majestic river. It was to be a canvas that could be unrolled for viewing by
audiences, a precursor of the newsreel and travelogue.

Banvard managed to accumulate enough capital by the spring of 1840 to purchase a
skiff and descend the river to make preliminary sketches. He rowed two thousand miles
alone in his open boat, crossing from one bank to the other to obtain the proper viewpoint for a sketch. He blistered his hands from the oars and the back of his neck from the
sun. Evenings he repaired to the woods to hunt for his food. At night he slept in a blanket
beneath the upturned skiff with his portfolio of drawings for a pillow. It took him 400
days to finish the journey.

Transferring the sketches to canvas required months. The finished panorama, Banvard claimed, was three miles long and was a smashing success. The canvas, unwound in
a darkened room, was spotlighted by a strong gas light. For two hours John Banvard
provided a running commentary. The spectator ascended or descended the river, depending on whether ·the painting was unrolled from left to right or from right to left. It

showed twelve hundred miles of river, from the mouth of the Missouri to the city of New Orleans. Longfellow was just finishing "Evangeline," an idyll of the Acadians in Louisiana, when he took in a showing of Banvard's moving panorama:

> This comes very *a propos*. The river comes to me instead of my going to the river; and as it is to flow through the pages of the poem, I look upon this as a special benediction. . . . One seems to be sailing down the great stream, and sees the boats and the sand-banks created with cottonwood, and the bayous by moonlight.

Longfellow was not the only one to approve Banvard's effort. Congress passed a resolution of endorsement, and on its European tour the panorama was shown at a command performance at Windsor.

Such popular success called forth a flood of imitators. First there was John Rowson Smith, then Samuel B. Stockwell, Henry Lewis, and Leon Pomarede. An advertisement in the St. Louis *Missouri Republican* on September 13, 1849 described the work of one of Banvard's successors:

> POMAREDE'S ORIGINAL PANORAMA of the Mississippi River and Indian Life, Painted in Oil, will be Exhibited at the Odd Fellow's Hall, commencing on Monday Evening, the 17th September. The painting comprises four sections, embracing Indian Scenery, War Dances, Buffalo Hunts, Dog Feasts, etc., etc., Dissolving and Moonlight Views, Prairies on Fire, Steamboats and Mechanical Moving Figures of Steamboats, Flat Boats and Indians. The fourth section will conclude with a beautiful dissolving view of the Great Fire at St. Louis, on the night of 17th May, representing that awful and terrific conflagration in all its fury, as it appeared to the distracted citizens. Gradually the devouring element subsides, and daylight appears, like a messenger from God, to stay the wreck of destruction. The river is seen gorged with half sunken wrecks and charred remains of 23 steamboats, and the district presents a sad spectacle, blackened and broken walls, and tottering chimnies rearing their summits, ghastly gloom over the smouldering ruins. . . .

By the late 1840s each copy was claiming to be the original panorama, and the longest. In fact Banvard's was probably a quarter to a third of a mile long, and the longest one might have stretched nearly a mile. We cannot know any lengths with certainty, because regrettably none of the canvases exists today.

A DECADE AFTER THE CIVIL WAR, people along the Mississippi watched open-mouthed as Nathaniel Bishop rowed past in a peculiar boat called a "sneak-box," a choice of craft that qualifies him as the river's best-prepared adventurer. A sneak-box, also known as a duck-boat, is a New Jersey invention created in the 1830s for creeping up on waterfowl. Pointed on the bow and squared on the stern, it looks like the result of breeding a rowboat and a kayak. It has a wide beam and a square cockpit with a cover that Bishop closed at night to create a wooden bivouac sack. With the hatch closed, the sneak-box was roomy enough for him to lie on his side. Propped on his elbow he wrote his journal by candlelight (a two-inch candle, so as not to scorch the wood).

Bishop, a veteran of eight thousand miles of solo trips in canoes, rowboats, and sailboats, rowed his sneak-box in 1875 down the Ohio to the Mississippi and on to the gulf and along the coast to the Suwanee River. He carried blankets, a gun and ammunition, and a small coal-oil stove that he highly recommended to boaters and canoeists. It could boil a gallon of water in thirty minutes, about as fast as today's backpacking stoves. It ran for ten hours at a cost of three cents.

Bishop rowed past occasional cotton plantations and squatters' cabins, but in 1875 most of the river he saw was nearly a wilderness. A mere thirty-five years later, the residents of Memphis were venturing on the Mississippi in gasoline cabin cruisers. The author of an article in a 1908 issue of *Recreation* magazine suggested combining a fall hunting trip with a motor cruise to New Orleans. The writer mentioned the Memphis Boat Club, "an unlovely structure built on a huge barge" (still in existence today), and reassured the reader that the river sported outing clubs (no longer in existence) with docking facilities all the way to the gulf. He spoke enthusiastically of great flocks of geese on sandbars, bear and turkeys in the woods, and quail in the corn and cotton fields. As for boats, most popular was the sixteen- to twenty-five-foot open launch with an eight-horsepower motor, the whole outfit costing as little as $250 new. But the article noted that using yachts or houseboats with forty to a hundred horsepower would allow taking servants.

Judging from the number of published accounts, long-distance canoeing was the adventure of the flapper years and the Depression. In the summer of 1937 a twenty-eight-year-old professor from Yale and two paddling companions sprinted down the river in forty-nine days to become the world's record holders. Today Gerald Capers is Professor Emeritus in the history department at Tulane University in New Orleans. He is the author of several books, including one on the history of his hometown, Memphis. At 70, he looks as trim as he did in photos from 1937. He still has the peppery spirit that kept him going for seven weeks, paddling fifty miles a day.

In 1931 his brother had canoed from the headwaters down to Memphis, so the professor had firsthand information on conditions. He and his two friends, one the former captain of their high-school football team and the other today the city prosecutor of Memphis, slept in cotton-picking sacks under a tarpaulin and mosquito bar. They carried drinking water but cooked with river water, which they boiled. "Let it settle," he says, "in a bucket overnight and it becomes clear." They went swimming the whole way but had typhoid shots and took quinine to prevent malaria. Their canoe was a seventeen-footer. They paddled in shifts, the man in the middle reading stories to the other two to pass the time.

The professor's forty-nine days remained in the *Guinness Book of World Records* until 1978, when a Royal Air Force team in three two-man canoes did the river in forty-two days and five hours. Professor Capers claims, however, that the British team had the enormous advantage of a land-based truck for supplies.

Today pleasure boating on the river below St. Louis is minimal, except around Memphis and during the spring and fall when northern boats are migrating. Few harbors and facilities are available. Driftwood is a threat to propellers, and the seas created by the large barge tows can be tricky. Even so we met an occasional adventurer. At Cape Girardeau in Missouri we came across Lee and Jackie Stahl, who were taking a 24-foot cruiser six thousand miles from the Florida keys up the east coast to New York City, from there up the Hudson River to Lake Champlain and the St. Lawrence Seaway, then across the Great Lakes to the Illinois River, into the Mississippi and down it to the gulf and back across to their home port. The whole trip, I later heard, took three and a half months. Another couple accompanied them as far as St. Louis, but then quit because of scare stories about the lower Mississippi.

Then there are a few nostalgic individuals who do the lower Mississippi on rafts. A theatrical troupe, the Otrabanda Company, makes an annual trek on a homemade raft from St. Louis to New Orleans. Supported by federal and state grants to the arts, the company puts on free shows in a red and yellow circus tent. A land crew does the advance work and drives the actors from the river to the towns, usually some distance from the banks. The troupe spends a frantic two or three days performing, then goes back to the river. They find the return to rafting an escape, "a lyrical interlude," a feeling we often shared.

The showboat tradition goes back to itinerant peddlers who floated downriver on flatboats selling patent medicines and whiskey and using music and acrobatics as come-ons. Floating circuses were popular in the 1850s, vaudeville by the late 1870s. Once steam had appeared, the showboats shifted from flatboats to steamboats. Steam-powered calliopes were played to attract audiences. One of the last showboats, the *Goldenrod,* was moored in St. Louis in 1937 by Captain Bill Menke and was still putting on shows until it burned in 1962. I remember it featured melodramas such as *Little Nell Still Alive.*

ONLY AROUND MEMPHIS did we find local residents frequenting the main channel. Memphis waterskiers and motorboaters picnic on Loosahatchie Bar or Chicken Island or Robinson Crusoe Island just north of the city, or cruise sixty miles down to Helena, Arkansas. A Memphis resident says, "There are thousands of sandbars along the Mississippi where in three-quarters of an hour you can be in a wilderness area." Unlike St. Louis, Memphis uses the river enthusiastically.

At present Memphis recreationists are feuding with commercial interests over whether boating facilities on McKellar Lake, a backwater of the Mississippi, should be expanded or the port kept clear for barge traffic. This seems to be the only instance on the lower river where pleasure boating is still actively competing with commercial traffic.

Plans for a riverfront park, Volunteer Bicentennial Park on Mud Island, include a canoe pull-out, since this sport is growing in popularity in Memphis. But on most of the lower Mississippi, today's canoe adventures are purely the province of long-distance paddlers. The most notable of these was the Bicentennial reenactment of La Salle's expedition. In 1682, René-Robert Cavelier, Sieur de la Salle, completed Marquette and Jolliet's journey by continuing all the way to the gulf and taking formal possession of the Mississippi Valley for France. In 1976 two dozen voyageurs, one to represent each member of La Salle's original crew, paddled from the Great Lakes down the Illinois to the Mississippi and to the gulf. The group was dressed authentically in knit stocking caps, called toques, linen shirts, knee breeches and leggings, bright-colored sashes, and moosehide moccasins. Making long portages because the Illinois River was frozen, the voyageurs wore out 368 pairs of moccasins.

All down the river we heard stories of people who ventured on the Mississippi in exotic ways. We heard tales of people who swam the whole way, waterskied it, or did it on horseback. The horseback rider, according to the park manager at Lake Itasca, filled a bottle of water in the gulf, rode upriver, and poured it into the lake at the finish. An even more apocryphal story, however, came to me from Pat Dunne, who for years was mayor of Greenville, Mississippi. Ten years ago he saw a raft going the whole way with power provided by a Chevrolet hooked up to a paddle wheel. The Chevy still had its wheels.

14

The Night Riders of Reelfoot Lake

WE HAVE THE FOLLOWING description of the Earthquake from gentlemen who were on board a large barge, and lay at anchor in the Mississippi a few leagues below New Madrid, on the night of the 15th of December. About 2 o'clock all hands were awakened by the first shock; the impression was, that the barge had dragged her anchor and was grounding on gravel; such were the feelings for 60 or 80 seconds, when the shock subsided. The crew were so fully persuaded of the fact of their being aground, that they put out their sounding poles, but found water enough.

At seven next morning a second and very severe shock took place. The barge was under way—the river rose several feet; the trees on the shore shook; the banks in large columns tumbled in; hundreds of old trees that had lain perhaps half a century at the bottom of the river, appeared on the surface of the water; the feathered race took to the wing; the canopy was covered with geese & ducks, & various other kinds of wild fowl; very little wind; the air was tainted with a nitrous and sulphureous smell; and every thing was truly alarm.

NEW ORLEANS *LOUISIANA GAZETTE,*
JANUARY 20, 1812

ACROSS THE RIVER FROM the Missouri bootheel lies a backwater lake that was born in violence, was saved by violence, and today is dying in violence. Reelfoot Lake, in the extreme northwestern corner of Tennessee, was formed in 1811 during one of the most powerful earthquakes in history. A century later, in 1908, the rare and beautiful Reelfoot was saved through the nefarious tactics of hooded night riders. Today, this shallow backwater is choking to death on Tennessee dust.

In 1811 the lower Mississippi Valley was experiencing a cold winter. North of Baton Rouge the valley was still a virgin wilderness, apart from a scattering of French and

Spanish settlements. East Tennessee had been admitted to the union a decade earlier, but the western part of the state remained Indian country. Although the Mississippi's shores were lightly populated, boat traffic was brisk. Farmers along the Ohio shipped their produce to New Orleans by flatboat. That cold December, as the river flowed through silent forests, the first steamboat on western waters was already making its maiden voyage. The Indians regarded it as an omen of evil.

At 2:00 A.M. on December 16, 1811, a great earthquake shook the Mississippi Valley. In Cincinnati, miles from the epicenter of the quake, chimneys toppled. Aftershocks struck every six to ten minutes. Near the village of New Madrid at the northern edge of the Missouri bootheel, fissures opened in the earth and the land visibly undulated in waves. Cabins were leveled, barns swallowed. Much of New Madrid caved off into the Mississippi.

During the following three months 1,874 additional distinct tremors terrified the survivors. The larger quakes were felt as far away as Boston and Quebec. Seismologist Emil Mateker believes that the New Madrid disturbance, in number of shocks and area affected, surpassed any recorded quake in the history of North America.

Four years after the cataclysm, a pioneer woman of New Madrid described her recollections in a letter:

> On the 16th of December, 1811, about 2 o'clock a.m., a violent shock of earthquake, accompanied by a very awful noise, resembling loud but distant thunder, but hoarse and vibrating, followed by complete saturation of the atmosphere with sulphurous vapor, causing total darkness. . . .
>
> The Mississippi first seemed to recede from its banks, and its waters gathered up like a mountain, leaving for a moment many boats, which were on their way to New Orleans, on the bare sand, in which time the poor sailors made their escape from them.
>
> Then, rising 15 or 20 feet perpendicularly and expanding, as it were, at the same time, the banks overflowed with a retrograde current rapid as a torrent. The boats, which before had been left on the sand, were now torn from their moorings and suddenly driven up a little creek, at the mouth of which they had laid, to a distance in some instances of nearly a quarter of a mile.
>
> The river, falling immediately as rapidly as it had risen, receded within its banks with such violence that it took with it whole groves of young cottonwood trees which had hedged its borders.

Eliza Bryan closed the letter by saying that "lately it has been discovered that a lake was formed on the opposite side of the Mississippi, in the Indian country."

The settlers thought that the river had overflowed during the quake and created Reelfoot Lake in a matter of hours. They believed that the lake, which connected with the river at both ends, would soon capture the entire flow of the Mississippi. Today geologists believe that Reelfoot filled gradually over a period of months after the quake. The northern section was a former channel of the Mississippi, an oxbow lake formed prior to 1811. The lower half was a swamp with a bayou flowing through it. The earthquakes of 1811–1812 caused entire land masses to sink; the Reelfoot swamp sank ten to fifteen feet and slowly filled with rainwater and water from the Mississippi River.

Waning electrical storm at Chester, Illinois.

Catfish at Tower Rock, Missouri.

Lily pads, Reelfoot Lake, Tennessee.

The Kress Building, Memphis.

At the helm of the J. Russel Flowers, *Baton Rouge, Louisiana.*

Facing page: *Cypress trees and duckweed in Reelfoot Lake.*

Twilight, Jackson Square, New Orleans.

Pirate Alley, New Orleans.

Facing page: *Water hyacinth, Louisiana bayou.*

A lugger boat in the delta.

The former swamp and oxbow lake is fourteen miles long and three to four miles wide. The formation of Reelfoot inundated twenty-seven thousand acres of cypress and walnut, leaving a jungle of logs and broken-off stumps. As the years passed, the old channel of the bayou was still visible, weaving through a watery landscape of dead trunks with truncated branches. A settler in the 1840s wrote of "tall, dead white timbers" standing so thick that it was difficult to see two hundred yards through the lake—"so weird, so ghastly, so lonely."

But not all the trees died. Here and there living cypress still stand in the water, more than 170 years old. Their wide trunks flare at the water's surface. Around the base, pointed woody growths protrude above the water. These "cypress knees" grow from the side roots of the tree and may help the submerged roots to breathe or perhaps provide support in the soft lake bottom. Resistant to rot, the wood was used by the early settler to build his house, his barn and fences, his boat. He was even buried in a cypress coffin. Down in New Orleans, hollowed cypress logs were installed as water pipes in 1798 and were still sound when removed in 1914.

The cypress of Reelfoot Lake stand among acres and acres of water lilies and American lotus. The lotus nearly chokes some of the shallow bays of the lake. Its gorgeous flowers, pale yellow beauties, bloom profusely in midsummer. But the scene is dominated by the cypress—an ancient, like its relative the redwood. The big trees brood silently, a primeval landscape that is a living reminder of the vast powers unleashed 170 years ago.

------------------◆------------------

THE PEOPLE WHO SETTLED the shores of Reelfoot Lake were farmers and fishermen. A fishing village, the town of Samburg, was founded in 1852. The fishermen and their families depended on the bounty of the lake: black bass, pike, catfish, carp, perch, buffalo, and gar. In the late 1800s their income was supplemented when a sporting club was built by men from Louisville, Kentucky. Local residents served as fishing guides, but they resented the intrusion on their lake.

In 1908 a group of businessmen called the West Tennessee Land Company claimed they owned legal title to Reelfoot and the land adjoining it. The company planned to build a canal and drain the lake. They would harvest the underwater timber and then farm the cleared bottom. The fishermen who looked to Reelfoot for their livelihood took the issue to court, but the judge sided with the land company. With no further legal recourse and with their families facing ruin, some of the squatters turned to drastic steps.

At first they merely intended to scare the officers of the land company. Riding at night, garbed in capes and hoods that ended in a point, they initiated a campaign of terror. Their threats escalated into whippings and then into house burnings. Though the majority of the population did not participate, most condoned the crimes because they believed the night riders served a just cause: "freeing" the lake from the land company.

Before long the crusade was completely out of control. Personal vendettas became the purpose of the violence as much as saving the lake. A family of blacks was massacred and the night riders lost public sympathy. For seven months the violence and bloodshed continued until the night of October 19, 1908 when the Klan-like riders abducted two of

CYPRESS SWAMP

the company's officials, Robert Z. Taylor and Quentin Rankin, at gunpoint. The mob carried the two captives deep into the forest and staged a fake hanging in an attempt to frighten Rankin into agreeing not to drain the lake. When he resisted, a shot rang out. In a moment he was riddled with bullets. The other prisoner, Taylor, wrested free of his captors and ran for a slough. He lunged into the bayou and swam underwater to a log, where he hid while the night riders fired into the water for fifteen minutes.

Taylor stayed put for an hour and then fled into the brush. The next day and night he stumbled through the swamps and across the bayous, scratched and bleeding from briars, thirsty and hungry. Finally the terrified man reached a farm twenty-five miles from the murder site.

The murder made front-page news as far away as New York. Sentiment ran against the night riders, but papers such as the *New York Times* concluded that a legitimate grievance had started the affair. The governor of Tennessee called out the state militia. A few of the night riders escaped by crossing the Mississippi on a steamboat, but the rest were apprehended by Pinkerton detectives. In the end, eight were convicted of murder. They appealed to the Tennessee Supreme Court and were set free on a technicality.

In its ruling the court also decreed that Reelfoot Lake was a navigable waterway and so belonged to the public domain. For the next decade and a half the state worked to acquire ownership. In 1925 the legislature authorized the purchase of a wide band around the lake, creating Reelfoot Lake Park and Fish and Game Preserve. Reelfoot National Wildlife Refuge, comprising 9,586 acres, was established in 1941. People in the area still thank the night riders for saving Reelfoot Lake, though the residents of Samburg and Walnut Log remain touchy about the subject. Many had fathers and grandfathers who were night riders.

A lawless spirit is still said to pervade the backwoods, and outsiders are viewed with suspicion. Steve Pardue, a young park ranger who grew up in Reelfoot country, conducted us on a tour of the lake, stopping on the way at the village of Walnut Log. We drove up a dirt road past a group of shacks. The road paralleled a bayou that was spanned by a swinging footbridge. Steve Pardue stopped the car and we walked up a path to the stream. But the ranger was nervous enough to ask one of us to stay with the car, and he encouraged us to keep the walk brief.

Visitors are welcomed, however, by the younger generation of businessmen and resort owners who wish to promote tourism. That evening the local merchants invited us to a banquet. Joe Holmes, our expedition photographer, was delighted by the improvement in our spartan camping diet: his appetite is forever struggling to fill out his lanky six foot, five inch frame. Clint Schemmer, a student from the University of Montana and the third member of our motorboat crew, helped Joe put away a Southern feast of home-cooked fried chicken, baked ham, fish, and hush puppies.

After dinner one of the businessmen explained how vital Reelfoot Lake is to the economy of the county. Not only do resort owners depend on it, but so do commercial fisherman. The Gooch family are fishermen who have made their living from the lake for years. Robert Gooch, 56, and seven of his brothers, uncles, and nephews go out in cold weather when the fish are "bedding up." They set nets around submerged stumps and cypress knees, holes where such fish as buffalo, catfish, and crappie congregate. Robert and his relatives, their hands often in freezing water, drag the bottom with a collection of metal and wire suspended on lines, driving the dormant fish into the net. The man handling the net wears cotton gloves. His hands are all right as long as they remain in the water, but if reaching the next hole takes too long, the gloves freeze to his hands.

Fishing is not the promising venture it used to be. The lake is suffering from a combination of stagnation and siltation. Until the turn of the century the Mississippi poured through Reelfoot during high water, and fish from the river spawned in the lake. But in 1901 a levee was built, and the flow of floodwater was cut off. Today the only fresh water that enters the lake comes from a couple of creeks. The lake is stagnating.

It is also filling with silt. West Tennessee is losing topsoil at a rate six to eight times the national average, at an incredible thirty to forty tons per acre per year. With every rain, fine loess washes into the creeks and down to Reelfoot. Ranger Steve Pardue walked us out onto a field of sawgrass that was open water only the year before. One of the businessmen mentioned a trailer court that stands today where ten years ago there was lake. One-half the original surface of Reelfoot Lake is gone.

Because Reelfoot is becoming so shallow from siltation, the Fish and Wildlife Service has raised the water level by means of a concrete spillway at the southern end of the lake. Now the water is too high for the deepwater beds the Gooch family once fished, and the shallow beds are covered with mud. Robert Gooch says that Reelfoot once supported a hundred commercial fishermen, but he doubts whether ten years from now three will be left.

The Reelfoot Refuge includes a swampy wilderness called "Cranetown," so remote that Ranger Steve Pardue has only penetrated the maze of cypress stumps twice. Once thought to be "the greatest colony of nesting birds in the interior of the United States," Cranetown was populated by great blue herons, cormorants, and American egrets. In 1932 a naturalist counted 450 nests; some of the big cypress trees contained as many as 20, with herons and cormorants nesting in the same tree. In 1951 parts of the movie *Raintree County* were filmed in the Cranetown wilderness. A canal was cut to bring in boats loaded with camera equipment. The film company left it to nature to close the ditch, so for a time sightseers found their way in. Some shot off firecrackers to relish the spectacle of five thousand cranes lifting off. The birds never returned.

Siltation no doubt contributed to the exodus as much as human disturbance. Old-timers can remember seeing egrets and herons perched on every stump, feeding or alert for fish. As the lake filled with silt and the water level was raised to keep Reelfoot from disappearing altogether, these perches have disappeared. Many of the herons and egrets found suitable habitat along the nearby Mississippi, but the cormorants simply declined in numbers.

Yet as long as some water remains, Reelfoot will continue to be an important winter haven for migratory waterfowl. In November and December of 1979 rangers counted three hundred thousand ducks—mallards, pintails, woodies, and teals—and in January a hundred thousand Canada geese.

Reelfoot is considered by many to have the largest wintering concentration of bald eagles in the Southeast. Nearly two hundred feed at the lake. To protect the eagles from casual disturbance and harassment, the state park initiated organized bus tours in 1974. Last winter four thousand people took advantage of the opportunity to view bald eagles under the close supervision of well-informed rangers. The Gooch family finds that the eagles are not too proud to ask for a handout. They come right to the back of the boat and feed on the rough fish that are discarded. Robert has had as many as twenty-five eagles following the boat like seagulls.

In 1968 federal, state, and local officials initiated a project to save the lake by damming the upstream creeks. Fifteen small dams, some already built, will serve for flood control and as catch basins for silt. Once the Reelfoot–Indian Creek Watershed project is complete, the sediment will settle out in the upstream reservoirs and only clear water will flow into Reelfoot.

The project is of course only a stopgap measure, for these dams will treat the symptom and not the cause. Steve Pardue remembers waterskiing on one of the siltation lakes built in 1968 that today is too shallow for boating. At that rate fewer than fifteen years will pass, once all the dams are built, before the lakes fill in and the dams become useless. Construction has proceeded very slowly, however, so it may be a race to see which is finished first—the watershed project or Reelfoot.

From the moment of their formation, all lakes are doomed. In the case of Reelfoot the inevitable has been greatly accelerated by the levee that stopped the flow of rejuvenating fresh water from the Mississippi. Herein lies a potentially tragic irony.

The New Madrid fault runs for 175 miles from southeastern Illinois to northeastern Arkansas, crossing the Mississippi at a point between Cairo and Reelfoot Lake. Many scientists believe that a major earthquake along the New Madrid fault would have the potential to inflict ten times the damage of the San Francisco quake of 1906. Unlike the San Andreas fault, parts of which lie exposed on the surface of the land, the New Madrid zone is buried beneath two to three thousand feet of river sediment deposited over the ages. Poorly consolidated alluvial deposits permit shock waves to travel much farther and with greater force than they would if the shock were confined, as with the California fault, to the immediate area of impact. The latter is comparable to dropping a stone on a rock pile; the former to throwing a rock in a pond.

Since 1974 more than eight hundred small earthquakes have been recorded in the New Madrid area. Should one occur having the magnitude of that of 1811, the cities of St. Louis and Memphis could suffer devastating losses. My hometown, with its rows of brick houses, could lose entire neighborhoods.

Little is known about the New Madrid fault zone. Scientists only began studying the fault during the past decade, and the Corps of Engineers has only begun to think about the effect of a severe earthquake on the levees that parallel the Mississippi. Should a major quake strike during high water, Reelfoot Lake may well receive more fresh water than it could ever need.

15

And the Waters Prevailed

We git up in de mornin' so doggone soon,
Cain' see nothin' but de stars and moon.
Cap'n, cap'n, will you sen' me some water?
Ain' had none since dis long mornin'.
Cap'n, cap'n, doncha think it's mighty hard?
Work me all day on 'lasses an' lard, O, Lawd.
I ask de cap'n what time o' day.
He look at me, an' he walk away.

LEVEE WORKERS SONG

*F*LOOD CONTROL ON THE MISSISSIPPI dates back to the selection of a flood-prone site for the city of New Orleans. In 1718 the governor of Louisiana, Jean Baptiste le Moyne, Sieur de Bienville, saw the desirability of establishing a town near the mouth of the Mississippi. A port thus strategically located could serve as the door to an entire continent. Bienville selected the highest ground available, an elevation along the east bank. The advantages of the location outweighed the fact that it was subject to frequent flooding.

As soon as the first rude cabins of cypress were erected, the French began building dikes to protect their dwellings. Within a decade they had constructed an earthen levee three feet high to restrain the river. The levee was eighteen feet wide at the top and exteile above and below Jackson Square, the heart of what is now called the French Quarter.

From that innocuous beginning, the campaign to control the Mississippi grew exponentially. Within another ten years the colonists had built forty-two miles of earthworks on both sides of the river. Each plantation owner was responsible for his own river frontage and was free to determine his levee's height and width. The dikes were constructed by hand, using wheelbarrows. This crude wall was no match for the Mississippi. In the flood of 1735 the river poured through numerous breaks.

The French colonial government soon passed an ordinance requiring landowners to complete their levees by January 1, 1744 or forfeit their lands. Flood control was already proving a financial drain. Slave labor was used initially, but as slaves became too valuable to risk in the river's malarial swamps, the planters shifted to Irish immigrants recruited in New Orleans.

Seventy years later, by the time Louisiana was admitted to the Union, the wall binding the river had elongated like a tapeworm. Twisting upon itself as it followed the convolutions of the Mississippi, it had multiplied until it reached all the way to Baton Rouge. In another thirty years, by the 1840s, segments of the dike extended nearly to Memphis.

By then levee districts had been created to spread the financial burden to include those who benefited from flood protection, but whose land did not front on the river. The levee organizations suffered from a chronic lack of funds, so by mid-century the land-owners were agitating for federal assistance. In the annals of flood control, every great flood stimulates a public outcry of sympathy and a response from government. Congress responded to the floods of 1849 and 1850 with the Swamp Acts. Millions of acres of swamplands were ceded to the states for public sale, the proceeds to be used for building levees and draining swamps.

The passage of the Swamp Acts initiated a pattern of association between flood control and wetland reclamation, a pattern that has persisted. Sometimes a levee is built first and then the newly protected wetland is drained for cultivation. Other times the swamp is drained first and then a levee built to protect the new cropland. Drainage works encourage levee building, and vice versa. Over the years, no matter which comes first, the wetlands disappear.

The Swamp Acts centralized the flood-protection program, with the states assuming a more active role than they had in the past. Yet construction of the levees remained piecemeal and inadequate. Some sections were too low compared to those upstream. During floods, as the river rose and the levee became saturated, the sections that were not up to grade were weak links in danger of collapse. Breaks, known in the idiom of the river as "crevasses," could also happen any place where the dike had been undermined by a burrowing muskrat or crawfish. Once water began seeping through, a hole or "sand boil" would form. Flood workers were alert for such trouble spots and would block them with sandbags. If not treated at once, the hole could enlarge, the levee collapse, and the river burst through in a torrent that would send workers fleeing for their lives.

Always those on one side of the river competed with their neighbors across the way to build the stronger levee. But the higher the dikes, the more the rising water was confined and the more pressure the river exerted. If the levee across the river caved in first, your farm was saved. Each community patrolled its own section to watch for sand boils and to ensure that the planters across the river did not take advantage of a dark night to sneak over with a spade and relieve the river's pressure. Levee building became a nineteenth-century arms race. If the other side was raised a foot, yours had to be built up two. Small dikes grew into large walls of earth.

A CREVASSE ON THE MISSISSIPPI

At this time the science of river hydraulics was in its infancy. Flood records were scanty, especially data on river stages—the heights the water reaches for varying amounts of rainfall. After the floods of 1849 and 1850, Congress appropriated funds for a technical survey of the river by Captain A. A. Humphreys and Lieutenant H. L. Abbot, officers in the Corps of Engineers. Their report, completed in 1861, is still considered by the Corps to be "one of the most authoritative documents ever published on Mississippi River problems." Humphreys and Abbot concluded that levees were the only practicable way to achieve flood protection, and this conclusion came to be accepted as the army's official position.

Civilian engineers attacked the "levees only" policy. Three alternatives were proposed. One opponent of the Corps' policy advocated dams on the tributaries as a more effective way of controlling downstream flooding. The reservoirs, by storing water, would hold back peak flows. Others argued for blasting artificial cutoffs across a few of the meander loops in the hopes that this would speed the floodwaters on their way to the gulf. The idea was to straighten—channelize—the river in order to flush out the water as quickly as possible. The third suggestion was spillways. The Mississippi had been bottled up, its escape routes blocked. The levees had walled off the floodplain swamps—temporary storage for floodwaters. Some engineers suggested that new outlets be created to give the water places to go. These spillways, also called floodways, would divert a portion of the flow, thereby lowering flood stages and relieving pressure on the levees.

Humphreys and Abbot rejected reservoirs as too expensive. They were sufficiently farsighted to see that cutoffs would depress flood stages upstream but increase them downstream. Their report did not consider emergency floodways—spillways that would be opened only if needed. They did investigate year-round outlets, but they felt these might capture too much of the Mississippi's flow.

Opponents of Humphreys and Abbot's "levees only" policy argued that further constricting the Mississippi with levees would raise the riverbed, because the sediment that formerly was deposited on the floodplain would instead be dumped in the channel. As the channel filled in, its carrying capacity would be reduced and flood heights would increase. Proponents replied that constriction would augment the velocity, and the faster water would dig out the riverbed. The deepened channel would be capable of carrying off the floodwaters that formerly spread into the swamps. Flood heights would not increase.

The Humphreys and Abbot report indicated that the Mississippi was scouring its banks rather than its bed. The study concluded that flood stages—heights—would increase as much as ten feet. Even so, the army officers opted for "levees only."

The debate continued among engineers, but meanwhile the Civil War broke out and the flood-control system collapsed from neglect. With the states distracted by the fighting, routine maintenance was impossible, and many of the levees washed away during floods. In the years immediately following the war, the South was too impoverished to rebuild.

In time the walls were to rise again. But no matter how high they were built, as one flood chronicler says, the river has found a way through. People who lived along its banks came to mark the years in terms of the great floods: 1867, 1882, 1884, 1890, 1897, 1903, 1912, 1913, 1922.

Throughout this period Southerners lobbied for federal help. But the rest of the nation was unwilling to foot the bill for building levees when the main benefit would be to increase property values for landowners along the river. However, since constriction by levees was thought to deepen and enlarge the channel, flood control was increasingly viewed as a desirable adjunct to navigation improvement. In 1879 Congress created the Mississippi River Commission with jurisdiction over navigation and flood control. The commission was composed of three army engineers, one member of the Coast and Geodetic Survey, two civil engineers, and one political appointee. The chief of the Army Corps of Engineers was given veto power over the commission's decisions. Its only job in connection with levee construction was to prescribe standard grades—specifications for height and width—based on previous flood heights. The commissioners recognized that levees increase stages, but they had faith in the ultimate deepening of the channel. That, together with their conviction that other flood-control measures were impractical, kept the commission committed to the "levees only" policy.

The Mississippi responded to increasing confinement by setting new high-water records. After each inundation, the river commission reacted by raising the levee grade. River and engineers were engaged in an escalating cold war. The commissioners, accused of a commitment to archaic ideas, replied that they were adhering to proven principles.

Meanwhile out on the river, the gargantuan task of raising the levees went on year after year. Men with wheelbarrows and mules with sleds dragged load after load up the steep slopes. In time of flood, men with shovels . . . men with sandbags . . . men with planks . . . shored up the low spots as the rising water surged at their feet. People became accustomed to the levees breaking. They lived with it. They built their cabins on stilts or they moved into the upper floors of their houses. Stores stayed open if the water rose no higher than the tops of the counters. Clerks would walk around on them, taking canned goods down from the shelves. Lyle Saxon, who grew up on a plantation at the turn of the century, tells of the family of a steamboat captain who took refuge in a church. Water came up to the tops of the pews and the family lived in the balcony with their chickens, dogs, and cats. To reach their home they rowed in, up the aisle.

He also tells how, when he was a boy, a crevasse forced his family to flee to the levee in the middle of the night. When the river rushed through a break, often the surviving levee was the only ground high enough to provide a refuge. As Lyle and his parents ran through the night, the rising water stampeded the plantation's cattle and mules. The Saxons and their black sharecroppers were nearly trampled. Once animals and humans had climbed to safety, chunks of the levee caved in, and the refugees were forced to move farther down. Lyle's mother cried when she saw the lights in the plantation house go out, since it meant that the water had risen high enough to extinguish the lamps on the marble-topped table in the hall.

The next day when the sun rose the Mississippi lay silent, a yellow sea pierced only by the treetops. The plantation house was askew, the whole building slanted sharply to one side. One chimney had fallen, and the water stood almost to the top of the front door. Lyle remembers that the flower garden and shrubs had disappeared. Only the trees remained, the current making a fan-shaped ripple behind their trunks.

———————◆—◆———————

HUMAN MEMORIES ARE SHORT and human optimism indefatigable. In 1922 a successful high-water fight raised hopes that the river commission had finally brought the Mississippi to its knees. That year crevasses were minimal, damages were light. In the state of Mississippi, people of the Yazoo Delta—a flat lowland at the confluence of the Yazoo and Mississippi Rivers—were for the first time hopeful for the future. Northern capital flowed in and the area developed rapidly. The Mississippi River Commission, joining in the prevailing mood, predicted that the end of the flood-control fight was at hand. The standard grade set by the commission had been attained all along the levee. No more would be spent on raising the height; the only task left would be maintenance.

Then came 1927. It brought the most destructive flood visited on the valley since the French began building dikes. In the spring of 1927 the rains were torrential. The tributaries filled and the main channel rose dangerously high. On April 21 the levee broke at Mounds Landing, just above Greenville, Mississippi, in the heart of the Yazoo Delta. Fifteen thousand fled to the levee as the water swept into the streets of Greenville at fifteen miles per hour. Cora Lee Campbell was one of the refugees:

> We stayed on the levee three nights and two days, and we didn't have nowhere to lay
> down. There was a lot of folks on the levee, my father and this child Roosevelt
> Campbell, my husband, his father, and all the rest of the other people around us. We

made little bitty little houses, just big enough for a child to get in, and I laid down there on a army blanket that I raised this child in and the water just come up on me, and I had to take him and lay him in my breast to keep him dry, from getting chilled. It didn't do me no good. Then, in three days a boat come and it took us to Rosedale, and the boat it like to sunk, oh Lord, it was a time.

Mounds Landing was the only major break on the east bank of the river, but it flooded 2,323,005 acres and left 172,770 homeless. So much levee caved in that one engineer estimated that the rate of water roaring through Mounds Landing was as great as that pouring over Niagara Falls. And the flood caused many lesser breaks. In all there were 42 large crevasses and 78 smaller ones. The flood tore down the river for a thousand miles, spreading as wide as a hundred miles. Seven states were inundated.

The Red Cross organized urgent rescue operations. Victims were clinging to roof-tops and trees, shivering in the rain on bridges and Indian mounds, huddled in boxcars. Thousands would die unless help came quickly. Those with boats searched for survivors. A resident of Greenville recalled the anguish:

> There was a house with seven people on it. I presume it was man and wife and five children. And I was heading over to this house. This was on my first hauling, the next day after the levee broke. And on the way getting to the house, the house was just moving along, you know, all of a sudden it must have hit a stump or something. And the house flew all to pieces. And I searched the boards and things around there for ten minutes, and you know I never saw a soul come up, not a soul.

Paddle-wheelers like the *Sprague* plucked refugees—some had been without food for three days—off levees and took them to hastily erected tent cities on high ground. Many of the residents of Greenville were transported to camps established in the rolling hills of the national park at Vicksburg. Others were housed in schools and warehouses. Red Cross nurses passed out millions of doses of quinine and administered mass inoculations for smallpox and typhoid.

In most great floods, more have died from disease and starvation than from drowning. In 1927, the deaths climbed to at least 250, evacuations to 700,000. Property damages would amount to $400 million—and that was in 1927 dollars. Herbert Hoover, then Secretary of Commerce and head of the 33,000 relief volunteers, labeled it "the greatest disaster of peace times in our history."

The cataclysm of 1927 led to a total review of flood-control policies. Hearings in Congress revealed how little the engineers knew. Today we would say the Mississippi had been remade with no notion of the impact such a massive project would have on the environment.

Two results of national importance came out of all the suffering. The federal government took over the financing and planning of flood protection. And the "levees only" policy fell. The Corps adopted a new flood-control plan that included elements of all the proposals that had been kicked around for seventy-five years. What seems obvious today and seemed obvious to many for nearly a century was that a mistake of gigantic proportions had been made. By caging the river, the levees had caused it to rise dangerously high before breaking out.

When the river was in a natural state and even after the first low dikes were built, the Mississippi's floods had been leisurely. The water came slowly and left behind fine silt rich in nutrients. Since the floods were not deep, they seldom lasted long enough to prevent plantation owners from getting in a crop. But by 1927, when thirty-foot-high levees crevassed, the waters poured through with tremendous force, leaving deep scour holes and ruining the land with gullies and infertile sand drifts.

Through 1927, $292 million is estimated to have been spent on levees. On May 15, 1928, Congress appropriated $325 million for construction of a new system called the Mississippi River and Tributaries Project. The new plan incorporated reservoirs, cutoffs, floodways and their control structures, floodwalls, pumping stations, and miles and miles of levees on the main stem and up the tributaries. The Mississippi River and Tributaries Project has been periodically updated and thus remains, after fifty years, still incomplete. From 1928 to 1979 the cost of the project mounted to $2.7 billion, and the Corps estimates that another $4 billion will be needed before it is finished. After that, annual maintenance will be required.

When complete, the project will not provide absolute protection against every possible flood. Our records cover only a moment in the Mississippi's long history, so we do not know what the greatest possible flood could be. And if we did, providing protection would be prohibitively expensive. Flood control is a misnomer. What the project provides is flood reduction.

 UNTIL THE 1930s the Mississippi's length was 2,552 miles, a tidy and easily remembered number. In 1932 Maj. Gen. Harley B. Ferguson, president of the Mississippi River Commission, took it upon himself to straighten a few meanders. By the early 1940s sixteen cutoffs had been made, including the Leland Cutoff, which left an oxbow lake connected to the river at one end, forming a slackwater harbor for the town of Greenville. Channelization shortened the Mississippi by 230 miles.

Differences of opinion developed as to the value of cutoffs, and no more have been made. Since the forties, the river has recovered some of its length through increased meandering, caused by bank erosion due to the heightened velocity of the water pouring through the cutoffs. To counteract this instability, the Corps embarked on a massive program to stop erosion of the riverbanks. Various materials were experimented with, everything from discarded automobiles to asphalt paving, plastic bags filled with sand, and flexible concrete mats or "revetment." On the upper river where rock is plentiful, riprap is used. Concrete, though it costs $1 million a mile, turned out to be the army's choice for the lower Mississippi. For camping, broken rock is slightly more appetizing,

Although straightening the Mississippi proved to be of questionable value, channelization is widely used on its tributaries as a flood-control measure. Sam Pearsall—native Tennesseean and director of the Tennessee Natural Heritage Program and a longtime friend—took me to see the Hatchie River, which empties into the Mississippi near Memphis. Designated a state scenic river, the Hatchie is the only remaining major tributary below Cairo that has escaped channelization.

Today, Sam told me as we stood on the banks of this secluded stream, the soybean may be the Hatchie's executioner. Farmers in western Tennessee, eager to grow soybeans for the foreign market, are after the Hatchie's fertile bottomlands. So anxious are they to take advantage of the high price of soybeans, they clear the river bottoms by bulldozing and then burning stands of furniture-quality wood: oak, black willow, sycamore—my favorite tree—and shagbark hickory.

Once crops are planted in the denuded floodplain, the farmers clamor for channelization. Just as with the Cache River in eastern Arkansas, and in fact with all the swamp rivers of the Southeast, landowners want the Hatchie ripped up by bulldozer and dredge to keep the soybeans dry. But straightening meanders, removing snags, and dredging the bottom destroys the stream's pools and riffles—the fish habitat. The damage is virtually permanent. At the same time, channelization defeats its own purpose. Increased siltation from erosion caused by clearing the banks destroys downstream wetlands, wetlands that once served as waterfowl habitats and as a sponge to soak up pollutants and floodwaters.

Channelization does reduce flooding on adjacent lands, but downriver the floods increase in size as the stream and its backwaters fill with silt. Soon the dredges are back to dig again. One admirer of the Hatchie River wonders whether children of the future will grow up believing that all rivers are straight. Will they believe that riverbanks grow only rye grass, fescue, and asphalt?

HUNDREDS OF FLOOD-CONTROL reservoirs for the Mississippi's tributaries were authorized in the 1930s. Most were constructed in the 1950s and 1960s, but some, such as the Meramec Park Dam in Missouri, aroused opposition. One of the last free-flowing streams in the state, the Meramec is one of those clear Ozark streams that is ideal for lazy float trips. It has been a favorite with St. Louisans for generations.

The Meramec was authorized to be dammed to control flooding at its confluence with the Mississippi. Opponents of the dam believe the farmland that would be flooded by the reservoir is just as valuable as the land that would be protected downstream. Instead of building an expensive structure to preserve one area at the expense of another, they suggest that the floodplain of the lower Meramec be turned into a park, a use compatible with periodic flooding. In this instance, few buildings would have to be relocated.

Flooding is natural. It is normal for a river to overflow its banks periodically. The floodplain is therefore a part of the river, as much as is the channel; in times of high water the bottomlands *are* the river's channel. Nonstructural flood-control measures, such as zoning to inhibit future construction in the floodplain, acknowledge the river's prior claim.

Floodways have been among the more successful flood-control devices, and not surprisingly, since they imitate nature. Storage for excess floodwaters was needed in the stretch between Cairo and New Madrid, so a spillway was built. A levee was set back five miles from the Mississippi paralleling the riverbank levee to form a strip of enclosed land called the Birds Point–New Madrid Floodway. As the river rises, water enters the flood-way from a low section of the levee called a "fuseplug." When the fuseplug "blows," water fills the floodway and then reenters the main channel at New Madrid. Pressure is thereby relieved on a narrow section of the Mississippi, a section where the levee and the bluff on the opposite bank are extremely close.

Farther down the river are the Morganza Floodway, the Atchafalaya Floodway, and, just above New Orleans, the Bonnet Carré Spillway. Birds Point–New Madrid has been opened only once, during the flood of 1937. Bonnet Carré has been opened a number of times—in 1937, 1945, 1950, 1973, 1975, and 1979. The soil at New Orleans cannot support higher levees; Bonnet Carré is the safety valve that has repeatedly saved the city. Morganza and the Lower Atchafalaya were used for the first time in 1973.

The use of cutoffs, reservoirs, and floodways does not mean the levee system has been abandoned. Far from it. In the present plan 1,608 miles of levees are authorized for the main stem alone, not to mention the tributaries. To date, only two-thirds or 1,094 miles are up to current specifications for grade. But in places the levee is now forty feet high.

Valuable urban land is often protected by concrete floodwalls, instead of levees. In Cape Girardeau, Missouri, we tied up to a dock at the base of a floodwall that towered about twenty feet above our heads. Steel steps led up one side and then down the other. Behind the wall the land rises; from the shore the Mississippi becomes visible only after you have walked back several streets up the hill. Without that rise in the land, the citizens of Cape Girardeau might well forget that they live in a river town.

In the levee on the main stem are gaps where the major tributaries enter. The volume of water confined by today's levees is so great that the river often backs up into these tributaries, flooding the lowlands at the confluences. The principal backwater areas are those of the St. Francis, the White-Arkansas, and the Red on the west bank and the Yazoo on the east. Levees protect the backwater lowlands from lesser floods, but are overtopped during major floods, making the storage capacity of the lowlands available.

The town of Greenville is in the Yazoo Delta backwater. In 1829 English and Scotch-Irish pioneers landed at Bachelor's Bend, near the present site of Greenville, and established a settlement in the cypress swamps. Bachelor's Bend was burned to the ground during the Civil War but rebuilt nearby in 1886. Mrs. Harriet Blanton Theobald had donated a portion of her cotton plantation for the new town, renamed Greenville.

By 1970 the population had grown to 41,802, and Greenville was thriving as a shipbuilding center. A number of towboat companies are based in Greenville because of its fine harbor. Though the town lacks the charm of Natchez and the beauty of Vicksburg's national park, it boasts more published authors than any other city of its size in America. It is the birthplace or home of a surprising number of Southern writers: Walker Percy, Pulitzer Prize winner Hodding Carter (father of the Hodding Carter formerly with the Carter administration), historian Shelby Foote, travel writer Bern Keating, Ellen Douglas, and William Alexander Percy.

At the Greenville levee we met a local farmer named Allen Clinkscales. He and his family were relaxing for the weekend on their houseboat. They invited us aboard for a steak dinner and then to visit their rice plantation forty miles southeast of Greenville. The Clinkscales have a thousand acres in rice and four thousand acres in soybeans, cotton, and wheat. The plantation employs twenty hourly laborers. Allen Clinkscales pointed out that since hand labor is a thing of the past, tenant farming is gone. Even so, many of his workers have been with him for twenty years, including his "rice man," a black who was supervising the harvest on the day we visited. Because school was closed for Labor Day, the rice man's small son was with him on the combine, learning the business.

Allen Clinkscales believes in the farm of the future. His equipment shed bulges with cotton pickers, combines, trucks, and tractors with air conditioning and AM/FM radios. The plantation has its own grain elevator where the rice is dried. Allen's Lincoln Continental has a two-way radio so that he can talk with his wife at the house, or consult with his son-in-law in the field, or direct operations on the family's other farm. He even has a laser beam for setting the height of the small levees that are used to maintain water on the rice fields. Each year these levees must be rebuilt. The laser, with a transmitter on a tripod and a receiver on a tractor, gives elevation readings.

In 1973 a major flood struck and the Clinkscales plantation was under water for six weeks. For most of that time a boat was their only transportation. Because the Yazoo Delta is so flat, a foot of high water will spread over a hundred thousand acres. The Clinkscales and their neighbors are very conscious of elevations. They know the exact heights of their homes and what river stage will mean disaster. In the spring of 1973 the Clinkscales' house was protected by sandbags. Had the water gone up another two-tenths of a foot, they would have started moving out the furniture.

The 1973 flood caught the people of the Mississippi Valley, and even the Corps of Engineers, by surprise. An entire generation had grown up during the dry decades of the 1950s and 1960s without experiencing a Mississippi flood. As in 1927, the valley had grown complacent. As the water rose, it became apparent that the capacity of the main channel had deteriorated seriously between 1950 and 1973. The army engineers at the Corps' hydraulic laboratory in Vicksburg—the Waterways Experiment Station—realized that the channel had silted in to such an extent that it could not handle the water that would soon come down the valley. A massive emergency program to raise the levees was started immediately. Workers began filling 14 million sandbags. By the time they had finished, they had filled enough to build up the levees along eight hundred miles of river.

Even so, several sections threatened to fail as the banks in front of them caved in. The Corps rushed to throw up "setback levees" to contain the water if the main dikes crevassed. They also spread sixty-eight hundred rolls of polyethylene to protect the levees from erosion, as waves built up across the wide expanses of water.

To help predict the course of the flood, the Corps consulted the Mississippi Basin Model at Clinton, Mississippi, a scale model of the river and its tributaries built in the aftermath of the 1927 flood. The largest working hydraulic model in existence, it covers 220 acres and is a mile long. The model, basically a gigantic relief map built of concrete, faithfully copies the original. Everything is there: miniature bridges, levees, highways, railroad embankments, and even folded screen wire to represent forests. Any size flood can be simulated on the model, depending on how much water the engineers turn on. I timed how long it takes to stroll from Memphis to Vicksburg in miniature, and it was nearly three minutes.

The Corps had decommissioned the model in 1969, believing it had served its purpose of helping to develop a comprehensive flood-control plan. But with the 1973 flood imminent, Maj. Gen. Charles C. Noble, president of the Mississippi River Commission, ordered the facility reopened and updated. Within hours a U2 plane was sent aloft to take infrared photos of the landscape. Vast tracts of bottomland forests that existed in 1950 were gone by 1973. Floodwaters are significantly slowed by anything in their path, so the model had to be altered to reflect the new, treeless world.

The miniature river helped the engineers determine the effect of opening the Morganza Floodway, which to that date had not been used, and helped them locate which levees were endangered. In this flood, the main stem was to hold, but the levees on the tributaries gave way. The lower Ohio, the St. Francis, the White, the Arkansas, the Red, the Yazoo, the Ouachita, and the Atchafalaya all left their banks. Three million acres flooded on the Yazoo Delta alone, as well as fourteen million acres of other tributary lands, more than went under in 1927. Losses mounted to in excess of $1 billion. Before it was over, twenty-eight people died and 45,300 were evacuated.

The flooding that occurred at the Clinkscales farm was backwater from the Sunflower River, a tributary of the Yazoo. Once the water receded, Allen was still able to make a good crop. "If the water stays out of the houses," he told me, "the floods are good for the fields." A farm north of him was ruined by sand in 1927 when Mounds Landing crevassed, but water that "kind of eases in," as Allen put it, brings fertile silt.

After the flood receded, the engineers were left with the task of figuring out what went wrong. Although the 1973 flood was one of the largest on record in terms of river stages—St. Louis experienced the highest in its history—the rainfall had not been heavy enough to account for these stages. Rainfall was only 21 percent above normal, but flood stages were twice that at many points along the river. The levees on the tributaries could not handle such excessive heights, and even the levees on the main stem would have crevassed had the Corps not scrambled to raise them.

Increasing urbanization perhaps contributed to the record stages. Parking lots, shopping centers, interstates—any kind of pavement builds a wall between the rain and the soil. Instead of soaking in and being stored, the water pours into the storm sewers. But the main effect of the water entering the river through the sewer system instead of as soil runoff is that floods peak more quickly, not that they rise higher. Nor can logging or farming be held responsible for the record heights. Destroying the ground cover does increase the damage caused by flooding—soil erosion—and does increase the frequency of small floods. But catastrophic inundations happen after the soil is saturated. After the earth contains all the water that it can, lack of ground cover makes no difference to flood heights.

What *did* cause the flood of 1973? The levees on the tributaries were simply not high enough, but what about the main channel? It had been thought adequate to handle rainfall of the magnitude experienced in 1973. But it was not, and its levees had to be raised with sandbags. The Corps attributes responsibility to silting in of the channel, caused by the cutoffs. The levee grades that were to prove inadequate in 1973 had been established by the Mississippi River Commission in 1950. At that time the channelization of the 1930s—the cutoffs made to speed the water to the gulf—was still effective. In the following years, however, the capacity of the river to handle floodwaters diminished as some of the gains from the cutoffs were lost. The river had meandered again and become braided, dispersed into shallow channels divided by sandbars and islands. With its capacity degraded by the meandering and braiding, the channel could not have handled the floodwaters, had it not been for the Corps' sandbags.

Today, with the channel's capacity reduced, the levee grade must once again be raised. The sandbags piled on top in 1973 were a temporary emergency measure; the levees must have a permanent buildup of four to five feet. As in 1927 and before, the Corps considered all the alternatives to a new levee grade: additional reservoirs, new cutoffs, and more floodways. This time, unlike 1927, the army opted for raising the levees as the least expensive choice. The Corps has reverted to the early days—the "levees only" policy of raising grades.

The obvious question is whether we will ever be done with building the dikes higher. To prevent further channel deterioration and a repetition of 1973, the Corps is relying on the channel stabilization program. Concrete revetments on bends subject to erosion will counteract future meandering and braiding. The engineers are in a race to finish the revetments before raising the levees becomes necessary again. But how long it will take to pave the channel the Corps cannot say.

Some hydrologists disagree with the army's cutoff theory regarding the cause of 1973's flooding. Loss of channel efficiency subsequent to the cutoffs cannot account for the record-breaking stage at St. Louis, because the city is upriver of the cutoffs. The dissenting scientists attribute the higher stages to the confinement of the river by levees—the same theory proposed by opponents of the "levees only" policy back in the days of the Humphreys and Abbot report. Dr. Charles Belt, a geologist at St. Louis University, agrees and goes even further, assigning part of the responsibility to wing dikes, which constrict the river's flow. Dr. Belt's research indicates that dikes reduce the discharge-carrying capacity of the channel during the initial stages of a flood; then, as the water rises, the levees increasingly become important in confining the floodwaters and raising stages. Dikes reduce the water storage capacity of the channel, and levees, that of the floodplain.

The Corps admits that deposition of silt behind the wing dikes narrows the channel, but they maintain that the result is increased velocity and bottom scour, enough to compensate for the reduced channel. The Corps' own studies, according to Dr. Belt, indicate that the data are insufficient to support this conclusion. Not only is the bottom resistant to natural scour, sections of it have become armored with a buildup of large particles that resist even the dredge.

All other factors being equal, according to a study done for the Corps by Professor Jerome Westphal of the University of Missouri–Rolla, narrowing the channel with wing dikes works against flood protection. Our program of improving the channel for navigation is competing with our program of flood control.

Not only do navigation works and levees reduce the river's flood-storage capacity, channelization on the tributaries contributes to higher stages by speeding water into the main river. A stream that has been straightened cannot store as much water as one that meanders. Channelization has sabotaged the natural storage of tributaries; wing dikes, that of the channel; and levees, the floodplain. All this loss of storage means larger and larger floods. Our programs of navigation and flood control are transforming moderate floods into big ones. The flood of 1973, Dr. Belt and others maintain, was a man-made disaster.

A reassessment is obviously in order. The Mississippi must be allowed to recover storage capacity. Floodplain zoning and floodways are successful measures because, by restoring lowlands to the river, they restore its ability to handle floodwaters. Rather than trying to control the Mississippi, they are means of living with it.

This is hardly a new viewpoint, but what is surprising is how long it is taking to gain acceptance. Had we listened a hundred years ago, we would have kept the floodplain free of buildings and never constructed a levee system. We would have devoted the bottom-lands to forests and such agriculture as its compatible with periodic flooding. Had we listened to Mark Twain, billions would have been saved in flood damages and control works:

The military engineers of the Commission have taken upon their shoulders the job of making the Mississippi over again—a job transcended in size by only the original job of creating it. They are building wing dams here and there, to deflect the current; and dikes to confine it in narrower bounds; and other dikes to make it stay there; and for unnumbered miles along the Mississippi, they are felling the timberfront for fifty yards back, with the purpose of shaving the bank down to low-water mark with the slant of a house-roof, and ballasting it with stones; and in many places they have protected the wasting shores with rows of piles. One who knows the Mississippi will promptly aver—not aloud, but to himself—that ten thousand River Commissions, with the mines of the world at their back, cannot tame that lawless stream, cannot curb it or confine it, cannot say to it, Go here, or Go there, and make it obey; cannot save a shore which it has sentenced; cannot bar its path with an obstruction which it will not tear down, dance over, and laugh at. But a discreet man will not put these things into spoken words; for the West Point engineers have not their superiors anywhere; they know all that can be known of their abstruse science; and so, since they conceive that they can fetter and handcuff that river and boss him, it is but wisdom for the unscientific man to keep still, lie low, and wait till they do it. . . . Otherwise one would pipe out and say the Commission might as well bully the comets in their courses and undertake to make them behave, as try to bully the Mississippi into right and reasonable conduct.

16

Watching the River Flow

"Jim, how did you run Plum Point, coming up?"

"It was in the night, there, and I ran it the way one of the boys on the *Diana* told me; started out about fifty yards above the wood pile on the false point, and held on the cabin under Plum Point till I raised the reef—quarter less twain—then straightened up for the middle bar till I got well abreast the old one-limbed cottonwood in the bend, then got my stern on the cottonwood and head on the low place above the point, and came through a-booming—nine and a half."

MARK TWAIN, *LIFE ON THE MISSISSIPPI*

*I*N 1811 THE *NEW ORLEANS,* the first steamboat on the Mississippi, was making her maiden voyage to demonstrate the feasibility of using steam on western waters. The paddle-wheeler reached the region of the 1811 seismic activity in December. Each time the earth shook, the vessel would lurch as if grounded, and many of the crew became seasick. One ghastly night an island that was used as a mooring caved in and disintegrated tree by tree. By morning nothing was left but open water. Despite "those days of horror," as one passenger referred to the journey through the New Madrid area, the steamboat *New Orleans* reached its namesake city, and it launched an era never to be forgotten.

Prior to the introduction of steam, a variety of vessels had been tried on the Mississippi. The flatboat or raft was the workhorse of early transportation, floating the produce of settlers down the Ohio and Mississippi to New Orleans. Cheaply built so as to be expendable, the flatboat was broken up and sold for lumber at the end of the journey. Many sidewalks in Baton Rouge and New Orleans were built from boards that once carried furs, hogsheads of bear grease, indigo, rice, corn, and tobacco.

A SHANTY BOAT

The upstream journey against the current was another matter. To return to his farm the flatboatman usually opted for an arduous and hazardous trip by land. Or he could take passage on a keelboat. The keelboat was a large vessel, seventy feet long, with a pointed bow and stern. On the upstream journey the crewmen rowed or poled, keeping the boat close to shore to avoid the current and to take advantage of eddies. If a clear path appeared on shore, the craft was towed by means of a long rope called a cordelle. Whether rowing, poling, or towing, gaining ground against the Mississippi's powerful current was backbreaking work.

Westerners were quick to see the advantages of steam. In 1810, the year before the first steamboat trip, port authorities in New Orleans counted the arrival of 679 flatboats and 392 keelboats. By 1814, only three years after the *New Orleans* made its historic voyage, 21 steamboats arrived at the southern port. By 1830 nearly 1,000 paddle-wheelers tied up at the levee, and a decade later nearly 2,000. But the steamboat never replaced the other modes of transportation, for no one kind of boat could keep pace with the growth of the country's interior.

After steam was introduced, woodyards soon lined the river to feed boilers greedy for cordwood. By the 1840s, as the banks were stripped and wood became scarce, coal was substituted. It required less space, was cheap, and eventually became the only fuel available.

The early steamboats were small, awkward, and often decrepit, hardly the graceful floating palaces we associate with the Mississippi's romantic age. Even by the 1850s—the flush days of riverboating—the shallow-draft sternwheelers that plied the tributaries remained simple, ungainly craft.

But on the main river, owners were putting as much as $200,000 into floating hotels that rivaled New York's best. Humanity has never come up with anything quite as fantastic as the steamboat in its heyday: the grand salon with its crystal chandeliers, oil paintings, Brussels carpeting, marble statues, and orchestra; the dining room with two dozen stewards, silver service, and a menu two feet long; the bar, the lounge, and the barbershop. Above the hurricane deck, the lofty pilothouse was embellished to look like a gazebo, the twin smokestacks were scalloped to resemble feathers, and the boat's name was painted in gold leaf. Calliope music echoed over the water as this fantasy steamed up to a landing, thrilling plantation and town dweller alike. Dickens thought the steamboats gaudy, Whitman rather liked them.

Despite their elegance, the paddle-wheelers were hazardous. Between 1810 and 1850 they caused four thousand deaths. One of those casualties was Twain's brother, Henry Clemens, who died in a steam engine explosion. Such explosions were not uncommon. When a boiler blew up, fatalities were especially high among the immigrants crowded together on the main deck. Those thrown in the water often drowned. Others were killed by flying wreckage, steam, and scalding water.

On February 24, 1830 an explosion on the *Helen MacGregor* drew this horrified account from an eyewitness:

> I advanced from my position to one of the cabin doors for the purpose of inquiring who were injured, when, just as I reached it, a man entered at the opposite one, both his hands covering his face, and exclaiming, "Oh God! Oh God! I am ruined!" He immediately began to tear off his clothes. When stripped, he presented a most shocking spectacle: his face was entirely black—his body without a particle of skin. He had been flayed alive. He gave me his name, and place of abode—then sunk in a state of exhaustion and agony on the floor. I assisted in placing him on a mattress taken from one of the berths, and covered him with blankets. He complained of heat and cold as at once oppressing him. He bore his torments with manly fortitude, yet a convulsive shriek would occasionally burst from him. His wife, his children, were his constant theme—it was hard to die without seeing them—"it was hard to go without bidding them one farewell." Oil and cotton were applied to his wounds; but he soon became insensible to earthly misery.

The average life of a steamboat was only four to five years. Besides boiler explosions, boats would collide or hit snags. Often the highly combustible cargo—cotton, hay, whiskey—would catch fire. Even the wrecks caused more accidents. The stretch between St. Louis and Cairo, notorious for sunken steamboats, became known as "the Graveyard." To recover valuable engines, insurance companies began financing salvage operations. The recycled machinery was used over and over in successive generations of riverboats.

The worst steamboat disaster in history had a larger death toll than that of the *Titanic*. On April 27, 1865 the *Sultana* took aboard twenty-five hundred Union troops just released from Confederate prison camps. The captain knew the boat was overloaded, but he was under orders.

The *Sultana*'s boilers had been neglected during the war, and the run-down engines had developed a leak. At Vicksburg the boat could barely get underway. At Memphis it stopped for repairs. A patch was applied and the boat went on, despite the engineer's objections. Crewmen of a gunboat, the *Grosbeak,* exchanged greetings with the happy passengers of the *Sultana,* as she resumed her journey north. The men on the *Grosbeak* watched the steamboat's gay lights dwindle as it disappeared into the darkness. Then they saw a flash of flame and a moment later heard a deafening explosion. This was followed by a fiery holocaust as the *Sultana* burned. Three-fifths of the soldiers—1,550 men—died.

America's first love affair with speed was responsible for a few of the disasters. In steamboat races safety precautions were flouted. The boilers were fed with the hottest fuel available—turpentine, pitch, pine knots, even sides of bacon. Safety valves were wired closed. Each company vied to prove it had the fastest service.

But in fact most explosions occurred when boats were setting out from port, not in races. Engines were poorly built and inadequately maintained. Careless or incompetent engineers neglected to watch the water level in the boilers, allowing them to overheat. In 1838 Congress passed a law requiring the hull and boilers to be inspected and running lights to be on at night. A decade later, the Steamboat Act of 1852 set quotas on the number of deck passengers and required stairs as escape routes from the main deck to the upper levels. The law also established a mandatory examination and licensing of steamboat pilots and engineers.

In 1856 a new kind of hazard appeared: a railroad bridge was built across the Mississippi at Rock Island. Two weeks after the first train puffed across, a packet hit the bridge and caught fire. The boat's owners sued the railroad, and in the ensuing lawsuit Abe Lincoln represented the defendants. He won. By 1886 fifteen railroad bridges spanned the upper Mississippi. Steamboat pilots, and today towboat pilots, regard the bridges as one of the worst hazards on the river. In high water, paddle-wheelers with high stacks were out of luck. Today's wide tows often squeeze through with only inches to spare between barge and bridge pier.

Before long the railroad began seriously competing for freight, a competition that was a century old by the time of the Locks and Dam 26 dispute. From the 1880s until well after World War I, the railroads won. Compared with river traffic, the trains were fast; they were not susceptible to seasonal shutdowns caused by ice or low water; they had the advantage of being able to expand into the hinterlands, running spur tracks right to the farm and factory doors; and they could lay routes that avoided the river's tortuous windings.

Other reasons existed for the victory of the railroad. Passengers, not to mention insurance companies, were hardly impressed by the steamboat's safety record. But also, the railroad barons, highly efficient and often ruthless, outmaneuvered the small and fiercely independent riverboat companies. Finally, the railroads grew fat on millions of acres of public land. Water transport could not survive federal subsidy of its competitor, any more than railroads today can compete with an inland waterway system maintained by the government.

Steamboats did not disappear, but they did decline drastically. In an effort to improve efficiency by carrying more freight, the river companies started using the steamboats to push loaded barges. In the 1930s another technological improvement was introduced: the diesel engine. The great era of steam ended and the modern towboat appeared.

The passing of steam is regretted by Captain Clarke Hawley, pilot of the *Natchez,* a steamboat in New Orleans operated for excursions. The *Natchez,* the ninth boat to bear that name, has a paddle wheel made of white oak that weighs twenty-six tons. Its boilers are fired with oil, instead of wood or coal as in the old days.

The boilers on the *Natchez* are fifty years old and will last another fifty, whereas diesels average a ten-year lifetime. Captain Hawley points out that steam engines burn less fuel. He also maintains they are safe when built and operated properly. If steam engines are indeed more durable and energy-efficient, why did towboat companies switch to diesel? At the time, fuel was cheaper than labor. No fireman was needed on a diesel boat. Even more important, the pilot of a diesel was not required to have a license. The pilot of a steamboat, by the Steamboat Act of 1852, is compelled to spend years obtaining a certificate. As the barge fleets grew, the companies needed pilots fast, so they opted for diesel. Captain Hawley hopes someday to see a return to oil-driven steam boilers to conserve fuel.

AT GREENVILLE, MISSISSIPPI, we switched from motorboat travel to towboats. We were to ride the *Jesse Brent* from Greenville to Baton Rouge, where a harbor tug would transfer us to the *J. Russell Flowers.* The *J. Russell* would take us to New Orleans.

It was late afternoon when Joe Holmes, Clint Schemmer, and I walked down the riverbank at Greenville and boarded the *Jesse Brent.* We climbed over the handrail, passing our packs and photographic gear to a deckhand. He led us to the galley, on the main deck right at water level. At the door a blast of cold air greeted us. A couple of deckhands were drinking coffee at the lunch counter and watching television, obviously reluctant to leave the air-conditioned galley for the hot deck of the barge.

In a few minutes a messenger arrived from Jesse Brent, the president of the towboat company that was our host. The company, based in Greenville, owns twenty-three towboats and most, like the *Jesse Brent,* are named after members of the Brent family. The messenger brought a stack of literature. Jesse Brent is active in Washington on issues that affect the towboat industry, and we had talked briefly about Locks and Dam 26.

I was glancing at the *Waterways Journal,* an industry publication, when Captain Dick Dedman arrived. The captain spoke in a drawl so heavy I was not surprised at his later revelation that he had picked cotton thirty years ago before taking to the river. He showed us our quarters. My cabin, on the third deck right below the pilothouse, was just large enough for a bunk, desk, and chair. It had a single window covered with a heavy curtain to shut out daylight.

Our next stop was the pilothouse. Most of a towboat is starkly functional, but the pilothouse is still alive with the spirit of Twain except that steering levers long ago replaced the traditional wooden wheel. While Joe took photographs, Captain Dedman left to supervise loading operations down on the barges. We watched from four decks up.

Barges are adapted for various types of cargo. Open-hopper barges carry coal and gravel; hoppers with covers are used for grain; and tank barges transport liquids, such as petroleum and chemicals. On this trip the *Jesse Brent's* tow would consist of four tank barges, which were being filled with petroleum. Three had single-skin hulls, but the fourth was the new type with a double hull to help prevent punctures and oil spills. A tow of eight tank barges carries 8.5 million gallons of oil. Few ocean tankers can handle as much. Up in the wheelhouse, a psychologically safe distance away, Joe and I could smell the fumes as the tanks were filled.

By evening we were ready to get underway. Captain Dedman came back to the pilothouse and took the controls. The small room high above the water is glassed in, giving a 360-degree view of the river. The captain has equipment at his fingertips Sam Clemens would have envied when he was training, a cub pilot. There is a radio phone, an intercom, a radar screen, a sonic depth finder (no more leadsman chanting "Half twain! Quarter twain! Mark twain!"), a swing meter, and a set of charts like the ones we had used in the canoes and motorboat.

The instrument panel includes controls for a pair of searchlights with a beam that can penetrate dark riverbanks three miles downriver. As Captain Dedman swung the lights back and forth searching for buoys, I remembered a sultry night upriver. I had lain in my hot-weather sleeping bag (a sheet sewn to form a sack), looking at the stars and a sliver of moon. A barred owl hooted with its dog-like bark, and in a moment the cry came again from the other side of the sandbar, beside the river. The night grew darker. Then came a familiar throbbing in the distance and the finger of light brushing the trees. For a moment I had felt myself drifting with the boat suspended in blackness.

Now, thinking of that campsite, I stepped out of the pilothouse onto the deck. In the close night air, I leaned against the railing and peered at the vague sandbars. The boat vibrated, then shook and rattled as the captain shifted the engines to half speed. On the deck below, an American flag and television antenna were both black with soot. As we passed the lights of Vicksburg, Joe Holmes came out of the pilothouse. He pointed out Polaris; it was much lower in the sky than it had been when we started our voyage in Minnesota.

We went back inside, where the only light was the glow of the radar screen. We sat on the high settee for visitors and listened as Captain Dedman chatted on the radio with an upriver tow. Both pilots observed old-time river courtesy:

"Good evenin', Cap'n. You want one whistle?"

"That'll be fine, Cap'n."

"All right. I'll blow one. Any traffic behind you?"

"Not that I know of. Have a good evenin', Cap'n."

One blast of our whistle meant we intended to pass on the left. As a tow heading downstream we had the right of way, because with the current behind us our boat was harder to control.

Breakfast was at 5:30 A.M., at the change of the watch. The crew members work six hours on, six off, putting in twelve-hour days. The cook, Bill Floyd, had risen at 3:30 A.M. to prepare breakfast for the ten-man crew. Like all the meals, it was lavish: eggs, bacon, sausage, pancakes, biscuits, and blueberry muffins. At lunch we had ribs, and for dinner, rib-eye steak. The cook bakes fresh pies and cakes every day. Soft drinks, ice cream sandwiches, and candy bars are always available to fill up people like Joe and Clint.

On his off-duty time Captain Dedman took us out on the barges of the tow, after fitting us with life preservers. We weaved our way through a snarl of ratchets, hawsers,

BARRED OWL

and steel cables, all equipment for fastening the barges together. The front of the tow was a fourth of a mile from the boat. As we walked, the captain remarked that he has seen his wife and children for only nine years out of the past thirty. But, he said, the river has been a good life. When he left his parents' home at age fifteen, he had twenty-five cents in his pocket. Now he earns twice as much as most college professors. We came to the foremost barge, and I was delighted with the quiet. On the towboat the pounding of diesels had become a subconscious irritation.

Too soon we left the peace of the river and turned back. The engine room, where the noise is deafening, was the last stop in our tour. I was surprised at the immaculate red floor and white walls—even the engines were painted white. The diesels consume four thousand gallons of fuel a day and fourteen gallons of oil. The used oil is pumped into the bilge and then into a holding tank, instead of the river. When the engines are idling, carbon builds up from incomplete fuel combustion, which explains the black soot on the antenna and flag.

With just four barges we were making fourteen miles per hour going downstream. A tow of normal size will do only eleven downstream and five upstream, though actual speeds may be faster or slower depending on the water level. In average conditions a downbound tow takes more than half a mile to stop. But "in high water," the captain drawled, "some of them jist cain't stop, period. They can slow down, but they cain't stop."

Piloting something that is longer than an ocean liner in a river that is sometimes wide and accommodating but often narrow and treacherously fast requires skill and experience and nerve. In Memphis we had met a riverboat captain who had gone into premature retirement because he felt the river was too risky. I asked Captain Dedman if he had ever had an accident. He replied that a few of the oldtimers have unblemished records, but "there's no way the younger generation can have one." Because the industry has grown so fast, he said, the demand for pilots has put a number of unskilled men in the wheelhouse. It is the hastily trained pilots who cause accidents.

Even a pilot with years of experience can have troubles. The steering may fail. An erratic current may seize the tow. A buoy marking a sandbar may be off-station, so that the boat will ground on an unsuspected shoal. The pilot may go around a bend and collide with some towboat whose captain has lost his bearings. "You go around a point," a pilot told me, "and there they are, when you expect them three or four miles downriver, according to the radio communication." Bridges are particular hazards; I asked one pilot if he had ever hit a bridge and he replied, "I've hit every damn one of them."

At Baton Rouge we transferred to the *J. Russell Flowers,* a new boat as luxurious as an ocean liner. The guest suite I occupied included a lounge with bar, television, and stereo. The *J. Russell*'s tow consisted of thirty barges loaded with coal and wheat. Joe and I were enjoying a sunny afternoon in the *J. Russell*'s wheelhouse when the relief pilot turned to us and said, "Folks, I'm afraid we're going to have some excitement here." We had just started around a 140-degree bend when the current caught us and swung our stern toward the bank.

The emergencies on the river, someone once said, are awful in their slowness. You can see what is going to happen but there is nothing you can do but wait. For ten minutes the pilothouse was silent. With the powerful current, the impact of hitting shore could knock the rudder off or even sink the boat. At the very least, the steel cables holding the tow together could snap and scatter thirty barges downriver. A cable whipping through the air can cut off a leg or send a heavy ratchet flying through the window of a pilothouse.

I thought of the times far upriver when our canoe had slammed into the bank when we were taking a tight turn in swift water. I was relieved this was happening on the *J. Russell* and not the *Jesse Brent* with its petroleum barges. I remembered a pilot we had met at a lock, who had told us about being on a towboat that burned so fast he had had to swim for shore.

We scraped by the bank, almost touching; "as close as you'll ever see without hitting," the pilot said. Towboat captains face such situations every day, and it shows in their faces.

During the next few months, a number of major accidents occurred on the Mississippi. In New Orleans a ship collided with three barges carrying butane. Several crewmen were killed, and pieces of the ship were blown over the levee. The heat was so intense that the roof of a car behind the levee melted.

In the Twin Cities a few days after our near miss, a barge leaked anhydrous ammonia and killed a Coast Guardsman; he inhaled the fumes, which caused him to suffocate and freeze to death. Fifteen others were hospitalized. The police chief reported a vapor cloud above the trees, and parts of a suburb were evacuated. A hundred thousand fish died.

THE MISSISSIPPI AT NEW ORLEANS, 1872

Three months later, again in New Orleans, a barge collided with a tanker. An eyewitness reported the initial explosion was like a "big ball of fire." It was visible miles away. "The whole river is on fire," said a state police trooper. Flames leaped three hundred feet into the air, as high as a thirty-story building. More than a hundred firemen battled related fires on the wharf. With 337,000 gallons of oil spilled, the water-treatment plant for St. Bernard Parish—a suburb of New Orleans—was put on alert to watch its water intakes. At a later inquiry, testimony indicated that the barge was unlighted and that the pilot of the tanker had tried repeatedly to radio the towboat without success.

Not long after that accident, network news carried the story of a Panamanian ore carrier that collided with a German ship, spilling 13.5 tons of a highly toxic chemical, pentachlorophenol (PCP), near the mouth of the Mississippi. Divers found loose sacks of PCP on the river bottom. The bags, made of four-ply paper with a plastic lining, were already beginning to rot. The Coast Guard closed the shipping channel to traffic for several days and used marine vacuums to suck up mud, water, and PCP onto barges. Authorities placed a ban on crabbing, shrimping, and oystering over 350 square miles of river delta. Two weeks later, the waters were expected to be reopened in time for the start of the shrimping season. Presumably the river had cleared up enough to be thought safe.

The industry's trade association—the American Waterways Operators—has published a list of chemicals carried by barges. It includes highly toxic substances such as chlorine, sodium cyanide, and anhydrous ammonia; flammable substances such as formaldehyde and carbon tetrachloride; corrosives such as hydrochloric acid; and carcinogens such as chromic acid and sodium dichromate. The association claims that "movements of bulk chemicals by barge have been increasing steadily and chemicals now comprise one of the largest movements of liquid commodities by water." On the Mississippi River, according to the Corps of Engineers, nearly one-third of all barges are carrying some kind of hazardous cargo, whether chemicals of some sort or petroleum products.

With the Mississippi's great potential for disaster, I wondered why those of us in the rest of the country seldom hear of accidents. The towboat industry claims that riverboats are one of the safest forms of transportation. But the pilots I asked said we don't hear because accidents often happen on remote stretches of the river. Lieutenant Commander Dick Carmack of the Marine Safety Detachment of the Coast Guard had another reason: "The Coast Guard likes to take a low profile when it comes to regulatory duties. So we're just not prone to notify the news media when something happens."

With large quantities of hazardous materials on the river, accidents also happen during loading and unloading operations. A faulty valve leaks or someone is careless. When a spill occurs, the current is so fast the substance often washes downriver before anything can be done. Many toxic materials are so soluble in water that we lack the technology to remove them.

Several accidents occur on the river every day. As was true for steamboats, ground-ings account for many of the vessel casualties, but unlike with the paddle-wheeler, explosions and fires rank relatively low in frequency. Collisions with fixed objects such as locks and bridges are more common on the upper Mississippi; on the lower river where traffic is heavy collisions between vessels account for a large percentage of the accidents. Because of the congestion in New Orleans, the Coast Guard in 1977 instituted the Vessel Traffic Service (VTS), a computerized traffic control. Unlike the old days, fatalities are now low, because deckhands are seldom out on the tow where the risk is greatest, and because fewer passenger vessels ply the river.

A new towboat costs $2.5 million to $3 million, so insurance costs are skyrocketing. Many companies with poor loss records have been forced to resort to European insurance companies, such as Lloyd's of London, which are more willing to take risks.

Statistics published by the Coast Guard indicate that human error is the primary cause of most accidents. In 1972 Congress passed legislation requiring that all towboat pilots obtain an "operator's" license by passing an examination administered by the Coast Guard. To sit for the test an individual must have three years of experience on a vessel, normally as a deckhand, and the company that employs him must certify that he has spent some unspecified amount of that time in the pilothouse. The law does not state that he must actually be given a turn at steering. How much experience he receives depends on how well he gets along with the captain.

Being cooperative seems to help a deckhand move up. An official at the National River Academy, a training school run by the barge industry, put it frankly:

> There's only one entity that makes a pilot, and that's the company. They are the ones who see what that man does under pressure, in tight situations. How steady he is—on showing up on crew change day. How willing he is to work over every now and then when there's a shortage. . . . Just how much he's willing to be part of the towboat life.

The towboat operator examination bears no resemblance to the test instituted for steamboat.pilots in 1852. The old-time pilot had to know the river so well that he could draw it mile by mile, including every bridge, every island, every chute, shoal, wing dam, buoy, and navigation light. It took him as much as three days to draw the section of river for which he wished to be certified.

The examination for a towboat operator's license is a multiple-choice test with 110 questions, of which 40 are open book. The Memphis pilot who retired from the river early, Captain Harold De Marrero, charges that anyone, whether they have ever been on the river or not, can pass the test after three days' study. Captain Mickey Crutchfield, president of the largest pilots' association on the Mississippi, agrees that no river experience is necessary, although he would put the study time at two weeks. I tried a sample test published by the Coast Guard and came close to passing with no study and without the open book.

Both Captain De Marrero and Captain Crutchfield believe that an actual driver's test on the river is the only way to determine whether a person is really a pilot. Captain De Marrero, members of whose family have been river pilots for four generations, believes that the industry opposed a stiff examination, because it was afraid of being crippled by a scarcity of pilots. The river companies, he says, used to be family operations run by people who were close to the crews and well informed about river conditions. But over the years these people retired and sold out to large corporations, who purchased the equipment but not the expertise. These conglomerates forced the industry's growth beyond the supply of qualified pilots.

Some believe that the license, inadequate as it may be, at least gives the Coast Guard a way of removing a pilot whose record reveals his ineptitude. But there is a Catch 22: many accidents go unreported because the pilot fears suspension or revocation of his license. When that happens, a barge damaged in an unreported accident goes unrepaired, later perhaps to leak benzene, styrene, or anhydrous ammonia.

Poor training and human error have a synergistic effect when combined with increasing congestion. The American River Pilots Association gives a grim assessment:

> The lack of a reliable channel report to navigate by, the influx of improperly trained government licensed operators into our profession, improperly buoyed channels, unmarked wrecks, unlighted and improperly moored barge fleets, missing and partially hidden bridge pier protection fences, together with the congestion created by the rapid buildup of barge line company fleets, have caused our great nation's inland waterways to be the most unsafe for navigation in the world today.

Captain Crutchfield urges that the size of tows be limited. Fifty and sixty barges at a time are already being pushed by boats with 10,500 horsepower. Some tows are so long, the stern must be backed or "flanked" around bends. Too often, Captain De Marrero agrees, a company assigns a pilot more than he knows is safe. No pilot, according to Captain Crutchfield, should ever agree to take more than thirty-five barges. Placing restrictions on tonnage moved would be tantamount to putting a limit on the future growth of the industry, but it is a limit that the towboat companies and the insurance underwriters know is coming.

Radar, licensing, and computerized traffic control can only do so much. Radar is line-of-sight and cannot show what is coming around a bend. A stricter licensing program would help, but better-trained pilots will still not eliminate the accidents caused by overcrowding. Computerized traffic control might increase the river's capacity, but not indefinitely. The river has limits, limits that may already have been reached.

FIVE

River of Oil

Baton Rouge to Venice

Atchafalaya:
A Second Chance

They were approaching the region where reigns perpetual summer,
Where through the Golden Coast, and groves of orange and citron,
Sweeps with majestic curve the river away to the eastward.
They, too, swerved from their course; and entering the Bayou of Plaquemine,
Soon were lost in a maze of sluggish and devious waters,
Which, like a network of steel, extended in every direction.
Over their heads the towering and tenebrous boughs of the cypress
Met in a dusky arch, and trailing mosses in mid-air
Waved like banners that hang on the walls of ancient cathedrals.
Deathlike the silence seemed, and unbroken, save by the herons
Home to their roosts in the cedar-trees returning at sunset,
Or by the owl, as he greeted the moon with demoniac laughter.

HENRY WADSWORTH LONGFELLOW, "EVANGELINE"

DURING THE FLOOD OF 1973, workers labored night and day to sandbag hundreds of miles of levees. Meanwhile an even more serious crisis developed as the rampaging river threatened to abandon its channel below Baton Rouge and adopt a new course to the sea. The Atchafalaya River—Mississippi distributary and floodway—was in danger of capturing the parent river's entire flow.

Water enters a floodway either through a fuseplug levee or a control structure. In the case of the Atchafalaya Floodway, Mississippi water comes in through the "Old River Control Structure," located on the west bank just above Baton Rouge. The facility is similar to a dam, but its gates are called on to handle a tremendous volume of water. During major floods close to half the Mississippi—mile-wide giant—pours down the Atchafalaya River and its associated floodways, taking a western path to the gulf.

In 1973, as the water rose higher and higher, the flooding river hurled its might at the control structure. Angry floodwaters surged against the concrete, and the dam began to vibrate. An approach guidewall collapsed. Maj. Gen. Charles Noble, in charge of directing the flood fight, visited the site to inspect the dam:

> The south training wall on the Mississippi River side of the structure failed very early in the flood, causing violent eddy patterns and extreme turbulence. The toppled training wall monoliths worsened the situation. The integrity of the structure at this point was greatly in doubt. It was frightening to stand above the gate bays and experience the punishing vibrations caused by the violently turbulent, massive flood waters.

The force of the water scoured a hole fifty feet deep beneath the foundation. The entrance to the floodway was in imminent danger of collapse.

The Mississippi was hammering away at its geologic destiny. Down through the ages the river has periodically selected one of its distributaries to be its new route to the gulf. In the past five thousand years the river has chosen no fewer than seven different exits. It has swung back and forth like a pendulum, first electing a passage well to the west of the present course, then swinging east back almost to today's channel, again to the west, then way to the east of the present route, back to the west, and finally, about 900 A.D., once again to the east, this time to the present course. Each channel, before being abandoned, deposited a delta; together the old deltas form the land surface of southern Louisiana.

The Mississippi is constantly in motion, snaking sinuously over its alluvial valley. Diversions to new channels occur as the meander loops migrate laterally across the floodplain. Occasionally a loop intersects a stream with an independent course to the gulf. If the stream is large enough, it becomes one of the distributaries for the water of the Mississippi. Should it happen that its path to the gulf is short, the stream will be steeper than the main river, and this gradient advantage will allow it to capture all the water, becoming the new channel.

The diversion takes time, for the new distributary must enlarge enough to accept the full flow. Completion of the process requires a century or so. In the initial stage the stream is too small and crooked to accommodate the huge river. But as water from the Mississippi pours down, the channel expands. A critical stage is reached once the new channel is taking about 40 percent of the flow during normal water. At that point the old channel begins to die.

In the old river, water moves more slowly than it does in the new, steeper one, with its gradient advantage. Just below the point of diversion, where the water first begins to slow, much of the sediment settles out, because slow-moving water has less energy for transporting suspended material. The old channel gradually closes in, plugged with silt, so that this former riverbed now receives water only during floods. The floods leave behind more sediment until nothing is left of the old channel except a saltwater estuary at the mouth of the river.

Such appeared to be the destiny of the Mississippi and the Atchafalaya. In 1973 the Old River Control Structure held, but it was seriously weakened. If it should give way in the future and the Atchafalaya become the new channel, Baton Rouge and New Orleans would be left stranded on a tidal backwater, cut off from their source of drinking water.

"BUT EVANGELINE'S HEART WAS SUSTAINED BY A VISION, THAT FAINTLY
FLOATED BEFORE HER EYES, AND BECKONED HER ON THROUGH THE MOONLIGHT."

Industries would have to be relocated, the harbor at New Orleans would require constant dredging, and the millions invested over the years in levees would be wasted. And in carving its new path, the Mississippi would destroy the Atchafalaya Basin: bridges, highways, oil and gas pipelines to the East, and a beautiful primitive swamp. As in 1927, the country would see a disaster as great as the Mississippi River is mighty.

The Atchafalaya is a young waterway, having formed about 1500 A.D. The name, pronounced "Ah chaf' uh lai' uh," or sort of like a sneeze, came from the Chitamachas word for "long river." It turned out to be an ironic name since the Atchafalaya wanders for only 142 miles before it reaches the gulf, giving it a substantial gradient advantage over the Mississippi, which takes 315 miles to make the same journey.

The Atchafalaya was still a stream of no consequence in the early 1800s when the area was settled. French-speaking Acadians were the first to arrive. Driven from Nova Scotia by the British in 1755, the Acadians found a refuge along the Atchafalaya's bayous and remote swamps. "Evangeline," the epic poem by Longfellow, is based on the true story of Emmeline Labiche, an Acadian woman who was separated from her betrothed at the time of the exile. She searched for him for years and is said to have found him, now betrothed to another, on the shores of Bayou Teche in the Atchafalaya Basin.

The Acadians, or Cajuns, survived off the land. Their descendants still live around the edges of the swamp, commuting by motorboat to their hunting and fishing grounds.

Most of us know the Cajuns best for their cuisine, which is rich in such delicacies as "boudin," a sausage filled with rice, pork, and spices.

After the Louisiana Purchase the Cajuns were joined by a few English-speaking settlers, who bought up the high ground to grow cotton and sugarcane. At that time the Atchafalaya was still a tiny stream, but its fortunes began to change in the decade just before the Civil War. Until then the Atchafalaya had been blocked at its northern end by a permanent logjam, a raft of logs twenty miles long that kept the waters of the Mississippi from pouring down the new distributary. In 1855 the raft was cleared away to make the Atchafalaya navigable. The channel immediately began to widen and deepen.

As more water poured down it, the Atchafalaya's floods increased in severity, and agriculture in the basin ceased. About the same time, canals were dug to float out the virgin cypress. Because of the swamp, the lumberjacks attached scaffolds above the waterline to stand on while they swung their axes. Still rising fifteen feet above the water are phantom forests of stumps—footprints left behind by the loggers.

By 1910 the vigorous young river carried a fifth of the flow of the Mississippi. In clearing the raft, the engineers had set a geologic process in motion that would be hard to stop.

After the flood of 1927, the Atchafalaya Basin was selected to be one of the new floodways, despite vigorous opposition. No landowner wished to see his property become the path for the Mississippi's excess water. Again and again as the engineers suggested possible floodways, local citizens screamed in protest. But in the case of the Atchafalaya, the decision had been made inadvertently long before, when the raft was cleared. Already a major distributary, it was a logical choice for a floodway.

A three-part system was eventually built: the West Atchafalaya Floodway, which has never been used and is to be flooded only in an extreme emergency; on the east, the Morganza Floodway, used for the first time in 1973; and the Atchafalaya Basin Floodway, or Lower Floodway, which receives water from the Morganza, the Atchafalaya River, and, if it is ever used, the West Atchafalaya Floodway. The three spillways, each section wholly enclosed by levees, are designed to carry half the combined floodwaters of the Mississippi and of a small river called the Red.

Although diversion was recognized as a possibility as early as the 1890s, not until 1950 did the Corps conduct a study to determine the rate of takeover. It was found that the critical stage of 40 percent would be reached by 1970 and, after that, closure would be rapid and diversion "relatively uncontrollable." Construction of the Old River Control Structure was begun in 1954, in order that flow down the Atchafalaya could be limited to a safe level of 30 percent during normal water and 50 percent during floods. The facility was completed in the mid-sixties—which was cutting it pretty fine. The flood of 1973 was the first high water to test the new structure.

THE ATCHAFALAYA BASIN, with 1.4 million acres of wilderness and farmland, comprises four distinct habitats. The northern section, the driest, consists of pastures, soybean fields, and bayous lined with oak, pecan, and sweetgum. To the south is the largest river-basin swamp in North America. Its bayous are bordered by land that is underwater

ANHINGA

much of the year, a swamp with tall cypress and tupelo trees standing among the remains of their ancestors. Below Morgan City—the largest town within the floodway—are miles of freshwater marshes stretching to the gulf. The final habitat is under formation in Atchafalaya Bay, where the new distributary is building its delta. The river's silt is constructing islands in what was once open water, islands that before long will join to form new marshland.

It is the middle basin—a half million acres of cypress swamp—that environmentalists predict will be the center of the next great conservation battle. Larger than the vast Okefenokee Swamp, the Atchafalaya is the nation's greatest forested wetland. The basin is the home of more than three hundred species of birds, including fifty thousand wading birds—egrets, herons, ibises, and anhingas. Endangered species thought to inhabit the swamp include the peregrine falcon, Bachman's warbler, and Florida panther. In 1971 an ornithologist believed he sighted an ivory-billed woodpecker, making the Atchafalaya possibly the final refuge of this magnificent woodpecker, believed by many to be extinct.

The alligator, another threatened species, lurks in the swamp's murky waters. The ancient reptile—Faulkner's "pleistocene nightmare"—symbolizes these black bayous as no other creature could except perhaps the anhinga, a reptilian bird that flies overhead with a distinctive flap, flap, flap, glide, a primitive bird in a primitive, haunting land.

I canoed these flooded forests with Charles Fryling, professor of landscape architecture at Louisiana State University in Baton Rouge. Charley and I, together with his eighty-year-old mother, set out on the Upper Flat, a canal that was initially dug for navigation. It was near the end of December, but winter this far south consists of nothing more terrible than a hint of chill by late afternoon.

As on the upper Mississippi, these southern wetlands are plagued by sedimentation. The silt flows in through such man-made canals as the Upper Flat. In addition to those

dug for navigation and logging, canals were dredged to oil and gas fields here and there in the basin. The Atchafalaya's lakes, once numerous, have dwindled to shallow waters filled with willows.

Charley, his hardy mother, and I branched off the Upper Flat into Bayou Sorrel. From there we turned off into one of the lakes that has filled with sediment. We pushed the canoe through thick stands of young willows, digging in wherever our paddles found enough water. Our destination was a cypress that Charley had photographed two years before and used for his Christmas cards the year we canoed to it. We had sat around his dining room table the night before our trip and talked while he addressed envelopes. The photograph on the cards showed a gnarled cypress standing in open water. What we saw the next day was the same tree nearly hidden by a tangle of brush. As the lake becomes solid ground, willows will completely replace the water-loving cypress.

With the Atchafalaya's backwater lakes silting in, the carrying capacity of the flood-way is seriously reduced. Today the Lower Floodway can handle only half the water it was originally designed to carry. At present it is capable of moving 850,000 cubic feet of water per second, far less than the 1.5 million cubic feet per second required as a crucial component of the Mississippi River and Tributaries Project.

One acre of wetlands can absorb and hold three-hundred thousand gallons of flood-water, retaining it for gradual release. Siltation can generate an increase in flood stages of as much as three feet—and a corresponding need to raise the levee grade. In the Atchafalaya, fighting sedimentation and the loss of backwaters with levees is a losing proposition. In the 1973 flood the dikes enclosing Atchafalaya Floodway were raised with sandbags, but a permanent height increase is a problem because swamp is a poor foundation. The levees settle, sinking in the ooze.

Sedimentation does have a beneficial side. In Atchafalaya Bay the river is forming productive marshland at a rate unprecedented for a geologic change. Only an earthquake or a volcano can mold the land with a speed to match what is occurring in the Atchafalaya. By the year 1990, the entire bay will fill in. Yet even in the bay, sedimentation brings its problems. This new marshland, though appreciated by wildlife, will plug the mouth of the floodway and block the release of water. With the engineers calling for nearly half the Mississippi to be flushed out through the Atchafalaya, the problem of what to do with floodwater is already critical.

It cannot go out the main channel, since the levees at New Orleans are as high as they effectively can be built, again because of poor foundations. The maximum flood the Mississippi River and Tributaries Project was designed to handle—a flood larger than the record flood of 1927—has a probability of recurring once every hundred years. Only by retarding sedimentation and restoring the Atchafalaya as a workable floodway can we hope to be ready.

Charley, his mother, and I turned away from the cypress and paddled back to Bayou Sorrel. As our canoe drifted down the winding stream, Charley spotted twelve cormorants roosting in a single tree. We turned off into the forest, paddling among the cypress trees and enjoying the sensation of finding our way without a stream for a path. Charley pointed out the first faint signs of spring returning to the Atchafalaya. When the rains of the new season come, the yellowtop *(Seneco glabelus)* blooms, and a paddle along the bayous becomes a float through fields of yellow.

The flower is soon submerged by rising water, which is the signal for the red swamp crawfish *(Procambarus clarkii)* to emerge from the burrow where it has taken refuge during the winter. The drowned flower provides food for the crawfish. The tiny crustacean, a freshwater cousin of the Maine lobster, becomes in turn lunch for largemouth and spotted bass, and for mammals and water birds. The yellowtop-crawfish-fish food chain, being short and simple, make the Atchafalaya Basin one of the most productive large aquatic ecosystems in America. Harvesting crawfish is a multimillion-dollar industry, and the 23 million pounds taken each year provide one of the basic ingredients in the Cajun cuisine.

The crawfish depends for its survival upon the seasonal overflow that is the swamp's lifeblood. The crawfish breeds in May and June while the water is still high, then in late summer burrows into the soft mud as the swamp recedes. The young are hatched in autumn and emerge in spring with the adults, when the water returns. The life history of the crawfish is intertwined with the swamp's wetting-drying cycle, the prerequisite for the whole food chain.

In the early 1950s the Corps began dredging the main channel of the Atchafalaya River, in an attempt to increase its carrying capacity and compensate for the loss of wetlands. Channelization disrupted the wetting-drying cycle, drying up backswamps that normally hold water in late summer. Bayous that formerly brought in fresh water were blocked by dredge spoil. Levees on the main channel isolated the swamps from overflow, turning them stagnant and sour. In especially dry years, the water is so low it is deficient in oxygen, and the crawfish crawl onto the cypress knees to breathe.

Together, sedimentation and channelization are destroying the Atchafalaya as a wetland, turning it into less productive terrestrial habitat. In the northern section, where the swamps have mostly filled in, commercial crawfishing has disappeared. Once again man has greatly accelerated natural sedimentation, and as the process moves down the basin, the outlook for the crawfish is grim.

In 1968 the executive vice-president of the National Wildlife Federation persuaded the chief of the Corps of Engineers to halt the dredging pending an environmental impact statement. A management plan was begun. In 1975 the Corps recommended the acquisition of easements from landowners, so the government could take measures to reduce siltation and restore the wetting-drying cycle. In addition to slowing the deterioration of the swamp, the easements would prohibit owners from clearing newly dried land and converting it to a soybean monoculture.

The United States Fish and Wildlife Service, participating in the planning, suggested outright acquisition instead of easements. The agency pointed to the ineffectiveness of easements in preventing logging in the northern part of the basin. To date, half the West Atchafalaya Floodway has been cleared for agriculture, despite flowage easements acquired by the Corps long ago. In the Morganza Floodway, where the full value of the land was paid to acquire comprehensive easements, 42 percent has been timbered. Simple flowage easements give the Corps the right to use the land as a floodway, while comprehensive easements in addition prohibit the construction of permanent buildings. Neither type has stopped the farmer with a bulldozer.

The Atchafalaya, the Fish and Wildlife people believe, is threatened by the same wholesale conversion to agriculture that destroyed the forested wetlands of the Mississippi River. In the Yazoo Delta, for example, where the Clinkscales grow their rice, half the original 4 million acres of swamp were gone by 1950. In the next two decades nearly half the remainder was cleared. Between 1970 and 1976 60 percent of the balance was lost, so that now only 500,000 acres are left.

Apart from irreparable damage to wildlife and fish, it is feared that conversion of the Atchafalaya to agriculture will lead to reluctance to use it as a floodway. During the 1973 flooding, to relieve the stress on the Old River Control Structure, the Corps of Engineers decided to open the Morganza Floodway. On March 21, 1973, the Corps sent telegrams to the owners advising them to remove all livestock, fences, and equipment within five days. Yet not until March 29 did the water enter the forebay of the floodway, and not until April 17 did the Corps actually open any gates. Louisiana conservationists believe that pressure from landowners delayed the opening. Major General Noble, president of the Mississippi River Commission, admitted that landowners pleaded with him not to use the floodway.

As more dry land is formed, then cleared and farmed, property values rise, population goes up, and investments within the floodway increase, all inhibiting its future use during floods. According to a 1972 census by the army, the West Atchafalaya Floodway contains 3,524 residences and 874 permanent homes, many of them brick. Industrial development is the next step in this relentless encroachment. Despite the existence of flowage easements, the Ventech Refining Company received a permit to construct an oil refinery in the middle basin and erect a levee around the installation, thus permanently eliminating that land from the floodway.

Easements will always leave the door open to legal contests. Typically landowners initiate a long string of court cases to test the easements and weaken the authority of their regulation. The alternative suggested by the Fish and Wildlife Service is public ownership of the middle and lower sections, which would provide unassailable, permanent protection for the Atchafalaya as a floodway and wetland habitat. Public acquisition would cost only 10 percent more than would be spent on comprehensive easements. The best way to ensure that the floodway will be used when needed is to keep it wet and wild.

Landowners in the Atchafalaya have opposed both proposals: easements they see as government control of private land, and public ownership, a land grab by environmental elitists. The Department of the Interior has replied that the public, if it is to pay to maintain the floodway, should be guaranteed the right of access to the basin. Acquisition would open thousands of acres to the people of Baton Rouge and New Orleans, who live in an area where opportunities for recreation are limited. Right now most of the Atchafalaya is closed to the public. Almost all the land is privately owned, held by four individuals and seven companies. Dow Chemical Company is the largest landowner.

In 1980 the governor of Louisiana suggested a compromise that has been well received by environmentalists. To prevent sacrifice of the floodway to agriculture and industry, development easements would be purchased for every acre in the basin, and access easements would be bought on 105,000 acres. Where owners are willing to sell, the land would instead be purchased. The aims of the Corps and the conservationists for once agree—preserving the Atchafalaya as a floodway and as wetlands—which augurs well for the governor's proposal.

WHATEVER HAPPENS TO this beautiful wilderness, vital to our flood-control program, the Corps still must deal with the Mississippi's urge for a new channel. After the close call in 1973, the Corps repaired the Old River Control Structure, but the facility is not as strong as it was. Fortunately, in the years since 1973, no large floods have come along to test the wobbly dam.

In 1980, after seven years of study, the Corps decided to build an auxiliary control structure to relieve pressure on the old facility. The new dam will be completed by late 1985, which will be none too soon. According to a Corps official, "It's been nip and tuck these last seven years." The engineers are confident that the $216 million project will keep the Mississippi in its present channel. But a recent report from Louisiana State University concluded that the shift will take place no matter what the Corps does. Professors Raphael G. Kazmann and David B. Johnson warn that the inevitable will happen sometime within the next forty years.

18

Arsenic and Old Lace

I CAME TO MR. R.'s plantation by a steamboat, late at night. . . . A little to one side of the house stood a large two-story, square dove-cot, which is a universal appendage of a sugar-planter's house. In the rear of the house was another large yard, in which, irregularly placed, were houses for the family servants, a kitchen, stable, carriage-house, smokehouse, etc. Behind this rear-yard there was a vegetable garden, of an acre or more, in [the] charge of a negro gardener; a line of fig-trees were planted along the fence, but all the ground inclosed was intended to be cropped with vegetables for the family, and for the supply of "the people." I was pleased to notice, however, that the negro-gardener had, of his own accord, planted some violets and other flowering plants. From a corner of the court a road ran to the sugar-works and the negro settlement, which were five or six hundred yards from the house.

FREDERICK LAW OLMSTED, 1861

*I*N THE EARLY 1700s A COLONIST from France hacked out a plantation in the canebrakes midway between the newly built fort of Le Baton Rouge and the infant village of La Nouvelle Orléans. The Frenchman built his house facing the river, near the bank where the land is highest. Three or four miles back, his fields of indigo sloped down to a swamp. In two straight lines from the river's edge to his new home, the Frenchman planted a double row of seedlings.

The original house was gone by 1837 when a sugar planter, Jacques Telesphore Roman, bought the plantation and built his own mansion. By then the twenty-eight seedlings, once spaced far apart, had grown into a magnificent procession of live oaks. Steamboats passed the plantation daily, and the passengers took to calling the twin row of trees "Oak Allée." The name stuck.

PLANTER'S HOUSE

Today the oaks, each more than twenty feet in diameter, are nearly 300 years old. Since all twenty-eight have survived, the stately avenue—Oak Alley—has no gaps. Jacques Roman's plantation house and sixteen hundred acres of sugarcane also remain, relics of the past in the center of the most industrialized section on the Mississippi.

The Jacques Roman house has had five owners since it was built, the latest being Zeb Mayhew and his brothers, sisters, and cousins. Zeb has opened the family home to the public, and he lives in the overseer's house, itself an antebellum home but on a small scale. The main house is an architectural eclectic. To match the oaks, twenty-eight Doric columns form a colonnade around the building, supporting an overhanging roof that shades a second floor porch and, at ground level, a brick veranda. The columns, brick covered with stucco, reflect the Classic style beloved by Southerners prior to the Civil War; the entrances are Federal; the veranda and gallery hint of a West Indian Creole ancestry. From a distance the mansion seems to stand as it did in its days of grandeur. It takes a close look, up on the veranda, to notice the chipped stucco and flaking paint.

The walls, also stuccoed brick, are as thick as a fortress, armored against the Southern sun. Inside, the cool rooms rise to an impressive height, and each has floor-length windows opening onto one of the porches, admitting a breeze but shaded to fend off direct sunlight.

A live oak standing alone in a field spreads out symmetrically, nearly as wide as it is tall. But those at Oak Alley are shaped to form an arch. The inside limbs curve overhead, reaching out toward each other and intertwining. The outside branches touch the ground, as if resting, then grow upward again like saplings. Each limb as it emerges from the trunk is itself as large as any ordinary tree.

Beneath this living arch, never bare of leaves, is an avenue of lawn stretching for a quarter of a mile. At the far end is a wrought iron fence with a sagging gate. Beyond the fence is a narrow road and beyond that the levee. Viewed from the top of the levee, the shores on both sides of the river are still wooded, despite the encroaching industry.

Other live oaks are scattered around the grounds. In gathering darkness I strolled through Oak Alley's formal gardens, following a walkway apparent only to my feet. Lush greenery had long since invaded the worn bricks beneath my shoes. The path led beneath palmettoes and orange trees dripping with moisture. My legs brushed against sweet-olive bushes and another plant with leaves so large it is called "elephants ear" *(Colocasia esculenta)*. Looking up, I could make out a rusty plantation bell on a tower silhouetted against the night sky.

I walked back toward the house. A yellow glow from its windows lit the live oaks, and a heavy fog was rising from the river bottom. Through the mists I could half hear the strains of a waltz and almost see the Creole gentlemen and belles in their hoop skirts pirouetting past the windows. Back in the swamp two hounds howled.

I walked to a nearby cabin, the home of Carol Hester, who has been living on the plantation for nearly a year to compile a history of Oak Alley. Zeb Mayhew soon joined us. Carol said that according to her research more than a hundred slaves worked the plantation in 1860. Our conversation turned from the past to the future. Zeb—thirtyish, slender, a moustached aristocrat—voiced his concern for Oak Alley. Many of the antebellum homes that graced the riverbanks until recently are gone, the plantations bought up by oil refineries and chemical plants.

After World War II, Louisiana, eager to attract the petroleum industry, passed a law granting new business a tax exemption for a period of ten years. The state soon ranked second in the nation for oil production. On the towboat we had passed Baton Rouge, the center of the industry, just at daybreak. A gray forest of smokestacks lined the shore. Here and there orange fire belched into the pale dawn. A chain-link fence surrounding a sulphur plant was stained yellow, and the ridged segments of a pipeline snaked over the levee, a gigantic earthworm.

As we talked in the cabin at Oak Alley, Zeb Mayhew was critical of the petrochemical industry. So many new companies are coming into his parish that the tax yield from the older plants is trivial compared to the revenue lost from exemptions. The parish has to supply water, police protection, highways, and other services, yet few jobs for local people have materialized. Once construction is finished, outsiders are brought in for the permanent work.

What made Zeb's moustache twitch, however, is the damage to the land. Louisiana is paying an ecological price for prosperity. Governor Edwin Edwards, the former head of state, once said, "In some instances we knowingly accepted environmental tradeoffs." Zeb, although he described himself as a small businessman and not an environmentalist, mentioned a live oak that formerly stood at a nearby chemical plant, one of the installations owned by Hooker Chemical and Plastics Corporation. Hooker is the company responsible for the horror at New York's Love Canal, where two hundred families were forced to abandon their homes after poisons seeped into their yards and basements from an abandoned chemical dump.

MOSS GATHERERS

The Louisiana Hooker plant is twenty-five miles above New Orleans and only a few miles downstream from Oak Alley. In April of 1979 a Congressional subcommittee acquired an internal Hooker report indicating company officials were aware that suspected cancer-causing agents had been buried at the facility near Oak Alley. The following summer, traces of asbestos, chlorinated hydrocarbons, and heavy metals were found in test wells. The company said the live oak on the property died from termites, but Zeb was skeptical. Everything else around the plant, he said, is dead.

Louisiana has more known chemical dumps than almost any other state in the nation. Most companies store or bury their wastes right at the site of generation. And if the landfill or lagoon is poorly designed, the toxic wastes readily leach into the ground and surface waters. The people at Oak Alley and the nearby town of Vacherie drink water that flows past dozens of refineries and chemical plants—more than sixty by the time the river reaches Venice, Louisiana. "Nobody knows," Zeb says, "what the end result is when you drink this every day for twenty years."

Scientists are cautious about assigning a direct link between hazardous chemicals and human health, so we cannot say with certainty that drinking Mississippi water is harmful. But medical statistics reveal that the river corridor between Baton Rouge and New Orleans is one of the nation's cancer capitals. Grocery stores in the city of New Orleans, which depends on the river for its drinking water, sell bottled water on the shelves and from coin machines. New Orleans has one of the nation's highest rates of bladder, stomach, and intestinal cancer. Tests by the Environmental Protection Agency reveal that the city's water supply contains forty-eight chemical pollutants and carcinogens, including one that is apparently introduced during chlorination.

Breathing the fumes of the petrochemical industry may be equally unhealthy. The rate of lung cancer in males in St. Bernard Parish, just below New Orleans, is an astonishing 140 percent higher than the national average. In Baton Rouge the rate is 50 percent higher than the national average, yet Louisiana has the lowest per capita sale of cigarettes of all the gulf states.

Zeb Mayhew and Carol Hester both recall waking with headaches one fine spring morning in 1979. When they looked out their windows, they saw a yellow cloud moving downriver from plantation to plantation. Carol phoned the police, who told her: "We don't think it's dangerous." Zeb fears that one day he will wake up to a permanent smelly cloud. Petrochemical interests want to put an oil refinery next door to Oak Alley. A grain elevator has been proposed as its other neighbor. Zeb is convinced that any new industrial growth will smother Oak Alley's live oaks, ruining an irreplaceable historical landmark.

Some believe air pollution has already destroyed the Spanish moss that used to drape the branches of Southern trees. A Northerner expecting to see live oaks festooned with long gray strands would be disappointed. Even in the backswamps of the Atchafalaya I saw almost none.

Gathering Spanish moss for stuffing mattresses and upholstering furniture used to be a two-million-dollar industry for the Cajuns of Louisiana. The cause for its disappearance is not known. The moss is an air-feeding plant, or epiphyte. It is not, as commonly thought, a parasite that lives off the tree. It derives its moisture and nutrients from the atmosphere. A fungus may be responsible for the moss's disappearance, but air pollution is a more likely bet. Some may not mourn the passing of Spanish moss, but I miss it.

Before breakfast the morning I left Oak Alley, I took a walk down the long avenue and out to the levee. I turned for a last look. As I stood there, the sun rose behind the fine old home. It touched the double row of live oaks, a Druid cathedral, with uncertain light.

SIX

Wilderness Endings

Venice to the Gulf

19

The Birdfoot Delta

THE WESTERNMOST ISLAND we visited was outside the national reservation, and that very morning it had been visited and plundered by a party of eggers. The eggs had been completely cleared from most of the island, gulls and terns had been shot, and the survivors were in a frantic state of excitement.

THEODORE ROOSEVELT, 1915

*A*T NEW ORLEANS THE RIVERBANKS are walled with warehouses; behind them are acres of crisscrossing tracks. Each street that runs perpendicular to the water ends with a wharf. At the water's edge, it is hard to locate a break in the wall of structures, a window where the river can be viewed.

In the French Quarter, however, city officials have provided an overlook on the riverbank in front of Jackson Square. It is small but designed with the sophistication that is New Orleans' birthright. Steps provide access over a floodwall, which is mostly hidden by trees, to a wooden promenade called the Moonwalk, after former Mayor Moon Landrieu. A stairway leads down to the water, which laps over the lowest step.

When the river is high, passing ships look down on the trees of Jackson Square, known as the Place d'Armes under the French flag and the Plaza de Armas when Spain ruled colonial New Orleans. Renamed after the Battle of New Orleans in the war of 1812, Jackson Square is rich with historic buildings. St. Louis Cathedral, the oldest active cathedral in the country, stands imposingly at the far end, flanked on one side by the Presbytère, or residence for the clergy, and on the other by the Cabildo, the town hall that housed the Spanish governing council.

Surrounding Jackson Square is the Vieux Carré—the French Quarter—where French and Spanish residency overlapped and created a unique Creole architecture characterized by enclosed courtyards and balconies with railings of iron lacework. The narrow streets are crowded with street artists and musicians. Residents rollerskating home mingle

CANAL STREET, 1883

with tourists sampling the shops and fine restaurants. Few changes seem to have occurred since the mid-nineteenth century when Walt Whitman wrote:

> One of my choice amusements during my stay in New Orleans was going down to the old French Market, especially of a Sunday morning. . . . I remember I nearly always on these occasions got a large cup of delicious coffee with a biscuit, for my breakfast, from the immense shining copper kettle of a great Creole mulatto woman (I believe she weigh'd 230 pounds). I never have had such coffee since.

Here, at the Mississippi's final urban gasp, the current clutches ocean liners and nudges them sideways as they round a bend, one of the turns in the horseshoe curve that cradles New Orleans and gave the city its nickname. The Crescent City is the third largest port in the world. At night the water reflects the lights of ships of many nations—Peru, Greece, Bulgaria, Norway, Guatemala. The river is alive with use.

At a wharf in New Orleans I boarded the *Delta Norte,* a freighter that would take me into the delta. I would stay on the ship for ten miles past Venice, the last town on the Mississippi connected to the world by road, and get off at Pilottown, a village accessible only by boat. Pilottown is located at the Head of Passes, where the river splits into a number of distributaries, or passes, for the final twenty miles of its journey to the sea. In those twenty miles, plus the ten from Venice to Pilottown, the Mississippi leaves behind the world of industry for the tangy breezes that sweep across miles of salt grasses.

Loaded with grain and automobile parts, the *Delta Norte* was bound for South America. On the return trip it would bring back a cargo of coffee. The *Delta Norte* is one of the new LASH vessels, the acronym standing for "lighter-aboard-ship." A lighter, as the river barge is called, is lifted aboard—fully loaded—by enormous cranes, and transported on the high seas to a destination such as Buenos Aires, where it is lifted off, attached to a towboat, and pushed upriver to its final port. Such marriages of river and ocean transportation speed up delivery and reduce the amount of expensive handling in port. The *Delta Norte* was carrying 74 barges and 288 loaded van containers—a marriage as well with truck transport. LASH ships are big, as big as anything on the ocean. The *Delta Norte* is 893 feet long, the equivalent of three football fields.

Because of the winding channel, shoals, and tricky currents, all ocean liners take on a river pilot to guide them up to the city or back down to the gulf. A "bar" pilot takes the helm for the twenty miles from the mouth of the river to Pilottown. From there to New Orleans a "crescent" pilot takes over, and then, if the ship is going on from New Orleans to Baton Rouge, a "NOBR" pilot. Paul Frolich, a crescent pilot, came aboard to steer the *Delta Norte* until he and I would leave the ship at Pilottown.

Nattily dressed in accordance with river tradition, Paul watched the traffic closely and in a quiet voice gave directions to the helmsman. He and the captain pointed out the sights as we left the port. We floated past the site of the Battle of New Orleans on the left and, just beyond it, the nation's second-largest primary aluminum producing plant. Paul, standing at the front of the bridge, called my attention to the burned-out hull of a ship moored at a drydock on the right. The ship was the victim of the collision with three barges filled with butane, the accident that happened just after I had ridden the towboats, and I recalled that twelve crewmen had been killed.

Traffic was heavy for some distance below the city. On shore, industries were interspersed with orange groves, all perched on the relatively high ground near the riverbank. Before the days of artificial levees the Mississippi overflowed every year. As the floodwater topped the banks it slowed, first dropping the heavier particles of sand and then, as it spread inland, allowing the silt to settle out. Over the centuries a natural levee formed, highest at the riverbank and sloping down to low swamps and marshes some distance back. Whereas man-made levees are tall embankments a few feet in width, natural levees are low ridges that vary from as wide as three miles in northern Louisiana and a mile across near New Orleans to, in the delta near Venice, a fifth of a mile. These narrow strips of solid ground were the first land settled in Louisiana.

Storm tides from the gulf sometimes flood the lowlands beyond the natural levees. In 1965 Hurricane Betsy inundated forty-eight hundred square miles and left 81 people dead. To protect the high ground along the banks, a second artificial levee parallels the one at the river. Behind this hurricane levee are vast uninhabited marshes interlaced with canals, lakes, miles of bayous, and bays. The delta, as one observer has said, is "a flat mysterious region, where water seems, in an indefinite flux, to become land, and land water. . . ."

The nearer the ocean, the saltier the water. Farthest upriver, the freshwater marshes are nurtured by rain from the uplands. Milfoils and cattails grow in the shallows, water lilies and duckweed in the deep pools, a few willows on the elevated islands. Downriver in the salt marshes, where the sea makes its way up a maze of canals and bayous, oyster grass is dominant but saltgrass and black rush also grow on the fertile mud. In between the freshwater and the salt marsh is the brackish marsh, which, being the ecotone, has the highest biological productivity. There wiregrass, coco-grass, and three-cornered grass are the typical cover. The size of these marshes is indicated by the fact that Louisiana contains one-third of the nation's remaining wetlands.

The marshes of the Mississippi's delta constitute one of the five or six major estuaries in the world. An estuary, the interface between sea and river, belongs to both and teems with life. The river contributes freshwater and nutrients; the tides circulate the nutrients, flush in seawater, and carry organisms back and forth from ocean to marshes. The mixing of the two ecosystems produces a habitat unmatched for its diversity and richness. The Mississippi's estuary is the nursery for the sea life of the Gulf of Mexico; the take from Louisiana's coastal fisheries is larger than anywhere else in the United States except Alaska.

A full quarter of the U.S. shrimp harvest comes from the coast of Louisiana. Besides shrimp, the state's commercial catch consists of catfish, crawfish, oysters, crabs, and menhaden. Catfish and crawfish depend on the river and its distributaries for their survival, and the others depend on the river's delta. In the case of the oyster, it spends its entire life cycle in the shallow inshore waters. Shrimp, crabs, and menhaden (a kind of herring used as a protein supplement for livestock) spawn offshore but require the estuarine bays to mature.

———————————◆———————————

WE ARRIVED IN PILOTTOWN around midnight. The *Delta Norte* slowed just enough so that Paul Frolich and I could climb a ladder down the side of the ship to a waiting harbor boat. Far below, the water was black and swift. Paul remarked as we started the climb, "I can count on one hand—no, on three fingers—the number of pilots who have fallen into the river and come out alive." Once we were down, the harbor boat ferried us to shore.

In the old days the pilots and their families made their homes at Pilottown, but today most prefer the conveniences of New Orleans. The town has dwindled from two hundred to thirty residents. The elementary school, down to only three students, closed in 1977.

We made our way from the dock to a shore house, with white clapboards and rocking chairs on the porch. The rambling house, maintained by the pilots association for the use of its members, provides space for resting between assignments, as well as a galley and dining room, guest facilities, and an operations room that was busy even at midnight. In the galley a supper was laid out for late arrivals.

The next morning I woke up early and took a walk to explore the village. Pilottown consists of a single row of houses paralleling the river for about a mile. The houses are built on stilts; there is no road, only a sidewalk raised on pilings above the marsh. Wooden walks lead to each home. The houses, some needing paint, are separated from the river by a narrow strip of marshy ground, and behind them are the salt flats. Pilottown is too small to support a store, so the inhabitants boat upriver to Venice for supplies.

In the early morning the wharf, the sidewalk, the marsh, all were dead still, not a soul in sight. I walked down to the dock. It suggests that each of Pilottown's thirty citizens is

PILOTTOWN, 1883

the owner of at least five boats. Every space was filled, mostly with fishing skiffs. Some of the townsfolk, like Kevin Nelson, whom I had met the night before, work for the pilots association but supplement their incomes with fishing and trapping. Kevin, eighteen years old, handles the boat that carries the pilots out to their ships and ferries them in when their jobs are finished. In his spare time Kevin, like other natives of Pilottown, traps an occasional nutria.

Louisiana is one of the world's great fur preserves. In addition to nutria, the Creole and Cajun trappers take otters, muskrats, a few beaver, and more bobcats for the overseas market than are killed anywhere else in the nation. Traps are set from December through February, after the marsh has been burned off to locate game trails and rejuvenate the grasses. An exceptional day for two men is sixty skins.

The nutria is a large aquatic rodent that looks like an oversized guinea pig, weighing about twenty-five pounds. In the 1930s, three hundred nutria were brought in from Brazil for testing as a replacement for their cousin, the muskrat. Muskrats had been the mainstay of delta trappers but had begun to decline. In 1940 a hurricane destroyed the pens containing the imported nutria and the colony escaped. By the early 1960s the exotic was so well established in the wild that it numbered more than fifty thousand and the state was offering a bounty. Today the nutria, no longer considered an outlaw, is worth $7.00 as a prime pelt. In the 1972–1973 season the catch was valued at $7.5 million, a happier ending than is usually the case with the accidental introduction of a new species to a natural ecosystem.

Lately, however, the nutria has found itself in trouble. Partly the decline is owing to loss of habitat and partly to the importation of yet another exotic. A beetle from South America was introduced in Florida to clear alligator grass from the navigable waterways. The alien beetle spread to Louisiana and destroyed the delta's alligator grass. The vacated ecological niche in turn gave a plant called *Bidens levians,* a daisy-like species indigenous to the delta, the chance to thrive. The thorns of *Bidens levians* prick the nutria's skin beneath its fur and cause infection. The animal then stops eating and dies. No doubt someone will soon propose scouring South America for an insect that eats *Bidens levians.*

AFTER BREAKFAST KEVIN NELSON ferried me two miles upriver across Cubits Gap—the entrance to one of the passes—to the headquarters of the Delta National Wildlife Refuge. The refuge, established in 1935 to protect the wintering grounds of thousands of water-fowl, contains forty-nine thousand acres of marsh.

The land in the delta was formed during the past millennium. The river, in the shallow, quiet water at its mouth, developed a number of distributaries, depositing its coarser load in the form of long sand fingers reaching toward the sea. The finer mud and silt was carried on out to the gulf and washed by shore currents into the bays between these distributary fingers. Salt marshes built up gradually in the bays, like the webbing on a duck's foot. The Mississippi's estuary is in fact called a birdfoot delta.

Over centuries of seaward growth, the river built three main distributaries—Southwest Pass, South Pass, and Pass à Loutre—as well as a number of smaller ones. The first two are navigable by ships, but Pass à Loutre and the others are too shallow for anything bigger than a shrimp boat.

Main Pass, one of the smaller distributaries, sprang into existence a mere century ago. I came across no fewer than three accounts of the formation of Cubits Gap, the entrance to Main Pass. By one story, a crevasse occurred during the flood of 1862, creating a gap in the natural levee that separated the river from a bay of the ocean. By another, a couple of schoolteachers took shovels and dug a channel to create an opening to the bay's oyster-fishing grounds. The third account has it that the navy cut a ditch to provide access to the bay for pursuing smugglers and privateers such as Jean Lafitte.

However Cubits Gap came to be, all accounts agree that the opening was originally narrow. In little more than a century, it enlarged to a half mile wide. A long distributary called Main Pass formed and the bay filled, creating thirty miles of new marsh. That geologically infantile land constitutes the considerable acreage of the wildlife refuge.

The headquarters of the refuge is built on sand that the Corps of Engineers dredged out of the navigation channel. In the wet season as many as a hundred deer at a time seek out this bit of high ground. In addition to an office, the compound includes three ranch-style houses, a shop and boathouse, and a radio tower that provides the link with the outside world and miraculously has withstood hurricanes.

Sam Henson, tall, lanky, and weathered, and his wife, Ev, were expecting me and invited me in for tea. The neat suburban house they inhabit, incongruous in the marsh, has been their home since 1969. Sam's boss, Ted Huer, soon joined us. Ted was recently sent to the refuge as manager. He and his wife, Beth, moved to the delta only one year after their wedding, bringing their furniture and cat, Oliver, downriver by barge. The Huers, like the Hensons, find much to like about life in this remote corner. Beth Huer showed me the vegetable garden she has painstakingly created, carrying in composted seaweed and filtering each bit of earth to remove shells.

Beth often joins Ted and Sam on their daily rounds. Unlike the practice at most refuges, no management techniques are employed at Delta to improve the wildlife habitat. Sam and Ted's primary job is law enforcement and, in addition, they spend four hours a day, seven days a week, banding ducks. The year before Ted arrived, Sam banded 12,500 birds.

Ted and Beth offered to take me out on a sample round. Beth's mother, who was visiting the newlyweds for the Christmas holidays, was eager to go along for the chance of seeing an unusual bird to add to her life list. The four of us donned hip waders and loaded sacks of grain into one of the runabouts in the boathouse.

Ted steered the boat out through a labyrinth of channels. The only solid ground was along the immediate banks, which were covered with low shrubs and phragmites, or Roseau cane, as it is called in the delta. Before long Ted ran the boat up on a mudbank and we climbed out. We walked over a low rise and waded through shallow water, Ted bringing up the rear with one of the heavy sacks.

Beth identified some of the plants we passed. There was elephants ear, which I remembered from Oak Alley, and a low ground plant called Delta duckpotato. We waded around a patch of water hyacinth, an aquatic plant brought from Brazil to New Orleans for the Cotton Exposition of 1884. The hyacinth escaped to clog rivers and canals all over the South. The Corps of Engineers has tried every form of control from sodium arsenite, back in the early 1900s, to the herbicide 2,4-D used for the past twenty-five years. Recently a moth that feeds on the leaves has been imported from Argentina.

Our destination was one of the traps for capturing birds to be banded. The trap was a wire cage tall enough for a person to stand up in and enclosing a patch of ground and some open water. Nearly two dozen ducks were swimming around and feeding on the grain that had been left as bait. Beth's mother and I were sent in to corral the now-frantic birds toward a wire box. The top of the box was an old rubber tire, which was slit so that Ted could reach in and pull out a duck. Each was identified by species, fitted with a leg band, and recorded by Beth. During the course of the afternoon we banded about fifty—pintails, gadwalls, American wigeons, and the diminutive blue- and green-winged teals—all ducks that are abundant in the delta in December.

As we went from trap to trap, we saw a great flock of snow geese lift off from the mud flats. From September to March, tens of thousands of these beautiful geese winter on the refuge, then migrate to the Arctic tundra to nest. Had I visited Louisiana a few months later, I would have seen flocks of songbirds on their annual flight from the tropics. From April through mid-May, more than seventy species cross the Gulf of Mexico: warblers, buntings, thrushes, vireos, grosbeaks, tanagers. Most set out just after sunset, fly across six hundred to eight hundred miles of open water in a single night, and alight at dawn along the coast of Louisiana.

After a period of rest they continue northward, using the Mississippi River to guide the flight. The river is one of the four continental avenues of avian migration. In 1948 these four migratory routes were designated for administrative purposes as "flyways," so that we have the Mississippi Flyway and the Pacific, Atlantic, and Central flyways. Although the designations are useful for the management of waterfowl, the flyways and the migration corridors do not everywhere correspond, since the travel patterns of some species cross the flyway boundaries. But a large number of birds do migrate along the major geographic features—the two coasts, the Rocky Mountains, and the Mississippi River.

During the afternoon we also passed beaches covered with shorebirds, including a few short-billed dowitchers, which Beth's mother was excited to add to her life list. We saw hawks, turkey vultures, egrets, herons, and gulls—but none of the Eastern brown pelicans that once were numerous in the delta.

In 1931 the coast of Louisiana had 85,000 brown pelicans, a spectacular bird with a wingspan of seven feet. By 1938 the breeding pelicans were down to 10,000, and by 1961 the population had plummeted to 200 pairs. A year later, 6 were left. Since then, none have been sighted.

The brown pelican, which ironically is Louisiana's state bird, was doomed by its diet. An expert diver, the pelican feeds on fish, using its throat pouch to separate the fish from the water. In the late 1950s and early 1960s massive fish kills occurred on the lower Mississippi, at least thirty large kills in the summer of 1960 alone. In November of 1963 an estimated five million catfish, a traditional food of the South's poor, were reported floating belly up. Other species were affected from Baton Rouge down to Venice, both freshwater fish and brackish-water species such as menhaden, mullet, and sea trout. The commercial fishing industry was devastated.

In 1964 the Public Health Service finally found the culprit hundreds of miles upstream. The Memphis plant of the Velsicol Chemical Corporation was found to be dumping large quantities of Endrin, a highly toxic chlorinated hydrocarbon insecticide, into sewers and waterways that drain into the Mississippi. Endrin, Rachel Carson said in *Silent Spring,* is "15 times as poisonous as DDT to mammals, 30 times as poisonous to fish, and about 300 times as poisonous to some birds." Traces were found in the drinking water of Vicksburg and New Orleans.

As with the well-known story of the bald eagle and DDT, the pelican responded to chlorinated hydrocarbons by laying eggs with shells so thin that the brooding bird crushed them simply by sitting on them. In 1970 the pelican was placed on the endangered list and a program was begun to stock the former colonies in Lousiana with young birds from Florida.

This is not the first time the brown pelican has had a brush with extinction. Around the turn of the century the pelican was much sought by hatmakers for its plumage. Excessive hunting, pesticides, and competition from imported species are three major causes for the species' decline. By far the most serious danger, however, is loss of habitat.

TO PROVIDE SANCTUARIES for migrating songbirds and waterfowl, a number of state and national wildlife refuges are spaced rather evenly along the Mississippi. Yet the lengthy Louisiana section, heavily industrialized, has only one until its southernmost reach, and then it has two side by side: Delta National Wildlife Refuge, which I had just visited, and the state-owned Pass-à-Loutre Waterfowl Management Area—sixty-six thousand acres at the very tip of the delta.

Allan Einsminger, Chief of the Fur and Refuge Division of Louisiana Wild Life and Fisheries, volunteered to show me the state refuge from a seaplane. Over the roar of the engine I strained to hear Allan's running commentary on some of the problems facing the delta. The situation at this end of the river is the reverse of that on the upper Mississippi, where the wetlands are being destroyed by siltation. In the delta, silt is considered not a nuisance but a precious resource, the foundation of new marsh.

With each storm the ocean's waves chew away at the beaches and marshes. New marsh built with the river's silt offsets land lost to the waves. In the past, sea and river have engaged in a delicate thrust and parry, always a close contest, but the victory over the long run has been awarded to the river as it slowly, with the patience of the geologic clock, has constructed the land of Louisiana.

Today, however, the Mississippi is unable to create land as fast as the sea is eroding it, because the river's load of silt is confined between levees built to protect the oil refineries and orange groves. The silt is channeled out to sea to drop off the continental shelf. Ten miles beyond the mouth of South Pass the water is a thousand feet deep. Much silt is saved by littoral currents—longshore currents that move along roughly parallel to shore—but the heavier material slides off the edge, wasted.

Historically, land loss in a decaying delta is compensated for by new marsh formed in the active delta. But today, with the waste of sediment caused by the river's confinement, loss in the delta is so great that the new Atchafalaya lobe is unable to keep up. Louisiana has the highest rate of land loss in the United States—forty square miles a year—and the rate is accelerating. In the past thirty years the coastal parishes have given up five hundred square miles, an area half the size of Rhode Island.

As we talked, Allan Einsminger turned the plane down South Pass to the mouth of the river. We emerged over open ocean and I finally saw the completion of a journey that had begun six long months before.

The day was foggy and we stayed close to the water. A hundred feet above the waves we flew over a low island called a "mudlump." Bare of vegetation, the mudlump was

SOUTHWEST PASS

sculpted into miniature mountains complete with ridges, peaks, and volcanoes. Up in the air, with nothing to refer to for a sense of scale, the waves could have been beating against the flanks of real mountains.

These mudlumps at the mouth of the river are intrusive clay masses that are squeezed up from hundreds of feet beneath the ocean floor. Over the centuries, as the Mississippi deposits its sediment and the river mouth advances seaward, the weight of the silt compresses the underlying clay. The compression is unevenly distributed, and this differential compression squeezes the cohesive mass of clay seaward. An impermeable layer of material underneath prevents the clay from being pushed downwards. Instead, it travels upwards, along a fault line, until it surfaces above the water. The mudlumps appear suddenly, then are slowly sculpted by the waves until they erode away. In the past, the development of a mudlump sometimes blocked sailing ships from entering the river for days or even weeks. But sea birds are more appreciative, finding the formations ideal for nesting sites.

We turned back to the channel and flew to the headquarters of the state refuge, landing the floatplane in a canal near the buildings. Shortly after we arrived, representatives of an oil company flew in by helicopter. They were looking for Allan to discuss a pipeline across the refuge. The waterfowl management area receives $4 to 5 million a year, the bulk of its revenue, from mineral leases for its rich deposits of oil, gas, sulphur, and salt. On the way to the headquarters, we had flown over an occasional well standing alone in the marsh.

Allan told me later that the oil spills that occur create no serious problems, but the canals dug to float in drilling rigs and lay pipeline are another matter. Many scientists agree with Dr. Sherwood Gagliano of Baton Rouge, an expert on the Louisiana coastal wetlands, who names the oil canals as the single greatest cause of the massive deterioration that the delta has suffered during the past thirty to forty years. The canals serve as conduits for the intrusion of saltwater into inland freshwater marshes. For plants and animals that cannot tolerate the increased salinity, saltwater intrusion means the loss of precious habitat. Primarily because of the canals, the oyster yield in Louisiana has dropped tenfold in the past thirty years. The shrimp catch has suffered a similar decline.

Both Dr. Gagliano and Allan Einsminger point out that recent technological improvements allowing narrower canals have reduced the impact of pipelines, but access canals created to float in drilling rigs are still dug destructively wide. And the damage from access canals is expected to increase, given the renewed wave of drilling activity necessitated by national pressure to locate new oil deposits.

Saltwater intrusion has been aggravated by three other human modifications of the delta: navigation canals, channelization, and levees. The Mississippi River–Gulf Outlet, a canal constructed in the 1960s for ships to use as a shortcut to the gulf, directly destroyed 23,606 acres of wetlands and exposed surrounding mashes to surges of saltwater. The canal is both an environmental and economic failure. Because of poor design, it has never received the use that was anticipated. Channelization is another reason for saltwater intrusion; in Lafitte's day the meandering bayous of the delta served as a refuge for pirates but also helped keep out seawater. Today many bayous have been straightened for navigation. Because saltwater intrusion is a synergistic effect of the sea being let in and the river being kept out, levees have contributed to the intrusion by cutting off the marshes from rejuvenating freshwater.

Freshwater could be piped over the levees into the marshes to help restore the balance by mimicking overbank flooding. But oyster fishermen are opposed to that because the river water is loaded with organic and toxic pollutants. Without corrective measures, the oysters will die from excess salinity. With river water siphoned in, they would probably be unfit for human consumption. The oyster fisherman is caught in a squeeze between urban pollution and saltwater intrusion.

Natural processes are partly responsible for the land loss and intrusion of seawater. Tectonic activity and downwarping of the gulf geosyncline from sediment loading are causing a slow subsidence of the Louisiana coast. Yet Dr. Gagliano and other scientists attribute the sudden deterioration apparent in the past thirty years to human activities: levees and canals. Even the subsidence is partly caused by humans. As the metropolitan area of New Orleans extends its levee system, the newly floodproofed wetlands are drained to provide space for subdivisions, airports, industrial parks, and power plants. Once dry, wetland soils compact. The organic material in the soil decays, causing further compaction, and the ground sinks. Subsidence caused by land reclamation can amount to as much as fifty inches. Sewers become exposed, unsupported driveways and sidewalks crack, and foundation slabs separate from the ground.

New Orleans was built on wetlands and has nowhere to grow except into more wetlands. It is a city shaped like a saucer, with high ground along the riverbank sloping down to former marshland that has compacted and settled, and is now as much as seven feet below sea level. By 1900 most of the dry ground had been used, and Orleans Parish began reclaiming wetlands on a large scale. Add urban encroachment to erosion, subsidence, and saltwater intrusion, and the sum is a great estuary dying.

THE DELTA IS A METAPHOR for the whole Mississippi. The problems are comparable—pollution, erosion, siltation, urbanization—though in the case of the delta they are concentrated in a region of wetlands so productive that the damage is more obvious. All down the river the loss of wetlands stands out as the prime ecological fact. In this the Mississippi is in turn a microcosm for the nation. Of the wetlands that remained in the United States in 1950, 40 percent have been destroyed.

The Mississippi has seen some hard use. We stripped its hillsides, mined its banks, and polluted its waters. Those changes need not be permanent, but when we take the soil from its shores and fill its side channels, and when we build barriers to slow its flow, and build other barriers to tame its waters, and when we straighten it and tidy up its banks, we make changes that will not easily be undone.

A resource as great as the Mississippi River must be used. You cannot go home again to the days of innocence. But with the economic base of the Midwest beginning to shift from agriculture to industry, pressures and conflicts will increase. More and more hands will be held out to what is, despite its size, after all a finite river. Since 1945, the barge companies have doubled their use of the waterway—in tonnage transported—every ten years. Old demands grow exponentially; new ones appear. Texans covet the water of the Mississippi to irrigate their high plains. The diversion is opposed by the people of New Orleans, who fear that a reduced flow would aggravate their troubles. Already, in dry periods, the city's drinking water sometimes tastes of salt.

But even as the demands grow, the understanding grows too. The omens, as they say, are good. With our increasing insight into the behavior of flowing water, we are coming to accept that the floodplain is part of the river. Even in Louisiana, which is sometimes accused of environmental backwardness, a recognition of the role of wetlands is growing. Many in New Orleans now appreciate that their marshes provide a buffer from the storms of the gulf, a barrier to the saltwater and eroding waves, just as upriver wetlands once served as buffers that absorbed floods.

In 1974 the city initiated a process of planning for the future of its wetlands. In so doing, as one observer has noted, the local government accepted that it has as much responsibility for protecting wetlands as it has for maintaining streets. The city set as a goal the restriction of development to no more than 10 percent of its remaining marsh.

St. Bernard and most of the other coastal parishes are similarly planning and thinking in terms of long-range values. St. Bernard has already begun the expensive process of introducing Mississippi water into its wetlands. In a decade, local government has gone from raising issues to implementation of solutions, both through zoning regulations as in New Orleans and freshwater siphons as in St. Bernard Parish.

In order to make use of the Mississippi, we have had to alter it to fit the patterns of an industrialized society. But as river systems become better understood, the grim side effects of human tinkering have emerged. Clarifying these has led to an analysis of natural processes, and to technological and social steps for imitating nature and so alleviating the problems. Unfortunately, compensations are expensive if done on a scale large enough to do any good. To correct any environmental ill is costly, whether it be creating floodways to replace lost wetlands, controlling erosion on Midwestern farmland, siphoning fresh water to revitalize dying marshes, or purchasing vital wetlands to protect them.

In 1973 the Army Corps of Engineers began a five-year study of the feasibility of building wetlands from dredge spoil. They constructed 352 acres in the delta, the largest man-made marsh attempted to date. Seeded by the wind and birds, the new land is growing witch grass and smartweed. Muskrats and herons have moved in. The man-made marsh mimics what natural overflow accomplishes. But it is a minor step compared to the losses from erosion. Marsh building and freshwater siphoning, if they are to have effect, require a commitment to large public works. Such expensive projects can be avoided in the future by learning the effects of changes before becoming married to them.

With a major river like the Mississippi, local and state planning must be preceded by regional efforts, such as the studies done by the Great River Environmental Action Team (GREAT) and its spinoff, the master plan nearing completion by the Upper Mississippi River Basin Commission. Environmentalists have led the way by taking local action and helping it to grow into regional action, and perhaps, someday, into a whole river concern.

The federal government can nudge local interests through legislation such as the National Flood Insurance Act. By this act, insurance is offered to those who adopt zoning regulations restricting future expansion into the floodplain. Insurance and federal disaster assistance are withheld from flood-prone communities that refuse to participate. The intent is that the taxpayer should not have to pay disaster relief funds to those who realize a profit from developing land that belongs to the river.

Many communities are refusing to adopt zoning, and encroachment continues. Yet the very existence of the flood-insurance program is an encouraging sign. Another is an experiment underway in Prairie du Chien, the Wisconsin town that was the center of the fur trade on the upper Mississippi. Severe flooding was an almost yearly occurrence for Prairie du Chien; the flood of 1965 hit especially hard. In 1974 the federal government and the town agreed that the best solution would be to relocate 130 private residences and commercial buildings out of the floodplain.

When our canoe expedition visited Prairie du Chien, the relocation was well under-way, with a number of structures already moved to vacant lots considered safe from flooding. A visitor center had been constructed, on stilts, in the evacuated land. The area will probably become a park, one of the many advantageous uses for a floodplain.

The movement toward establishing riverfront parks, both for the Mississippi's urban shores and for its wilder lands, is another cause for optimism. From the pristine upper reach that is a candidate for wild and scenic river status to the wildlife refuges below the Twin Cities, to a suggested Upper Mississippi National Recreation Area, to the riverfront parks of town and city, to the great swampland of the Atchafalaya, to the Jean Lafitte National Historical Park near New Orleans, to a proposal for a national park at the delta for viewing the mudlumps and wildlife, and finally to the Great River Road stretching along the whole twenty-three hundred miles, the signals indicate that a new interest in the Mississippi River is at hand.

WHEN I THINK of the Mississippi I see a fragile marsh with a narrow stream winding through tall strands of wild rice. I see it widen and lose itself in broad lakes, only to narrow again and flow where the paddles of another people echo, and willows touch overhead.

I see it—a river now—grinding the wheat of the Scandinavian immigrant. I hear it whisper as it passes a once thriving, deserted town. Another day south and the river murmurs past the home of a man whose pen evoked its sweet summers. I see the Mississippi of symbol, the magnificent incarnation of our nostalgia for a simple, carefree time.

Below are miles and miles of an immense lonely river, imprisoned, its surface home only to those who sign on to riverboats in hopes of finding that time. Alongside is a rich and heavy land where the river's oldest trees brood over the ancient life in its waters and remember the year when the riverbed groaned. Then comes a sad land where the oaks gasp for air. And at last the lush and ephemeral gift of river's end.

INDEX